**Umberto Santino** is the founder and director of the Centro siciliano di documentazione in Palermo, which was the first centre for research into the mafia and was established in 1977 and then named after Giuseppe Impastato, a leader of the antimafia movement who was assassinated by the mafia in 1978. He is one of the most authoritative experts on the mafia and has been a leading figure in the antimafia movement over the past few decades. He has lectured at university level and spoken at conferences, seminars and other events in numerous countries.

*"Mafia and Antimafia: A Brief History* helps bring our knowledge of the mafia up to speed with thinking on the front-line, in Sicily. But it also fills a gap in our appreciation of the civic and political importance that research into the mafia has, and of its profound relationship with the antimafia movement. Umberto Santino, perhaps more than anyone else in Sicily, is the living illustration of how the forces ranged against the mafia power system have developed their understanding through a constant encounter with the mafia's horrifying reality."

– John Dickie, Professor of Italian Studies at
University College, London

# MAFIA AND ANTI MAFIA

UMBERTO SANTINO

Foreword by John Dickie

BLOOMSBURY ACADEMIC
LONDON • NEW YORK • OXFORD • NEW DELHI • SYDNEY

BLOOMSBURY ACADEMIC
Bloomsbury Publishing Plc
50 Bedford Square, London, WC1B 3DP, UK
1385 Broadway, New York, NY 10018, USA
29 Earlsfort Terrace, Dublin 2, Ireland

BLOOMSBURY, BLOOMSBURY ACADEMIC and the Diana logo
are trademarks of Bloomsbury Publishing Plc

First published as *Breve storia della mafia e dell'antimafia* (Trapani: Di Girolamo, 2008, 2011)
This paperback edition published by Bloomsbury Academic in 2022

A catalogue record for this book is available from the British Library.

A catalog record for this book is available from the Library of Congress.

ISBN: HB: 978-1-7807-6667-6
PB: 978-1-3503-2767-2
ePDF: 978-0-8577-2694-0
eBook: 978-0-8577-2902-6

Typeset in Garamond Three by OKS Prepress Services, Chennai, India

To find out more about our authors and books visit
www.bloomsbury.com and sign up for our newsletters.

# CONTENTS

# LIST OF ILLUSTRATIONS

## Maps

## Figure

## Plates

14. Garibaldi's entry into Palermo. The battle of the Ponte dell'Ammiraglio. *(Luigi Lavini,* Combattimento del Ponte dell'Ammiraglio, lithograph. *From Giuseppe Cesare Abba,* Da Quarto al Volturno. Noterelle di uno dei Mille, *Palermo: Sellerio,1993 (original edition 1880), p. 51.)*

15. Nino Bixio, a leading member of Garibaldi's Mille. *(Nino Bixio,* lithograph, Fratelli Terzaghi, *Milan, from Giuseppe Cesare Abba,* Da Quarto al Volturno, *p. 26.)*

16. On 1 October 1862, 12 people were stabbed in Palermo, the anonymous drawing shows the execution of one of those condemned. *(Salvatore Mannino,* I pugnalatori di Palermo del 1862, *Palermo: Il Vespro, 1976 (original edition 1903).)*

17–18. An old edition of the popular comedy *I mafiusi di la Vicaria di Palermu. (G. Rizzotto and G. Mosca.* I mafiusi di la Vicaria di Palermu, *Piazza, Palermo, no date;* I mafiusi di la Vicaria di Palermu, *Palermo: Editrice Reprint, 1994.)*

19. Bust of Giovanni Corrao, a general in Garibaldi's army. *(Bust of Giovanni Corrao in the Villa Garibaldi, Palermo. Photograph by the author.)*

20. Cover of Giuseppe Pitrè, *Usi e costumi, credenze e pregiudizi del popolo siciliano. (Giuseppe Pitrè,* Usi e costumi, credenze e pregiudizi del popolo siciliano, *vol. II, Palermo: G. Barbera editore, 1939.)*

21. Student of folk traditions, Giuseppe Pitrè. *(From the Italian Senate, www.senato.it.)*

22. The Palermo Prosecutor Diego Tajani. *(From Nando Russo (editor),* Antologia della mafia, *Palermo: il punto edizioni, 1964.)*

23. The text of the bill on the parliamentary inquiry in Sicily in 1875. *(Ibid.)*

24. From the cover of Leopoldo Franchetti and Sidney Sonnino, *Inchiesta in Sicilia. (From the cover of Leopoldo Franchetti and Sidney Sonnino,* Inchiesta in Sicilia, *Florence: Vallecchi, 1974 (original edition 1877).)*

25. Emanuele Notarbartolo, the mayor of Palermo and a director of the Banco di Sicilia. *(From Leopoldo Notarbartolo,* La città cannibale. Il

memoriale Notarbartolo, *Palermo: Edizioni Novecento, 1994 (original edition 1949).)*

26. Leopoldo Notarbartolo, son of Emanuele. *(Ibid.)*

27. Raffaele Palizzolo. *(Ibid.)*

28. The Marquis Antonio di Rudinì. *(Ibid.)*

29–30. The cover of Salvatore Francesco Romano, *Storia dei Fasci siciliani,* and a drawing depicting the trial against the leaders of the Fasci. *(Salvatore F. Romano, Storia dei Fasci siciliani, Bari: Laterza, 1959.)*

31. The engraving shows the women of Piana dei Greci in the province of Palermo, who took part in the peasant struggles. *(From L'Illustrazione italiana, in Nicola Barbato, Scritti e documenti, II, Caltanissetta Rome: Documenti, Salvatore Sciascia Editore, 1995, p.194.)*

32. Francesco Crispi, a leader of the Italian Risorgimento and prime minister. *(Leopoldo Notarbartolo, La città cannibale, p. 38.)*

33. Palermo police chief, Ermanno Sangiorgi. *(Giornale di Sicilia, 8-9 maggio 1901 and J. Dickie, Cosa Nostra. A History of the Sicilian Mafia, London: Hodder & Stoughton, 2004.)*

34. The first page of the report by Ermanno Sangiorgi, 1898. *(Central State Archive.)*

35. The trial based on Sangiorgi's reports. (L'Ora, *3-4 May 1901.)*

36. Joe Petrosino, the Italian-American policeman killed in Palermo in 1909. *(Copyright unknown.)*

37. Lorenzo Panepinto, the socialist leader killed in 1911. *(Copyright unknown.)*

38. Bernardino Verro, the socialist mayor of Corleone killed in 1915. *(Copyright unknown.)*

39. Giuseppe Rumore, the socialist activist killed in 1919. *(Copyright unknown.)*

40. Nicolò Alongi, the socialist leader killed in 1920. *(Copyright unknown.)*

41. Giovanni Orcel, the socialist trade unionist killed in 1920. *(Copyright unknown.)*

42. Sebastiano Bonfiglio, the socialist mayor of Monte San Giuliano killed in 1922. *(Copyright unknown.)*

43. A peasant demonstration in the 1920s. *(Copyright unknown.)*

44–46. Cesare Mori, the prefect of Palermo from 1925 to 1929. A demonstration at the swearing of the gamekeepers' oath on 13 May 1926. *(By kind permission of Giovanna Terranova; Cesare Mori, Con la mafia ai ferri corti, Milan: Mondadori, 1932.)*

47. Allied landing in Sicily, 10 July 1943. *(Salvo Di Matteo, Anni roventi. La Sicilia dal 1943 al 1947, Palermo: Denaro editore, 1967.)*

48. Calogero Vizzini, the mafia leader at Villalba (Caltanissetta). *(Filippo Gaja, L'esercito della lupara, Milan: Maquis editore, 1974.)*

49. Special issue of *La Voce comunista* and *La Voce socialista*. *(Centro Impastato Archive.)*

50. Mafiosi leading a separatist demonstration in Palermo. *(Salvo Di Matteo, Anni roventi.)*

51. The bandits Salvatore Giuliano and Gaspare Pisciotta. *(Petix Archive, from Angelo Vecchio, Salvatore Giuliano, il 're' di Montelepre, Palermo: Antares Editrice, 1998.)*

52. A manifesto, signed by Giuliano. (Portella della Ginestra 1947-1997: tra storia e memoria, *Palermo: 1997, p. 32.*)

53–54. The Minister of Agriculture, the communist Fausto Gullo and an occupation of uncultivated land. *(Copyright unknown; Scafidi Archive, from* Portella della Ginestra 1947–1997: tra storia e memoria, *p. 16.)*

55–56. Leaders of the peasant struggles killed by the mafia: Nicolò Azoti, Accursio Miraglia and Epifanio Li Puma. *(Nicolò Azoti by kind permission of the relatives; Copyright unknown.)*

57. May Day 1947: the massacre at Portella della Ginestra. *(Salvo Di Matteo, Anni roventi.)*

58. Sicilian election results. *(Contemporary newspapers.)*

59–62. Leaders of the peasant struggles killed by the mafia: Epifanio Li Puma, Placido Rizzotto, Calogero Cangelosi and Salvatore Carnevale. *(Copyright unknown.)*

63. The mother of Salvatore Carnevale, Francesca Serio, with the writer Carlo Levi. *(Copyright unknown.)*

64. The funerals following the Ciaculli massacre of 30 June 1963. *(www. vittimemafia.it.)*

65. Cardinal Ruffini and Pope Pius XII. *(wikipedia.org.)*

66. The Waldesian Pastor Pietro Panascia. *(www.chiesavaldesetrapani.com)*

67–68. Salvo Lima and Vito Ciancimino and the building speculation in Palermo. *(Angelo Vecchio, Storia illustrata della mafia, Palermo: Antares editrice, 2005, p. 31; Massimo Picozzi, Cosa Nostra. Storia della mafia per immagini, Milan: Mondadori, 2010, p.180.)*

69. Giuseppe 'Peppino' Impastato, a Nuova Sinistra activist killed in 1978. *(Centro Impastato Photographic Archive.)*

70. The journalist Mario Francese, killed in 1979. *(Copyright unknown.)*

71. Deputy Police Chief Boris Giuliano, killed in 1979. *(Copyright unknown.)*

72. The magistrate Cesare Terranova, killed in 1979. *(Copyright unknown.)*

73. The President of the Region of Sicily Piersanti Mattarella, killed in 1980. *(Copyright unknown.)*

74. The communist leader Pio La Torre, killed in 1982. *(Copyright unknown.)*

75. The Prefect Carlo Alberto Dalla Chiesa and his wife Emanuela Setti Carraro, killed in 1982. *(Copyright unknown.)*

76. The magistrate Rocco Chinnici, killed in 1983. *(Copyright unknown.)*

77–78. The *pentito* Tommaso Buscetta and the 'maxi-trial' in Palermo. *(Massimo Picozzi, Cosa Nostra, p. 233; Felice Cavallaro (ed.), Mafia. Album di Cosa Nostra, Milan: Rizzoli, 1992, p. 142.)*

XII MAFIA AND ANTIMAFIA

79–82. The magistrates Giovanni Falcone and his wife Francesca Morvillo, killed with their escorts in the massacre of Capaci, on 23 May 1992. The magistrate Paolo Borsellino, killed with five policemen, in Via D'Amelio on 19 July 1992. *(Copyright unknown.)*

83. The businessman Libero Grassi, killed in 1991. *(Copyright unknown.)*

84. Rita Atria, who killed herself after the murder of Paolo Borsellino. *(Copyright unknown.)*

85. The parish priest Pino Puglisi, killed in 1993. *(Copyright unknown.)*

86. The arrest of the mafia leader Toto Riina in January 1993. *(Olykom. From Bruno Vespa (editor),* Storia d'Italia. Un racconto fotografico. Crimini e scandali, *Milan: Mondadori, 2007, p. 236; Crimini e scandali, Milan: Mondadori 2007, p. 236.)*

87. The massacre in Florence on 27 May 1993. *(www.misteriditalia.it.)*

88. The arrest of the perpetrator of the Capaci massacre, Giovanni Brusca, in May 1996. *(Copyright unknown.)*

89. The arrest of the mafia leader Antonino Giuffre in April 2002. *(Copyright unknown.)*

90. The arrest of the supreme leaser Bernardo Provenzano in April 2006. *(Copyright unknown.)*

91. The arrest of the mafia leader Salvatore Lo Piccolo in November 2007. *(Copyright unknown.)*

92. The mafia members involved in the 'Old Bridge' operation in February 2008. *(Copyright unknown.)*

93. The mafia leader Matteo Messina Denaro, still on the run. *(Copyright unknown.)*

94. A national demonstration against the mafia to mark the first anniversary of the murder of Giuseppe Impastato, 9 May 1979. *(Centro Impastato Photographic Archive.)*

95. Antimafia initiatives in Sicilian schools. *(I colori della speranza, Comune di Palermo, 1996.)*

96. On fields confiscated from the mafia. *(Photograph by Giulia Bucca, Arci Sicilia.)*

97. Anti-racketeering demonstration. *(Addiopizzo committee.)*

98. The bandit Salvatore Giuliano and the Italo-American mafia leader Vito Genovese. *(Filippo Gaja, L'esercito della lupara.)*

99. Lucky Luciano in Palermo. *(Publifoto, Centro Impastato Photographic Archive.)*

100. Cinisi (Palermo) in the 1950s. The mayor and some mafiosi. *(Centro Impastato Photographic Archive.)*

101. The mafioso Joe Valachi, who revealed the secrets of Cosa Nostra in America in 1963. *(Angelo Vecchio, Storia illustrata della mafia, p. 131.)*

102. The first page of the 'ndrangheta code seized in Reggio Calabria in 1987. *(Nicola Gratteri and Antonio Nicaso, Fratelli di sangue, Milan: Mondadori, 2008, p. 363.)*

103. A page from the code seized by the Canadian police from the home of an 'ndrangheta member. *(Ibid, p. 81.)*

104. The murder of Giuditta Levato, a leader of the peasant struggles in Calabria in the 1940s. *(Painting by Mike Arruzza. perlacalabria.wordpress. com.)*

105. The communist activist Rocco Gatto, killed in 1977. *(Copyright unknown.)*

106. The magistrate Antonino Scopelliti, killed in 1991. *(Copyright unknown.)*

107. Francesco Fortugno, vice-president of the Regional Council of Calabria, killed in 2005. *(Copyright unknown.)*

108. Raffaele Cutolo, head of the Nuova Camorra Organizzata. *(Gigi Di Fiore, La camorra e le sue storie, Turin: Utet, 2005.)*

109. Carmine Alfieri, head of the Nuova Famiglia. *(Ibid.)*

110. The Christian Democrat Mayor of Pagani (Salerno), Marcello Torre, killed in 1980. *(Copyright unknown.)*

111. The journalist Giancarlo Siani, killed in 1985. *(Copyright unknown.)*

112. The priest Giuseppe Diana, killed in 1994. *(Copyright unknown.)*

113. Silvia Ruotolo, killed during a camorra shootout in 1997. *(Copyright unknown.)*

114. The Mayor of Pollica (Salerno), Angelo Vassallo, killed in 2010. *(Copyright unknown.)*

115–125. Children killed by the mafia: Giuseppina Savoca (1959). Simonetta Lamberti (1982). The twins Giuseppe and Salvatore Asta killed with their mother in 1985. Claudio Domino (1986). Marcella Tassone (1989). Nicholas Green (1994). Giuseppe Di Matteo (1996). Stefano Pompeo (1999). Valentina Terracciano (2000). Annalisa Durante (2004). Domenico Gabriele (2009). *(Copyright unknown.)*

126. Serafina Battaglia. *(Copyright unknown.)*

127. Franca Viola. *(Copyright unknown.)*

128. Felicia Bartolotta, the mother of Peppino Impastato. *(Photograph by Gabriella Ebano.)*

129. Demonstration of the Associazione delle donne siciliane per la lotta contro la mafia (Association of Women in Sicily against the Mafia). *(Centro Impastato Archive.)*

# ACKNOWLEDGEMENTS

For the English language version of this book, I wish to thank Roger Dean, who kindly took on the task of translating it, and the generous cooperation of John Dickie, with whom I have been in a prolonged dialogue about historical research into the mafia.

Anna Puglisi, my life partner, is co-author of this book rather than a collaborator. Her contributions include the maps and tables and the layout of the photographs.

Vincenzo Pinello, a member of the Centro Impastato and editor of the periodical *Espero*, assisted in reconstructing the present composition of Cosa Nostra in the province of Palermo.

Many thanks to Alice Orton, Azmina Siddique and Sophie Campbell for their kind cooperation.

# FOREWORD

The history of the Sicilian mafia, and of the fight against it, has many lessons to teach us. One of the most important lessons concerns the close relationship between reality and representation: between, on the one hand, what the mafia does, and on the other hand, the way the mafia has been studied by academic researchers, described by journalists, seen by photographers and film directors, and talked about by politicians and the general public. Throughout its history, the Sicilian mafia has succeeded in shaping what the world thinks of it. Indeed this power to shape perceptions is one of the many things that make the mafia much more than just a bunch of crooks. In other words, the mafia has an ideology – a vision of itself, of Sicily, and even of Italian history – that it needs to pass off as the truth.

At the simplest level, the mafia spreads that ideology when it needs to escape justice: on countless occasions, defence lawyers, recruited to defend *mafiosi*, have argued that the mafia is not criminal, and still less a criminal organisation, but rather an ancient attitude embedded deep within the psyche of every Sicilian. Or that violent struggles between mafia factions are merely disputes within and between families. But the mafia's ideology has purposes that are far more ambitious than the exigencies of the courtroom. The mafia is a network that stretches from the street-corner thug up through the social classes to the corrupt doctor, entrepreneur or statesman; it needs to win the passive or active support of a significant section of the population; it needs to infiltrate the political, administrative and economic system; it needs to confuse the public and discredit its enemies: for all these reasons, the mafia is a power system, and as such it has an ideology to both disguise and legitimate itself. The mafia ideology is certainly false; it is also frequently jumbled and unsophisticated. But one measure of its insidiousness is the fact that a number of academic researchers have produced work that, to a greater or lesser extent, naively elaborates some aspects of that ideology.

So it is appropriate that Umberto Santino begins his *Mafia and Antimafia: A Brief History* with a critique of the 'stereotypes and paradigms' which for so long shaped thinking about the mafia, and many of which have more or less distant origins in the mafia ideology. But this translation of the text is appropriate for a profounder reason: for its author, perhaps more than anyone else in Sicily, is the living illustration of how the forces ranged against the mafia power system and its ideology have, like their enemy, blended reality with representation – in this case by joining research and writing with activism.[1]

Santino was born in the Sicilian interior in 1939. After roughly a decade of militancy in the New Left milieu, he left politics in 1977 and, with his wife Anna Puglisi, founded the Centro siciliano di documentazione (Sicilian Documentation Centre) an independent and self-financed library, archive and research hub based in Palermo. A long season of intense intellectual activity began at that point: *Mafia and Antimafia: A Brief History* is a synthesis of the many important works written by Santino as part of his work with the Centre.[2] While Anna Puglisi has written a series of influential studies of mafia women, Santino's research output has ranged from a survey of mafia murders, to analyses of Sicilian organised crime's links to the economy and politics, to globalisation and narcotics trafficking, to the history of the mafia's earliest manifestations and of the antimafia movement from its origins to the present day. His work is distinguished by its ability to blend a range of disciplinary approaches in what he himself has suggested could be called a 'socio-history'.

Santino's prolific research activity was conducted in a climate of rapid change, controversy and, above all, bloodshed. The years following the foundation of the Centro siciliano di documentazione were to be the most violent and dramatic in the Sicilian mafia's history. Propelled by narcodollars, and shielded by its close relationship with sections of the ruling Christian Democrat party, Cosa Nostra embarked on an unprecedented and savage attack against anyone who stood in its way:

police, magistrates, politicians, journalists, professionals and activists. Indeed, the mafia murder of one young activist would draw Santino and the Centre into the first, longest and most significant of the many campaigns that have run alongside their intellectual activities.

Peppino Impastato was from Cinisi, the seaside town near Palermo airport which was a strategic base for the powerful boss Gaetano Badalamenti and his transatlantic drug trafficking. Impastato was from a family profoundly immersed in the mafia: his father was an affiliate, and his paternal uncle was the boss before Badalamenti. Rebelling against this background, Impastato became a passionate and eloquent, if occasionally tormented, advocate of a range of left-wing causes. He was unrelenting in his denunciation of the mafia, whether it be in his writings, in the satirical broadcasts he made through Radio Aut (a station he founded), or through a public exhibition showing the mafia's damaging impact on the local landscape. On the night of 8/9 May 1978, just after that exhibition, Peppino Impastato was kidnapped, tortured and then left by a railway track with dynamite tied to his body.[3] Just as the boss Badalamenti had intended, his death was dismissed in the press as a terrorist attack gone wrong: 'Leftist fanatic blown apart by own bomb on railway track', was one headline. The police and judicial authorities took the same highly improbable line on Impastato's death.

Although Umberto Santino and Anna Puglisi had not known Peppino Impastato personally, they were immediately convinced that the mafia was responsible for his death. Together with Peppino's mother and brother, they embarked on a tireless and courageous effort to get the case reopened, and expose a mafia cover-up. The Centro siciliano di documentazione was renamed after Peppino Impastato in 1980, and is now universally known as the Centro Impastato. One of the first magistrates to take the Impastato case seriously was Rocco Chinnici. Until Chinnici's assassination in 1983, the Centre's relationship with him became a model of many future practical and intellectual collaborations between magistrates committed to prosecuting the mafia and intellectuals committed to trying to understand it.

After more than two decades of dogged efforts, the campaign on the Peppino Impastato case finally achieved results. In December 2000, a Parliamentary Commission of Inquiry stated that the investigation into the murder of the activist had effectively supported the killers' attempts to cover their tracks. In April 2002, the Cinisi boss Gaetano Badalamenti was at last convicted of ordering the murder.

The years between Peppino Impastato's murder and this final verdict were marked by bloody milestones in the history of the mafia and the antimafia. In 1982, against the background of the worst mafia war in history, there was the passing of the Rognoni-La Torre law, which defined the mafia in the penal code for the first time, and gave the state new powers against it; the politician who proposed the law, Pio La Torre, was murdered for his efforts. In 1984 came the decision by the *mafioso* Tommaso Buscetta to become a 'supergrass', thus providing crucial insider knowledge of Cosa Nostra for both the authorities and for scholars. In 1986–7, the 'maxi-trial' against Cosa Nostra, prepared by Giovanni Falcone and Paolo Borsellino, unfolded in Palermo's 'bunker' courthouse. In 1992, Falcone and Borsellino were themselves murdered by mafia bombs. Throughout these years, Umberto Santino and the Centro Impastato always took a leading role in the frequently heated debates that accompanied the growth of a civic and political opposition to the mafia. Among the most important of their activities has been their work in schools, and in preparing educational material for teachers as part of an 'education for legality' drive.

Of the extraordinary research done on the Sicilian mafia in Italy by Umberto Santino, Anna Puglisi and others since the mid-1980s, surprisingly little has been translated into English. As a result, readers outside Italy are often left with a distorted and even confused idea of the mafia and its place in Sicilian society. The translation of *Mafia and Antimafia: A Brief History* is an important step towards increasing our knowledge. But it also fills a gap in our appreciation of the civic and political importance that research into the mafia has in Sicily, and of its profound relationship with the antimafia movement, in all its manifestations.

John Dickie
University College London
June 2015

# ORGANIZED CRIME IN ITALY

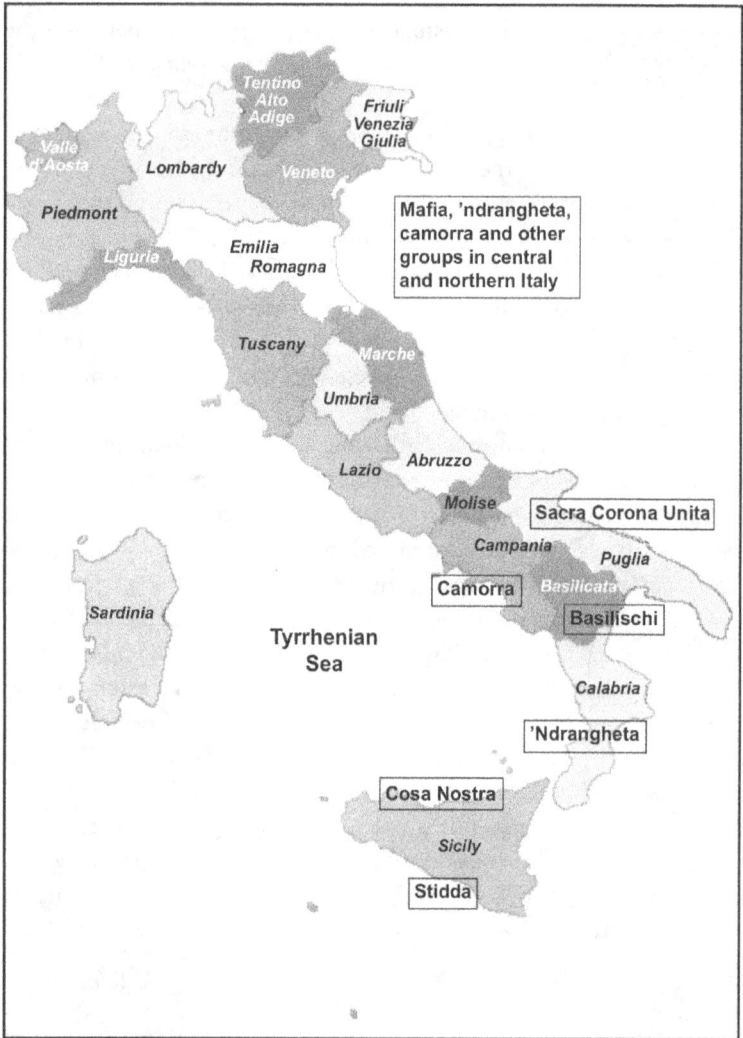

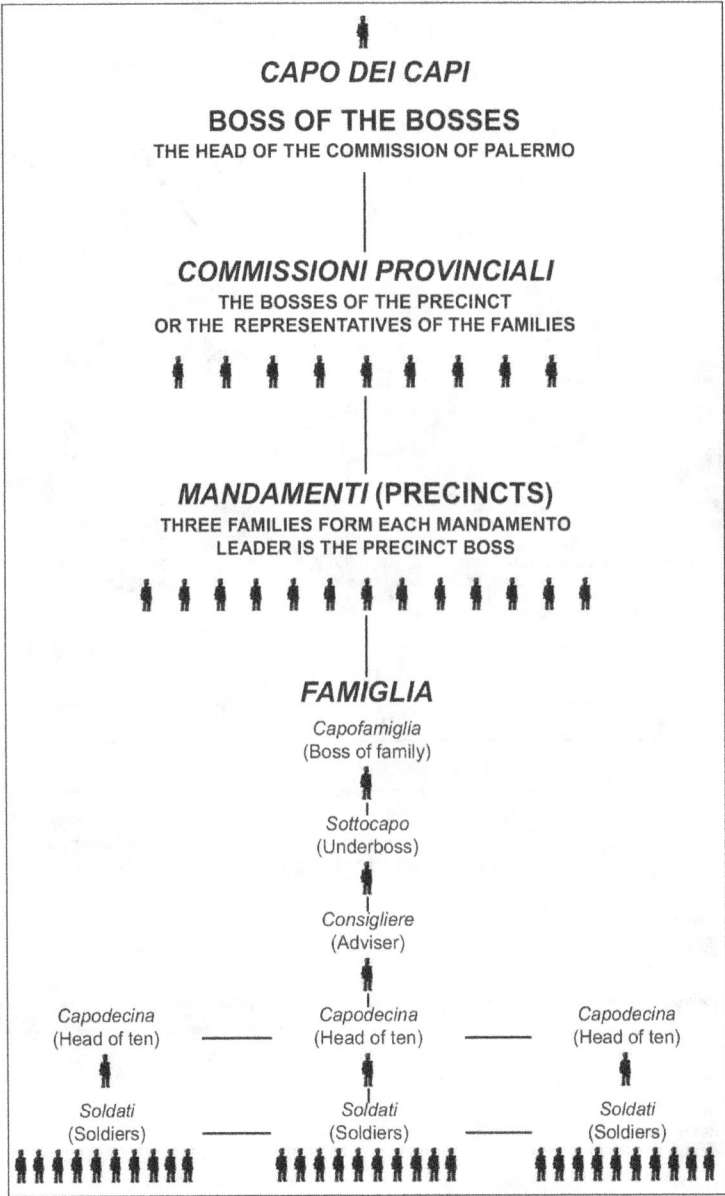

**CAPO DEI CAPI**

**BOSS OF THE BOSSES**
THE HEAD OF THE COMMISSION OF PALERMO

**COMMISSIONI PROVINCIALI**
THE BOSSES OF THE PRECINCT
OR THE REPRESENTATIVES OF THE FAMILIES

**MANDAMENTI (PRECINCTS)**
THREE FAMILIES FORM EACH MANDAMENTO
LEADER IS THE PRECINCT BOSS

**FAMIGLIA**

Capofamiglia
(Boss of family)

Sottocapo
(Underboss)

Consigliere
(Adviser)

| Capodecina | Capodecina | Capodecina |
| (Head of ten) | (Head of ten) | (Head of ten) |

| Soldati | Soldati | Soldati |
| (Soldiers) | (Soldiers) | (Soldiers) |

**The structure of Cosa Nostra**
According to Tommaso Buscetta, 1984

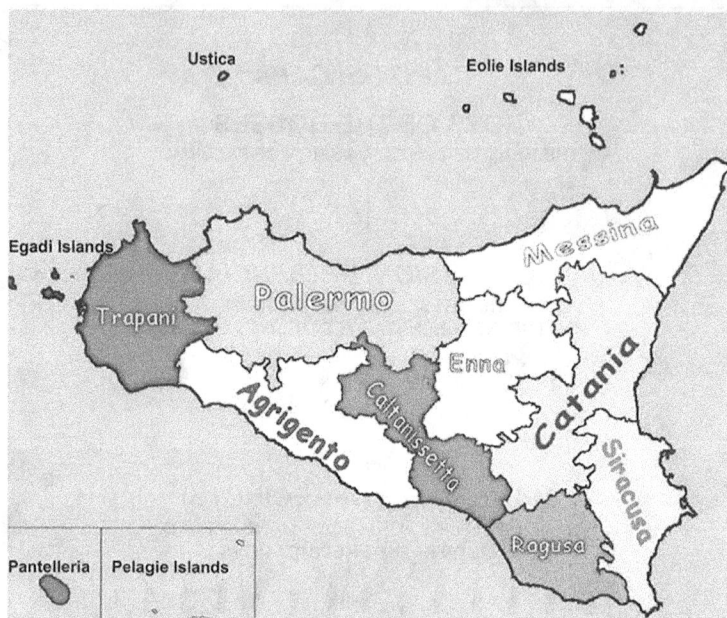

# Mafia in Sicily

## Agrigento

| Towns | Families | Bosses |
|---|---|---|
| Porto Empedocle | Messina – Salemi | Messina Francesco – Salemi Pasquale |
| | Albanese | Albanese Giulio – Putrone Giuseppe |
| | Grassonelli (Stidda) | Grassonelli Salvatore – Grassonelli Bruno |
| | | Grassonelli Giuseppe |
| Canicatti | Ferro – Di Caro | Ferro Antonio – Di Caro Calogero |
| | | Guarneri Antonio – Paci Antonio |
| | Avarello (Stidda) | |
| Palma di Montechiaro | Napoli – Ribisi – Allegro | Napoli Croce – Burgio Angelo |
| | | Lauria Giuseppe – Rizzo Calogero |
| | | Ribisi brothers |
| | Allegro | Allegro Francesco |
| | Bordino (Stidda) | |
| Sciacca | Di Gangi | |
| Siculiana | Cuntrera – Caruana | Their local representatives |
| Licata | Alabiso | |
| Campobello di Licata | Bove | |
| Ravanusa | Ciraulo (Stidda) | |
| Favara | Barba | |

## Caltanissetta

| Towns | Families | Bosses |
|---|---|---|
| Gela | Locolano | Locolano Salvatore – Laglietti Diego |
| | | Lauretta Crocifisso – Schembri Salvatore |
| | | Tuccio Gaetano |
| | Madonia | Madonia Giuseppe – Iannì Francesco |
| | | Passaro Giovanni – Scerra Orazio |
| | | Trubia Nunzio |
| | Paolello (Stidda) | |
| | Di Giacomo (Stidda) | |
| Niscemi | Spatola | Spatola Bartolo – Arcerito Gaetano |
| | | Calcagno Salvatore |
| | Russo (Stidda) | Russo Salvatore – Allia Sebastiano |
| | | Campione Vincenzo – Moscato Gaetano |
| Riesi | Riggio (Stidda) | |

## Catania

| Towns | Families | Bosses |
|---|---|---|
| Catania | Santapaola | Santapaola Benedetto – Ercolano Sebastiano |
| | | Ferrera Francesco |
| | | Cannizzaro Francesco – Mangion Francesco – |
| | | Rapisarda Giovanni |
| | | Campanella Carlo |
| | Pillera – Cappello | Pillera Salvatore – Piacenti Carmelo |
| | | Cappello Salvatore – Ferone Giuseppe |
| | | Sciuto Biagio – Puglisi Antonino |
| | Cursoti 'catanesi' | Garozzo Giuseppe – Mazzeo Santo |
| | (Stidda) | Privitera Salvatore |
| | Cursoti 'milanesi' | Miano Luigi – Campisi Salvatore |
| | (Stidda) | Giuffrida Orazio |
| | Di Mauro 'Puntina' | Di Mauro Giuseppe – Di Mauro Angelo |
| | | Di Mauro Paolo – Favara Corrado |
| | | Favara Antonino |
| | Laudani | Laudani Sebastiano, Laudani Alfio, |
| | | Laudani Giuseppe |
| Misterbianco | Pulvirenti 'Malpassotu' | Pulvirenti Giuseppe – Castorina Giuseppe |
| | | Lanzafame Alfio – Licciardello Salvatore |
| | | Scuderi Francesco – Grazioso Giuseppe |

## Catania

| Towns | Families | Bosses |
|---|---|---|
| Bronte – Adrano Biancavilla | Santangelo – Scalisi | |
| Giarre – Randazzo | Campo | |
| Scordia | Di Salvo | Their local representatives |
| Acireale – Mascali Giardini Naxos | Santapaola – Vadalà | |
| Fiumefreddo Piedimonte Etneo | Cantarella – Fresta | |

## Enna

| Towns | Families | Bosses |
|---|---|---|
| Barrafranca Pietraperzia | Messana – Privitelli | Messana Calogero – Messana Sebastiano Privitelli Gaetano – Bonaffini Salvatore |
| Enna | Raspa (Stidda) Seggio (Stidda) | Raspa Giuseppe |

## Messina

| Towns | Families | Bosses |
|---|---|---|
| Barcellona Pozzo di Gotto | Chiofalo Milone | Chiofalo Giuseppe – Gulli Domenico – Imbesi Salvatore Milone Carmelo – Milone Giuseppe Torre Carmelo |
| Tortorici Capo d'Orlando | Bontempo Scavo Galati Giordano | Bontempo Scavo Cesare, Carmelo, Sebastiano Galati Giordano Sebastiano, Orlando, Calogero |
| Messina | Sparacio | Sparacio Luigi – Sparacio Rosario – Castorina Pasquale Munafò Orazio – Vitale Giovanni |
| | Mancuso Leo Ferrara Marchese | |
| Brolo | Cipriano | |
| Milazzo | Sottile | |

## Ragusa

| Towns | Families | Bosses |
|---|---|---|
| Ragusa Vittoria | Carbonaro – Dominante | Carbonaro Claudio – Dominante Carmelo<br>Giannone Giovanni – Interlici Emanuele<br>Ventura Filippo |
| Comiso | Cappello | Cappello Giovanni – Ferreri Salvatore<br>Campanella Umberto |

## Siracusa

| Towns | Families | Bosses |
|---|---|---|
| Siracusa | Urso (Stidda) – Bottaro<br><br>Schiavone – Aparo –<br>Provenzano | Urso Agostino – Bottaro Salvatore<br>Cannizzaro Gioacchino – Sparatore Angelo<br>Schiavone Salvatore – Aparo Antonino<br>Provenzano Orazio A. – Salafia Nunzio<br>Mauceri Concetto |
| Lentini | Nardo | Nardo Giuseppe – Nardo Sebastiano<br>Restuccia Placido |

## Trapani

| Towns | Families | Bosses |
|---|---|---|
| Marsala | D'Amico<br>Zicchitella | Piccione Michele – Patti Antonino – Raia Gaspare<br>Zicchitella Giuseppe – Zicchitella Ignazio<br>Genna Pasquale |
| Alcamo | Sciacca – Milazzo<br><br>Greco | Sciacca Francesco – Sciacca Baldassare<br>Milazzo Vincenzo – Maltese Baldassare<br>Greco Lorenzo – Greco Domenico<br>Badalamenti Isidoro |
| Mazara del Vallo | Agate | Agate Mariano – Asaro Giovanni<br>Mangiaracina Vito – Bastone Giovanni<br>Riserbato Antonino |
| Castellammare del Golfo | Buccellato | Buccellato Antonino – Bonventre Vito<br>Calabrò Gioacchino – Scuderi Salvatore<br>Magaddino Sebastiano |
| Partanna | Accardo<br>Ingoia | |

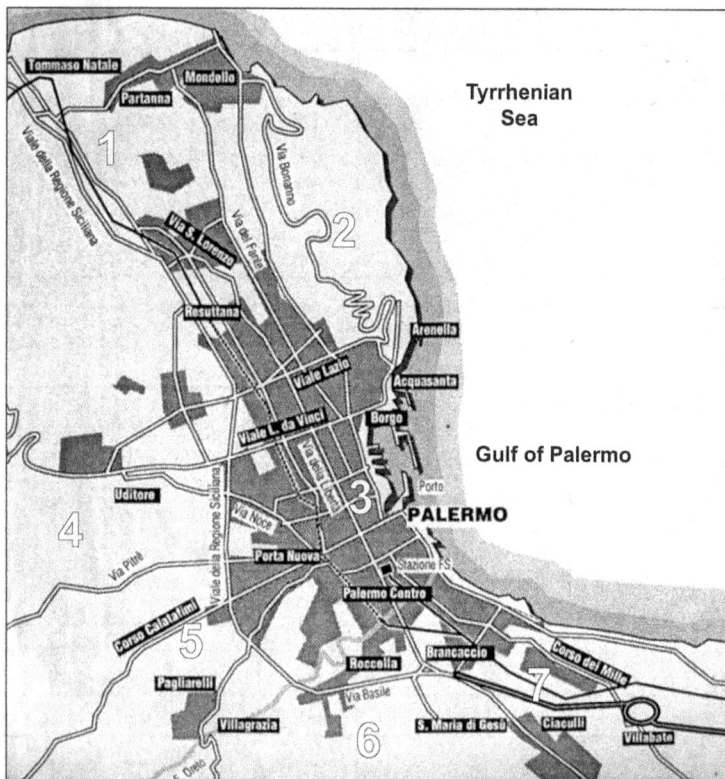

## MANDAMENTI IN PALERMO

### 1. San Lorenzo
*Families:*
San Lorenzo
Tommaso Natale
Partanna Mondello
Carini
Villagrazia di Carini

### 2. Resuttana
*Families:*
Resuttana
Viale Lazio
Arenella
Acquasanta

### 3. Porta Nuova
*Families:*
Porta Nuova
Palermo Centro
Borgo Vecchio

### 4. Passo di Rigano
*Families:*
Passo di Rigano
Uditore
Noce

### 5. Pagliarelli
*Families:*
Pagliarelli
Borgo Molara
Corso Calatafimi

### 6. Santa Maria di Gesù
*Families:*
Santa Maria di Gesù
Villagrazia

### 7. Ciaculli
*Families:*
Ciaculli
Brancaccio
Corso dei Mille
Roccella
Belmonte Mezzagno

## MADAMENTI IN THE PROVINCE OF PALERMO

| Villabate | Bolognetta | San Giuseppe Jato |
|---|---|---|
| *Families:* | *Families:* | *Families:* |
| Villabate | Misilmeri | Monreale |
| Ficarazzi | Baucina | Altofonte |
| Bagheria | Ciminna | Piana degli Albanesi |
| Casteldaccia | Bolognetta | San Giuseppe Jato |
| | Marineo | Camporeale |

| Cinisi | Partinico | Corleone | Caccamo |
|---|---|---|---|
| *Families:* | *Families:* | *Families:* | *Families:* |
| Capaci | Balestrate | Cefala Diana | Trabia |
| Cinisi | Borgetto | Corleone | Termini Imerese |
| Terrasini | Partinico | Prizzi | Caccamo |

## THE COMMISSIONE PROVINCIALE OF PALERMO

| | | | |
|---|---|---|---|
| Aglieri Pietro | S. Maria di Gesù | Montalto Salvatore | Villabate |
| Calò Giuseppe | Porta Nuova | Bono Giuseppe | Bolognetta |
| Buscemi Salvatore | Passo di Rigano | Di Maggio Procopio | Cinisi |
| Motisi Matteo | Pagliarelli | Geraci Nenè | Partinico |
| Lucchese Giuseppe | Ciaculli | Buscemi Salvatore | San Giuseppe Jato |
| Madonia Antonino | Resuttana | Riina Salvatore | Corleone |
| Gambino Giuseppe | San Lorenzo | Intile Francesco | Caccamo |

Source: *Il Sole - 24 ore*, 17 October 1992.

# CHAPTER 1

# THEORIES AND REALITIES

## Prologue

After decades in which its existence was denied, in recent years the mafia has become, and remains, a topic of discussion in newspapers, on television and even in schools. This is largely due to the spectacular crimes attributed to it. Many people remember or have heard about the large number of deaths that occurred in Palermo in the early 1980s, during the so-called 'mafia war', which also involved many crimes outside the mafia groups. The massacres in 1992, which saw the deaths of the magistrates Giovanni Falcone and Paolo Borsellino (we too often forget that others died alongside Falcone: his wife Francesca Morvillo, herself a magistrate, and Rocco Dicillo, Antonio Montinaro and Vito Schifani; and alongside Borsellino, the police officers Agostino Catalano, Walter Cosina, Emanuela Loi, Vincenzo Li Muli and Claudio Traina), and those in 1993 in Florence and Milan, with ten victims, also made headlines around the world.

These and other crimes gave rise to talk of an 'emergency', suggesting that the mafia exists only when it is shooting and is headline news when it kills famous people. Since those years saw attacks on representatives of state institutions (the police, magistrates, politicians), the mafia was also seen as 'anti-state'.

These views of the mafia – as a murder machine; as operating outside and against the State – are among the most widespread, but we should ask how accurate they are and whether they provide an adequate description of the phenomenon that is the mafia.[1]

We also need to question ideas about the antimafia that have gained currency. It is said that the struggle against the mafia began only in recent years, and we remember the efforts of certain magistrates, particularly those who were killed, the demonstrations that have been held and still take place, and the work done in schools. In fact, as we shall see, the struggle against the mafia started long ago and is as old as the mafia itself: we may see it as beginning in the 1890s, with the first peasant struggles (the Fasci siciliani).[2]

## Methodology

To understand the mafia and the antimafia correctly, we must first examine the ideas now circulating to establish whether or not they are correct. This preliminary phase, the assessment of current ideas, or inspection of the collective imagination, must be followed by a second, formulating a definition, and inevitably a third, verification of this through research. This methodology is valid for any subject, but is particularly relevant to one such as the mafia and the antimafia, around which so many wrong and often misleading ideas have accumulated over time.

## Current Ideas: Stereotypes and Paradigms

I shall divide the current ideas on the mafia into two groups: stereotypes and paradigms. Stereotypes are the most widespread current ideas, the clichés trotted out without reflection or documentation, which are derived from and perpetuate a mass consensus, are accepted thanks to a lack of thought and passed on through force of habit. The assessment of these ideas requires their demystification, through comparing them with an accurate representation of reality. This operation is fairly easy at a cultural level but difficult to put into practice, since many of these notions about the mafia have been adopted by the media and also underpin the legislation in force today.

I shall call paradigms those ideas that have some claim to be regarded as scientific, in that they are derived from the collection and interpretation of a certain mass of data. As we shall see, the most widely accepted paradigms (the mafia as a typical criminal association and the mafia enterprise) describe only part of the mafia phenomenon, and so raise the question of how we can incorporate other aspects that have not been fully considered or have been ignored.

## The Most Widely Accepted Stereotypes: Emergency and Anti-state

I have already mentioned the idea of the mafia as an emergency and as an anti-state body. The stereotype of the mafia as an emergency is based on the view that it is mainly or primarily a murder machine. Whenever there is a murder that can be ascribed to the mafia, the press and television talk of the 'revival' of the mafia phenomenon, as if in between crimes the mafia ceased to exist and proof of its existence consists only, or mainly, in its carrying out of murders. If there are many such crimes, and particularly if well-known people are targeted, we talk about an 'emergency'. This is a view that sees the mafia as alive only when it is shooting, as a phenomenon that is of importance and concern when it generates *cadaveri eccellenti* ('eminent corpses', a brutal expression that it would be better to avoid) and becomes a *questione nazionale* (a 'national issue', to quote the headline in the *Corriere della sera* of 5 September and *La Repubblica* of 6 September 1982), if it kills men such as Dalla Chiesa, Falcone and Borsellino. By this reckoning, if the mafia does not kill it ceases to exist — or it is as if it has ceased to exist, and deserves no attention; if it does not aim high, it is merely a local phenomenon that gives no grounds for concern.

This stereotype is undoubtedly the most prevalent: held not only by ordinary people, it is a favourite of the mass media and is also shared by Italian legislators. All the antimafia laws in Italy were passed following major crimes and massacres: the law of 13 September 1982, which stated for the first time that the mafia is essentially a criminal phenomenon, was passed ten days after the assassination of General Prefect Dalla Chiesa, a figure well known nationally and internationally as a result of his long career and in particular for his efforts to combat terrorist groups; the anti-racketeering law was passed following the assassination in 1991 of the businessman Libero Grassi, who had opposed extortion and who also had a high profile following his appearance on television; the laws introducing strict imprisonment (Article 41bis) and providing rewards for mafia members who cooperated with the authorities (the so-called *pentiti*: 'turncoats') followed the massacres of the magistrates Giovanni

Falcone, Francesca Morvillo and Paolo Borsellino with their protectors in 1992. Some legislative provisions adopted in response to mafia violence have subsequently been watered down or abrogated. For example, limitations were placed on cooperation by the *pentiti*, who have to make their statements no later than six months after they start to cooperate.

The mafia is not a phenomenon that comes and goes, as the 'emergency' stereotype would have it, and it is not merely a murder machine; it is a structural and ongoing phenomenon, and its activities are legion and not limited to the planning and execution of murders.

The stereotype of the mafia as 'anti-state' is based on a reading of the crimes against those working for the institutions as a 'war on the state'. In reality, these are crimes carried out against individuals who are particularly committed to the struggle against the mafia and who are often isolated within the institutions and offices to which they belong. This stereotype argues that the mafia, as a criminal entity, will always be other than the state and its institutions; in other words, their adversary. In fact, the relationship between the mafia and the institutions is much more complex, ranging from aversion to complicity. As we shall see, the link with sectors of the institutions is part of what characterizes the mafia phenomenon (we shall consider below the mafia as a political actor).

### 'Mind Your Own Business'

We have not exhausted the list of stereotypes. One of the most common expressions is: 'The mafiosi simply kill each other. If you mind your own business, they won't bother you.' Here the underlying belief about the mafia is quite clear: mafia crimes are an internal affair, which is considered a natural phenomenon. The resulting moral is equally clear: mind your own business, keep your eyes closed, live quietly, curled up in your own shell, because this is the only way of keeping out of it, certain not to become involved and a target.

For decades the mafia has killed trade unionists, leaders and ordinary activists in the peasant struggles and opposition parties. But none of this should be of concern to ordinary people, who are happy with their own lives and firmly anchored to their own self-interest – or so the stereotype implies. Society is seen as a series of closed boxes, not communicating and having preordained roles that cannot be altered. Why should I care what happens to other people? My family and I keep to ourselves, not looking beyond the ends of our noses or our own concerns.

As a result of the murders of people working for public institutions – magistrates, police officers, journalists and government politicians – this stereotype has begun to lose ground, but it has survived thanks to a twist: it is *their job*, their professional duty, to deal with the mafia, that is what they are paid to do. And – some people think this but do not say it, some think it and say it – almost all those killed were too enthusiastic, they pushed themselves forward, and that is why they became the targets of mafia violence.

In the early 1980s, when the toll of the killings in Palermo amounted to hundreds a year, a lady 'assailed continuously by the deafening sirens of police cars escorting the various judges' wrote a letter published in the *Giornale di Sicilia* on Sunday 14 April 1985, asking for the magistrates most at risk, whom she described as 'those eminent officers', to be transferred to 'villas on the outskirts of the city', in order to preserve 'the peace and quiet of those who live and work' and to ensure 'the safety of all of us who, in the event of an attack' could be 'involved for no reason (as in the Chinnici massacre)'. The lady's moral position was quite evident: the mafia problem is one for the magistrates, a sort of war between gamekeepers and poachers; it has nothing to do with the ordinary 'workers and citizens', who should not therefore suffer the consequences. The removal of the most committed magistrates to the suburbs follows from this logic and this moral position: they, not the mafiosi, are the public danger, better to keep well away from them.

## The Mafia as a Subculture

In academic language, the term 'subculture' does not imply a value judgement: it refers to codes and models of behaviour that are specific to sectors or segments of society and that constitute a deviation from or opposition to the prevailing culture. In everyday language, however, the term does imply a judgement: the behaviour to which it relates is viewed negatively while the dominant behaviour is regarded positively. Using this term about the mafia means considering it as the product of factors that are negative, deviant or minoritarian, whether culturally or socio-economically (backwardness and underdevelopment).

If we use the term subculture in an anthropological sense, we are simply saying that the mafia has its own distinct culture, as do particular social strata and those who belong to specific professions (doctors, teachers, businessmen, etc.). This does not expand our understanding in any way. If we use it in the non-academic sense, the mafia is seen as a deviant, minority phenomenon, which is and can be isolated. This means ignoring fundamental factors which integrate the mafia phenomenon into the body of society as a whole. For this reason I propose the term 'transculture' to describe the behavioural aspects of the mafia. In my view, this term is better able to embrace the complexity of mafia behaviour, which includes aspects ranging from the archaic to the modern or, as is often said, post-modern. I shall come back to this point later.

## 'All Sicilians are Mafiosi...'

This is a clearly racist stereotype, which sees all Sicilians, to a greater or lesser extent, as mafiosi, behaving as mafiosi, having a mafia mentality and so on. This stereotype extends to other regions of southern Italy where phenomena similar to that of the mafia exist, albeit with certain specific features: the 'ndrangheta in Calabria, the camorra in Campania and, in recent years, the Sacra Corona Unita in Apulia.

This stereotype stems from anti-southern prejudice: the Mezzogiorno is seen as a 'paradise inhabited by devils', a land of brigands and criminals, of idlers and parasites, a lead weight chained to the foot of Italy.

There is also a contrasting stereotype, one that makes excuses and offers a defence: so-called *sicilianismo*, the defensive regional pride that sees the mafia as invented by northerners to denigrate Sicily; this interprets the mafia not as a criminal association but simply the result of an inflated ego and overdeveloped sense of honour. This leads to the demand by Sicilians for the state to intervene and provide resources to make up for the 'wrongs' done to Sicily. Similar are certain forms of *meridionalismo* ('patriotic *meridionalismo*') that ignore or underestimate the bad points of the South, which certainly include criminal organizations, and stress primarily or solely the responsibilities of central government and its prejudices against southerners.

The first of these stereotypes extends the presence of the mafia and criminal elements to a whole region and the entire Mezzogiorno, identifying an entire population with the mafias. The second stereotype replies with excuses, or by denying the reality of the mafia and other criminal phenomena. Both stereotypes are equally without foundation. The mafia and other forms of organized crime certainly exist, but the whole of Sicily is not mafia, nor is the entire Mezzogiorno criminal: this is clearly demonstrated by the substantial efforts made to combat the mafia, particularly in Sicily. And the stereotype of excuses or denial is generated and fostered by the mafia itself and other similar organizations, nurturing pro-mafia and pro-criminal ideologies in order to minimize or camouflage criminal activities and pursue the interests of one part of the population by presenting them as the interests of all. I shall return to this point again, with particular reference to the events (the trial resulting from the Notarbartolo murder) that gave rise to *sicilianismo*.

## 'The Mafia is Everywhere', or 'Everything is Mafia'

It is often said that the mafia exists throughout the world, and equally frequently the term 'mafia' is employed as a generic description of criminal activity, corruption, arrogance, aggression, abuse of power, favouritism and bad behaviour, ranging from bullying in schools to the use of *raccomandazioni* (the practice of securing jobs for relatives or friends by recommending them to potential employers or appointing authorities).

The effect, whether intentional or not, is a tendency to obscure or underestimate the presence of the mafia in Sicily by reducing it to a sort of global or cosmic mafia, vague, unknowable and impossible to get to grips with. Look elsewhere, not here, is the watchword of this viewpoint, while historical reality and the present day clearly show that the mafia is both *here* and *elsewhere*, and before it took root elsewhere it grew and developed here. The indiscriminate use of the word 'mafia' for virtually anything bad creates the impression that the mafia is the ultimate evil, for which there is no remedy other than some improbable cosmic regeneration.

## Mafia as an 'Octopus'

The most recent media version of this stereotype is *La Piovra*, a famous television series that has achieved higher foreign sales than any other

Italian production. The various episodes show omnipresent and omnipotent mafiosi in conflict with a positive hero who is a police chief or magistrate. The clash between lawlessness and the law is in reality a clash between two forms of violence: the illegal violence of the mafia and the legal violence of the police, a media portrayal that frequently boosts the stereotype of the 'godfather' as a charismatic personality who is more attractive than the positive hero. Following the recent TV series *Il capo dei capi* (*The Boss of Bosses*) I heard teachers observing that children identified more strongly with the mafia boss than with the hero fighting against the mafia.

The mafia is said now to be active throughout the world; in fact, for some time there have been various groups around the globe that resemble the Sicilian mafia model in the complexity of their activities and relationships. But there is no single mafia or supermafia, as certain journalists like to argue. Fighting these groups needs not a single hero but a concerted collective effort.

## 'There Used to be the Mafia, Now There're Only Criminals'

One stereotype which concerns in particular the mafia's historical development argues that in the past it was possible to speak of the mafia as a more or less organized body of men who had a sense of honour, followed certain rules – for example, no killing of women and children – and administered a sort of people's justice when official justice was absent or perverted, but at some point it changed into mere criminality. This stereotype promotes the idea that, once upon a time, the mafia served a useful purpose, or was at least reassuring. It goes on to argue that more recently this mafia has ceased to exist and there are now only common criminals who kill, threaten, extort and undertake a variety of illegal acts, knowing no rules and possessing no sense of honour. In reality, the mafia has been a criminal association since it began: it has always operated within a system of relationships and has developed by adapting itself to its context and changes therein, often showing great flexibility alongside a formal rigidity that is more talked about than practised. We shall see that the history of the mafia, as of all long-term phenomena, is a mixture of continuity and innovation.

It is well known that mafiosi call themselves 'men of honour', suggesting that their behaviour is underpinned by a set of values such as sincerity, courage and the family, and that respect for these traditional values is the reason for the prestige they enjoy in the society where they operate. In reality the fundamental 'value' of mafia behaviour is the capacity for violence, and at the centre of the oath taken when subscribing to the mafia association there is, as we shall see, the acceptance of violence as a punishment for betraying the pact with the group.

## The Stereotype about Origins

The origins of the mafia, and more generally the events leading to the creation of the oldest and most long-lasting forms of organized crime, are sometimes ascribed to the vacuum left by the state and the public authorities, to the inadequacies and failings of the market, and to the shortage of legal opportunities. This portrays the mafia as an archaic and feudal hangover, suggesting that it survives because there is still work to be done on modernization, because the state is absent or too weak, and because the market is not following the rules of mature capitalism. But this stereotype avoids any consideration of how the state and the market actually operate, of how the mafia has developed historically and is still evolving – both in outlying or underdeveloped areas and in central or developed areas, in the countryside as much as in the cities. Indeed, the mafia has not only been able to survive in its original areas of operation, but has also put down roots in situations different from those in which it emerged and has integrated itself into the dominant social and political groups. An explanation of these processes requires ideas that match up to all the complexities and contradictions inherent in the actual situation rather than relying on less effective models.

As we shall see, the history of the mafia in Sicily shows that it took root and grew in situations characterized by a whole network of relationships underpinning production and the ongoing pattern of domination and subservience rather than just by a vacuum and shortages.

## Paradigms: A Criminal Association of a Mafia Type

In 1982, ten days after the killing of General Prefect Dalla Chiesa, his wife Emanuela Setti Carraro and the officer Domenico Russo on 3 September, the 'antimafia law', combining the drafts tabled by Pio La Torre, communist MP, and Virginio Rognoni, Minister of the Interior, was approved. Law No. 646 of 13 September 1982 added to the Penal Code Article 416bis which for the first time defined mafia-type association:

> An association is of a mafia type when those taking part in it use both the power to intimidate that derives from the association itself, and the resulting conditions of subjection and secrecy, in order to commit crimes or to acquire, directly or indirectly, the management or any other form of control over economic activities, concessions, authorizations, contracts and public services so as to secure unjustified profits or advantages for themselves or for others.

Simple criminal association as defined by Article 416 of the Penal Code requires three conditions to be met: an associative bond, an organizational structure and a criminal plan. A mafia-type association includes specific additional characteristics, namely: the intimidatory nature of the association; and the subjugation and *omertà* (law of silence) that that intimidation generates. A mafia organization imposes a tacit obligation of obedience on its members and demands silence, i.e. a refusal by both its members and those outside to cooperate with justice, so that there is a sort of collective subjugation. Failure to comply with these obligations results in threats and the imposition of punishments that often include death (for the mafia, murder is not a crime but a penalty, a punishment for violating a rule of the mafia code).

The antimafia law defines the purposes of a mafia association as: (1) carrying out typical crimes, such as extortion and the related crimes of damage, kidnapping, murder and massacres; (2) acquiring management and control over economic activities – a legitimate goal made illegitimate by the methods: threats, intimidation, physical violence and the other means habitually used by mafia-type organizations; (3) securing unjustified profits or advantages: a very broad formula that seeks to cover the gaps left by the first two purposes.

The second and third purposes of a mafia association contain elements of the paradigm that regards the mafia as an enterprise, i.e. an organization engaged in economic activities for profit.

For the first time, the antimafia law provided for the sequestration and confiscation of goods obtained as a result of illegal activities. Sequestration is a temporary measure while confiscation is permanent.

The provisions of the 1982 law were subsequently updated by Law No. 109 of 7 March 1996, which streamlined the procedure and provided for confiscated goods to be used for social purposes: municipalities, charitable bodies, voluntary organizations, social cooperatives, therapeutic communities and centres for the rehabilitation of drug addicts.

## The Mafia-as-Business and the Mafia Enterprise

The business paradigm stresses the economic role of the mafia association; within it we can identify two approaches: the mafia-as-business and the mafia enterprise.

The mafia is a business in the sense that mafia activity may be regarded as a rational combination of means and ends used for the purpose of securing wealth. For example, trafficking in drugs and other illegal goods is undertaken precisely to accumulate capital and make profits by controlling production and marketing and stimulating demand.

Economic activities that are strictly speaking legal become mafia enterprises when one of the following elements is present: the person heading the enterprise, whether nominally or in practice and even if covertly, has been condemned or indicted for mafia activities; the capital used has been obtained illegally; competition uses illegal means, such as violence or threats.

## A Preliminary to the Paradigm: The Mafia Mentality

For a number of years now, psychoanalysts and psychologists have been looking at the mafia phenomenon and have come up with concepts such as the 'mafia psyche' and the 'mafia mentality'. These cover psychological and anthropological aspects that are no doubt relevant, but these experts regard them as the result of unconscious, or pre-reflective, thought, widespread throughout the population of Sicily and transmitted by the members of the same family. This both generalizes the mafia phenomenon and sees it as deriving from unconscious impulses. As we shall see, even cultural (or transcultural) features of the mafia are the product of history, not an unconscious predisposition. But the idea of the 'mafia psyche' threatens to cast something that is recent in its present constitution, something against which struggles have been and can still be waged, as a perpetual and basically unchangeable phenomenon. These academic theories are useful, but their limitations mean that they may be regarded as a sort of pre-paradigm: they are studies that require substantial further work and an appropriate presentation of the problems.

## Demystifying the Stereotypes and Completing the Paradigms

Any useful study of the mafia must seek to overturn accepted ideas if these prove misleading, like the stereotypes, or require further work, even if they contain partial truths, as in the case of the paradigms.

As I have noted, demystifying the stereotypes is fairly simple: it is not difficult to show that the mafia does not go on holiday between one murder and the next, that it is not merely a murder factory but engages in a variety of activities, and that it is a constant, permanent presence, even when it does not occupy centre stage in the news. It can similarly be shown that the mafia's relationship with politics and institutions is not always one of opposition, but has been and frequently remains one of interaction; that the mafia is not a private organization but concerns everybody; that it is not a marginal subculture but a body that weighs heavily on life and social relationships; that not all Sicilians are mafiosi; that the mafia's activities on the international stage have not led it to abandon its roots; and that there is no 'octopus' extending its tentacles worldwide but a number of different groups operating in many countries.

The problem is that the most pervasive stereotypes do not exist only in the minds of ordinary people; they are constantly renewed and reinforced by the media and, as already noted, also underpin legislative measures. As we shall see, this is true of the concept of the 'mafia bourgeoisie', originally regarded as the fruit of extremist views and now presented either as mass criminalization or a sample of isolated cases. The work of demystification is usually undertaken by individuals or groups who are marginal and discriminated against.

The paradigms of the mafia as a typical association and of the mafia-as-business cover two basic aspects of the mafia, just as the study of cultural aspects provides considerable assistance in understanding what the mafia is. But these aspects (organization and the economic and psychological profiles) do not fully explain all the complexity of the mafia and its various strands. The paradigms therefore need to be expanded to take account of other factors that they either ignore or regard as of secondary and marginal importance.

## The Paradigm of Complexity:
## Criminal Association and the System of Relationships

To generate a useful picture of the mafia, I have produced what I call a 'paradigm of complexity' – the mafia is seen as a polymorphic organization, the result of a number of interrelated aspects: crime, accumulation of wealth, power, the cultural code and consensus. The suggested definition is:

> The mafia is a complex of criminal organizations, the most important of which is Cosa Nostra, although this is not the only one. These operate within a system of relationships, undertake violent and illegal activities, as well as some which are formally legal, for the purpose of enrichment and the acquisition and management of positions of power, follow a cultural code and enjoy a degree of social consensus.

### The Cosa Nostra Association

The starting point is the organization, the associative structure, as defined by the antimafia law. The organization is secret, at least in principle (in fact, it has never been hidden and we know quite a lot about it), and admission to it is by means of an oath-taking ceremony. It was only following the revelations of Tommaso Buscetta in the 1980s that the older and more powerful mafia organization began to be known as Cosa Nostra; in the United States, the term Cosa Nostra appeared in the early 1960s with the statements by the mafioso Joe Valachi, who had cooperated with the McClellan Committee (1963). In Sicily, there are other minor groups: the Stidda (Star) in the provinces of Caltanissetta and Agrigento, the non-Cosa Nostra clans in the Catania area, operating alongside, and sometimes in conflict with, Cosa Nostra.

Cosa Nostra has a complex organizational structure: at the bottom are the families, not necessarily blood-related: family ties are of fundamental importance for the mafia, as for all social groups, but links go beyond blood ties and leadership is not hereditary, even if there are often actual dynasties.

The mafia families have a varying number of 'soldiers', the self-styled 'men of honour', organized in tens, and a boss, an underboss and a *consigliere* (adviser); three or more close families form a *mandamento* (precinct) with its own boss. Representatives of the *mandamenti*, not necessarily the heads of the families, form the *commissione provinciale* (provincial commission) or *cupola* (dome). The supreme leader (the boss of bosses) is the head of the Palermo provincial commission. Cosa Nostra has long been established in the four provinces of western Sicily (Trapani, Palermo, Caltanissetta, Agrigento); more recently it has spread into eastern Sicily.

Within Cosa Nostra, appointment to positions of responsibility is by election, or at least those mafiosi who cooperate with the authorities say that was so until the arrival of the Corleonesi, the mafiosi from Corleone, in the province of Palermo, who secured internal positions of power through the physical elimination of their opponents and the construction of alliances. The Corleonesi imposed a sort of dictatorship, killing several members of the committee and installing first Totò Riina and then Bernardo Provenzano as leader.

In more recent years, following the arrest and conviction of leaders and ordinary members, a more moderate line (the so-called *mafia sommersa*: 'submerged mafia') has gained the upper hand in Cosa Nostra. This marked a departure from high-profile crime and the setting up of a collective leadership.

Members come from various social strata, with a large number of professional people (particularly doctors and lawyers), but the leaders almost always come from the lower strata. The two most famous *capimafia* in recent decades, Totò Riina and Bernardo Provenzano, were from peasant families and completed only the early stages of elementary school. This inevitably raises the question of how men with no educational qualifications and experience limited to the area around Corleone and Palermo achieved their positions in a variety of sectors, from public works to health, without links to professionals and others able to map out and implement the complex strategies rightly attributed to the mafia, in both the recent and more distant past.

The final report of the parliamentary Antimafia Commission in February 2008 put the number of members of Cosa Nostra in the provinces of Palermo, Agrigento and Trapani at about 4,500. With the members of the other provinces the total is over 6,000.

## Women and the Mafia

The mafia organization formally admits only one sex (men) but in fact women have played and still play a part, at least in practice. In any case, male dominance is not specific to the mafia, it merely reflects the attitudes of the society in which it exists (until only a few years ago, women were excluded from certain professions and still may not become priests in the Catholic Church). Since the mafia has no ideology and its continuing existence in different situations may be explained by its combination of rigidity of form and flexibility in practice, it is not surprising if once again it adapts to a society in which women are playing an increasingly important role. Recently a female member of a mafia family in Partinico, in the province of Palermo, who cooperated with the authorities after her arrest, stated that she been appointed as head of a *mandamento*.

## The Oath

Admission to Cosa Nostra entails an initiation ceremony comprising the introduction of the applicant by a member of the association, unveiling of the existence of the association and disclosure of its rules, the choice of a godfather, the cutting of a finger (the *punciuta*) so that a few drops of blood fall and the uttering of the words of the oath while a holy picture is burned between the prospective member's hands.

This initiation ceremony has remained basically unchanged over time, with some unimportant modifications. At times the cut has been made in the right thumb, or the index or middle fingers of one hand, usually the trigger finger. The blood-oath has some variants, but the words always reiterate the irrevocable nature of the bond it forms. One example is the oath sworn by the new members of the Favara (Agrigento) Fratellanza (Brotherhood) in 1884:

> I swear on my honour to be faithful to the brotherhood, as the brotherhood is faithful to me, and as this picture and these few drops of my blood burn, so shall I shed all my blood for the

brotherhood, and as these ashes and this blood cannot return again to their former state, neither can I leave the brotherhood.

This is the oath taken by the doctor Melchiorre Allegra in 1916: 'I swear to be faithful to my brothers, never to betray them and always to help them, and if I do not, may I burn and be lost, as this picture turns to ashes and is lost.' In 1948 Tommaso Buscetta swore: 'May my flesh burn like this picture if I do not remain faithful to the oath.' A different formula was used around 1980 and 1981 in the ceremony when Salvatore Palazzolo entered the Cinisi (Palermo) family headed by Gaetano Badalamenti: 'As paper I burn you, as an image I adore you and I swear to be faithful to this oath and never to betray it, if necessary shedding my blood for my brothers.'

The initiation ceremony is designed to employ the symbolism of baptism, with explicit reference to Catholicism and the use of a holy picture sprinkled with the applicant's blood and then burned between his hands. This is a sort of ritual rebirth, giving the new member the status of a 'man of honour', which will remain throughout his life (in practice, there have been cases of expulsion, the most famous being that of Gaetano Badalamenti) and establishing a new family relationship between the members. As we have seen, the words of the oath refer specifically to the punishment that awaits anyone who betrays the alliance: the member knows that in such circumstances he will be condemned to death. This acceptance of violence, to be perpetrated (the trigger finger is cut) and suffered, has been an essential part of becoming a member of the mafia up to the present day.

## The Stidda and the Catania Clans

During the 1980s, the provinces of Agrigento, Caltanissetta and Enna saw the rise of a new mafia-type criminal organization, the Stidda, formed by refugees from Cosa Nostra and others who, in the late 1980s and early 1990s, had fought with Cosa Nostra in bloody clashes for territorial supremacy. In subsequent years, Stidda and Cosa Nostra managed to coexist and cooperated on various activities, ranging from extortion to drug trafficking, while the Stidda's networks spread throughout Italy and the rest of Europe.

In Catania, there are various clans operating both inside and outside Cosa Nostra. The most famous is the Santapaola family, at the head of Cosa Nostra, which split into two branches following the arrest of the *capomafia*. Other groups, including the Cursoti (inhabitants of a lower-class area) and the Carcagnusi (very poor people), names that clearly reveal their plebeian origins, operate outside Cosa Nostra and are made up of criminals who over time have assumed the characteristics of mafiosi by controlling territory, practising extortion and trafficking in drugs. During the 1980s, internal disputes within Cosa Nostra and among the various groups resulted in a series of murders. Almost all the groups succeeded in building a network that ranged from relationships with highly placed individuals, through the infiltration of the public administration, the subversion of tendering procedures and the involvement of politicians, to marginal sections of the population in town centres and more or less run-down suburbs, often organized into sports fan clubs.

## The Relationships System:
## The Social Bloc and the Mafia Bourgeoisie

The system of relationships that is the real driving force behind mafia-type criminal groups gives rise to what can only be described as a real social bloc, cutting across society from the lowest to the highest strata. Usually the lower strata provide the criminal manpower, who carry out activities ranging from extortion to drug trafficking in exchange for a share of the profits, the greater part of which remains in the hands of the members, and especially the leaders. It is estimated that this social bloc comprises hundreds of thousands of people.

The hierarchy includes individuals operating both outside the law (the *capimafia*) and within it; together they form the mafia bourgeoisie. Its members are professional people: surveyors, architects and engineers, who undertake activities connected with building; lawyers, notaries and even magistrates, who are concerned with aspects relating to the law; bankers, financial consultants and computer experts, who are engaged in recycling dirty money; doctors, who are particularly well represented even among the members because of the extensive networks their profession enjoys and the enormous range of interests concerned with public and private health; teachers, particularly in regional and private schools; religious men, such as Father Coppola, who was a member of

# Mafia and the relationships system

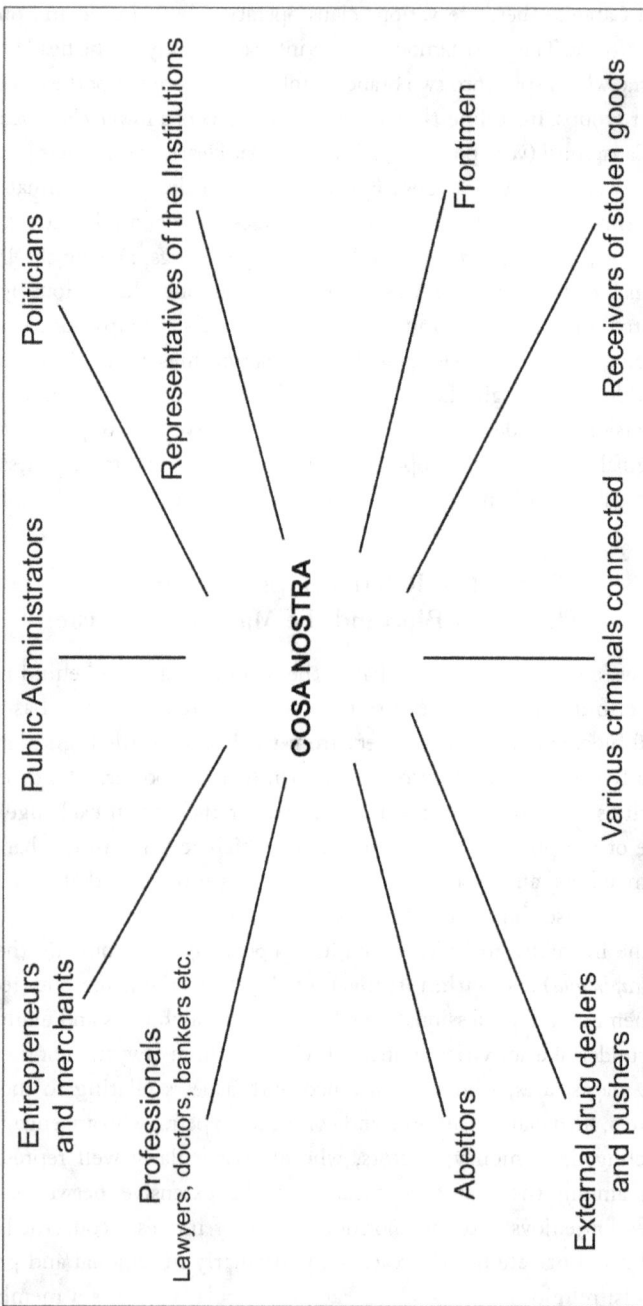

Politicians

Representatives of the Institutions

Frontmen

Receivers of stolen goods

Public Administrators

**COSA NOSTRA**

Various criminals connected

Entrepreneurs
and merchants

Professionals
Lawyers, doctors, bankers etc.

Abettors

External drug dealers
and pushers

**Social block and mafia bourgeoisie - Underworld and Upperworld**

Cosa Nostra, and those attending the *capimafia* while they were on the run; retailers and businessmen engaged in various areas of activity, from supermarkets to construction; public administrators, who ensure the satisfactory resolution of matters of concern to the mafiosi and their allies; politicians and representatives of the institutions in a relationship with the mafia, which might entail anything from the supply of votes in exchange for the granting of contracts and favours to the adoption of laws and regulations favourable to mafia interests.

The size of the mafia bourgeoisie may be put at several tens of thousands of people.

Freemasonry plays an important part in the system of relationships, with many *capimafia* being members of Masonic lodges. Where, for example in the Trapani area, the Masonic lodges exercise real, deep-seated and substantial power, the mafiosi make them their allies by joining them or by creating relationships of various kinds. In other, more frequent, instances, the mafia takes on the guise of Freemasonry in order to give itself an acceptable appearance on the social stage.

## How the Mafia Acts

In common parlance, the activities of the mafiosi and their relationship with their society, from economics to politics, are considered in terms of the separation and the connection, whether clear or opaque, between two different worlds. The term most used is, in fact, 'infiltration'. Instead of thinking in terms of separation and infiltration, I believe that a view based on unity and distinction, so combining an analysis of the background with the identification of specific characteristics, would be closer to reality.

This can be done if we avoid two temptations: generalization – everything is mafia: capitalism, the economy, the state, politics, all is mafia – and reductionism, which confines the mafia to a peripheral and marginal role. We must remember that the mafia has its own characteristics, which derive in particular from the private use of violence, but it would be an unfathomable mystery if we merely described its practice without tackling the question of how it forms part of society, the historical process and current reality. Hence, when we study mafia violence, the mafia economy, mafia political action and the other aspects of the mafia, we need to look both at the specific data and at the dynamics governing its interaction with its surroundings.

## Mafia Violence

The main characteristic of the mafia is its private use of violence and its non-recognition of the State's monopoly on the use of force.[3] Violence underlies both the struggle for internal command and competition with the outside world, as well as the imposition of the mafia's domination of society, daily life and economic and political choices.

Violence is used to select leaders and renew the command structure and, whether practised or threatened, to bring to heel disobedient outside businessmen and to assert the mafia's own interests at a political and institutional level. This explains the use of murder and massacres during the peasant struggles and, more recently, when there was a need to prevent political and institutional choices that could run counter to or restrict the interests of the mafiosi and of those individuals with connections to them.

For a long time the use of violence has been legitimized by the lack of punishment; it is only in recent years that the use of violence against individuals active in politics and the institutions (police officers, magistrates, politicians in government) has evoked a reaction from the authorities, although always in the context of an emergency – that is, in response to mafia violence boiling over. The cases we have already noted are typical: the assassination of Dalla Chiesa and the massacres that resulted in the deaths of Falcone and Borsellino.

Mafia violence is an *instrument*; that is, it is a means of achieving the objectives essential to mafia activity and it forms part of a view that sees as legitimate the execution of one's own justice without recourse to the state.

Examination of the most serious form of mafia violence, murder, reveals the following: murder by the mafia is in the main planned (*omicidio-progetto*) rather than the fruit of an uncontrolled blood-lust and a marginal subculture. It is motivated by strategic reasons since it: (1) is the way of resolving competition between mafia organizations or individual mafiosi that cannot be settled by other means; (2) is the main instrument, or one of the chief instruments, for resolving struggles for hegemony, both internal and external; (3) smooths the way for the control of activities managed by mafia organizations, whether legal or illegal; (4) is a way of intervening in and altering the social, political and institutional set-up.

So far, violence has been an essential attribute of the mafioso and one of the main things he must learn; skill in the use of violent means is a prerequisite for a career as a criminal. It is not only followers who are engaged in killing; the leaders, too, whether the so-called 'moderates' or the Corleonesi, kill viciously and in cold blood.

Stefano Bontate, the heir to a mafia dynasty, was regarded as a 'moderate' but there is written evidence that he strangled people with his own hands; the ferocity of the Corleonesi, from Luciano Liggio to Totò Riina and Bernardo Provenzano, is well documented by reports and by television screenplays, which usually portray these individuals as heroes of evil, more interesting and attractive than their opponents.

The use and culture of violence mean that murder is not regarded as a crime to be punished but rather as a death penalty to be enforced, as sanctioned by the words of the oath. It is carried out by a member who is judged and assessed for his criminal abilities – just as military orders have to be obeyed without question.

This is the basis for the mafia's double view of the state. On the one hand, it is *outside* and *against* the state, since it has its own penal code and its own machinery for administering justice, that is, an apparatus for imposing penalties on those who transgress; on the other hand, it is *within* and *alongside* the state, as a result of a series of activities, ranging from concessions to contracts, which require the use of and interaction with institutions.

Mafia violence takes the form of programmed violence, which in practice has a variety of forms. We can distinguish the following types, which may be further divided into subtypes: *internal violence*, perpetrated within the world of the mafia in the course of conflicts concerning the whole organization or individual groups; violence designed to *administer crime*, against individuals in the criminal world dependent on the mafia organization, or like the *transverse vendetta*, against the relatives or persons in some way linked to mafiosi with whom it is in armed conflict.

*External violence*, against the world outside that of the mafia, may be divided into *political-mafia violence* when it is aimed at leading politicians, representatives of institutions or those engaged in attempting to suppress it; *economic-mafia violence*, directed at businessmen and economic operators in competition or conflict with activities managed directly or indirectly by the mafia; and *exemplary violence*, by which the mafia imposes its domination by attacking those whose behaviour is seen as insubordinate or lacking in respect for its power.

Both internal and external crimes seek to assert mafia dominance; they usually achieve their aims and are legitimated by the absence of punishment. None, or virtually none, of the crimes perpetrated against those active in and leading the peasant struggles or against opposition politicians have been punished, since they served to defend and perpetuate a system of power. More recently, crimes against members of the institutions (politicians, magistrates, law and order officers) have had a boomerang effect and triggered reactions resulting in legislation and trials which have imposed heavy sentences on mafiosi at all levels. Once again, the responsibility of instigators who might be outside the mafia but are linked with it has remained unclear. This scenario has been repeated, to take only the postwar period, from the Portella della Ginestra massacre to those in Capaci, Via D'Amelio, Florence and Milan. Crimes and massacres are the most obvious manifestations of political-mafia violence and are one of the most striking pieces of evidence demonstrating that the mafia is a political actor, in that the use of violence is designed to have a substantial influence on the social and political life of the community.

## The Mafia Economy: Parasite and 'Producer'

The mafia's activities may be criminal and illegal (murder, extortion, trafficking of prohibited goods and so on) or legal (the management of businesses, firms and financial companies). It takes its cut of economic activities by demanding *pizzo* ('protection money') and engaging in usury, but it also manages firms that have been established legitimately, either in its own name or through frontmen.[4] From a purely economic point of view, even the most reprehensible activities, such as the production and marketing of narcotics, may be considered productive, if by production we mean, in the broad sense, any process that increases the assets of the producing individual (i.e. enriches him), or, in a narrower sense, turns the factors of production into a product (i.e. creates new economic goods that can be traded on the market, irrespective of whether or not they are legal).

Hence the mafia economy acts as both a predatory parasite, as in the classic case of extortion, and a 'producer', particularly of goods and services which are strictly speaking illegal but which are in great demand by consumers on the local, national and international markets.

We rightly focus on the parasitical and predatory nature of the mafia, but it should not be forgotten that various strata of the population, and indeed whole countries, base their economies on illegal production and trade. Even though the masses of capital accumulated in this way are often overestimated, the sums involved are substantial, with predictable effects on the financial system through the recycling of dirty capital, and on the whole economic system through the investment of a large part of this capital in the legal economy.

Recent research has attempted to calculate the 'costs of illegality'. Crime boosts expenditure on the forces of law and order and on justice, depletes resources and discourages investment. It has been argued that without the presence of criminal organizations the pace of development in Sicily and the regions of southern Italy would be the same as in the rest of the country. For example CENSIS (Centro Studi Investimenti Sociali, the Centre for the Study of Social Investments) estimates that criminal organizations absorb about €7.5 billion per year and, by depressing the GDP of the southern regions by 2.5 per cent, account for the gap between the Mezzogiorno and the rest of the country.[5]

If the mafia, or the mafias, were merely parasitic and predatory, if they were only a heavy and detestable burden on the communities in which they operate, it would be easier to isolate and defeat them, despite the fear created by their acts of intimidation and their presence; things become much more complicated when we think of the conveniences offered by illegality in societies where the legal economy is weak and wealth is concentrated in only a few hands. The mafias operate with two hands: with one they take and impoverish, with the other they produce and spread around some of their income, even though their revenues end up mainly in the pockets of the leaders and their allies. This is excellent business for the highest social strata, provides channels of social mobility and guarantees a survival income for the poorest strata. The result is a social mix resembling transclassism, but decidedly favouring the privileged and dominant strata.

## The Problem of Development

Economists have raised the problem of whether the mafia generates development or is an obstacle to it. A correct response to this question must start from an appropriate definition of the concept of development. If development means solely or mainly an increase in GDP, that is an increase in productive activities, with no account of *what* is produced and *how* it is produced (even goods dangerous to health or produced in conditions of complete exploitation result in growth, in the sense of increased GDP); if what is meant is consumption by a privileged sector of the population, while the most basic needs of the poorest (from work to health and from housing to education) remain unsatisfied; if 'growth' is the only model on offer for countries defined as 'developing', while in fact they are condemned to underdevelopment by market forces, these ideas can have many points in common with the illegal accumulation of wealth. These include: individual success using any means, competitiveness at any price, a tendency to bend standards and break rules, or to distort the rule-making process in order to impose regulations to protect the interests of a few, and seeking the avoidance of punishment.

If, however, we take development to mean an improvement in the overall living conditions of the members of a community, as accepted for a number of years now by international bodies such as UNDP (United Nations Development Programme), which in its 1996 Human Development Report introduced a Human Development Index (HDI) based on the three criteria of a long and healthy life, literacy and an income that provides a certain standard of living, it is clear that mafia activities run counter to this concept. They inculcate a get-rich-quick culture, which despises work and relies on abuse and domination by violence, social inequality and blind obedience to the orders of the leaders and the interests of the criminal organization. This is quite the opposite of a society whose citizens live together in conditions ensuring that they can all develop their potential harmoniously.

Recently, the term 'development' itself, along with some associated adjectives (the most common is 'sustainable', referring to the precarious condition of the planet that is overexploited to an extent that threatens the very survival of the species to which it is home), has been subjected to radical criticism with talk of 'post-development' and 'negative growth', suggesting the prospect of a society that sets limits to production and consumption.[6] This analysis makes the criminal economy the most conspicuous expression of a financial system based on the waste of resources, which is leading to global catastrophe.

## The Mafia as a Political Actor

There is a lot of talk of the relationship between mafia and politics. It is documented in books that reconstruct the links between mafia leaders and politicians, and there is a report by the parliamentary Antimafia Commission, approved by a large majority in 1993, but there has been no satisfactory scientific research into this link, which must be regarded as fundamental to the mafia phenomenon, from its origins to the present day.[7] The mafia is a political actor in two ways:

1.  As a criminal association, it is an organization exercising power and a political organization as defined by the German academic Max Weber, since it possesses the basic characteristics of (a) a series of rules (order), (b) a territorial dimension, (c) physical force, (d) an administrative staff able to ensure compliance with the rules and exercise physical force.

2.  The mafia, as a criminal association and with the social bloc of which it forms part, constitutes a broader power system and is a source generating politics in the fullest sense, in that it determines or helps determine decisions and choices on the management of power and the distribution of resources.

Weber, one of the fathers of sociology, in his first volume of his work, *Economy and Society*, concerned with *The General Theory of Sociological Categories*, defines a political organization as follows: 'A "ruling organization" will be called "political" insofar as its existence and order is continuously safeguarded within a given territorial area by the threat and application of physical force on the part of its administrative staff.'[8]

The mafia organization has all these characteristics. It exercises what I call *signoria territoriale* (territorial dominance), a dictatorial type of domination that extends, or seeks to, to all activities taking place in a particular area, from economic to social and the private life of individuals, such as marriage and the choice of relationships and friends. This entails a detailed control of resources, either by taking them over, by co-managing their use, or in other ways that may be less direct but are nevertheless effective and permanent. This dominance is the basis for its broader political role, exercised directly and through the system of relationships, via interaction with the administrative machinery and the centres of decision-making.

On the basis of these general indications, we may talk about how the 'mafia generates politics'. It does so, first, through the political use of violence. As we have seen, the so-called political mafia crimes, the massacres, from Portella della Ginestra to Capaci and Via D'Amelio, constitute an intervention on the political scene; they may be the result of a convergence of interests with others and they involve a number of different people in their planning and implementation. Then there is its contribution to the formation of institutionalized representation (the collection and control of votes, direct or indirect participation in electoral campaigns). Finally, there is the mafia's influence over government institutions. This influence takes various forms: exchanges of favours between mafiosi and politicians or administrators; infiltration of institutions by the mafia and even complete control over them. The result can be regarded as a formal or informal 'criminocracy'.

We may also speak of the 'politics generating mafia', in the sense that politics generates the mafia by helping it develop through a guarantee of freedom from punishment and by consenting to activity linked to institutions and the expenditure of public money or the institutionalization of mafia methods (whether or not partially the responsibility of the mafia). These include the use of crime and massacres when the ebb and flow of politics puts certain power centres in danger. Examples include the terrorist-type crimes and massacres that have led to slaughter in Italy but have remained virtually unpunished (to list but a few, those in Piazza Fontana in Milan, Brescia, and Bologna railway station).

The social sciences stress that the monopoly of the legitimate use of force is an attribute which the state cannot renounce. However, the historical experience of Italy demonstrates that, while the state has always retained its formal monopoly on force, this has been undermined in the legal field as elsewhere. This is demonstrated by the considerable delay in defining mafia association as criminal, something for which penalties were not introduced until the September 1982 law.

This has led to the identification of two dichotomies, applying to both the mafia and the state. Unlike normal criminal activity, the mafia does not defy the law but *denies* the law: we have seen that it is outside and against the state, because it does not recognize the state monopoly of force and regards the use of murder as its own form of justice; but as regards its activities relating to the use of public money and its active participation in public life, it is inside and within the state.

Just as the mafia has a dual nature, so does the state because of its partial renunciation of its monopoly of force and its delegation in practice to the mafia of law-enforcement duties. This is manifested by the state's failure to punish criminal behaviour that protects the power of the ruling classes, whenever intervention by the state was either impossible, because it would have been flagrantly illegal, or would not have been as swift and brutal as mafia action.

These points recall reflections on the 'dual state' resulting from the dynamics of the relationship between national and international politics in the postwar period, which instilled in leaders a dual loyalty: towards their own country and towards the international alliances created following the division of the world into two blocs. This analytical hypothesis should be used with caution but may help us to understand the violent and unpunished massacres that have taken place in Italy.[9]

## The So-Called 'Third Level'

In recent years the expression 'third level' has often been used to describe the relationship between the mafia and politics. It was used by the magistrates Giovanni Falcone and Giuliano Turone in a report on mafia crimes presented in June 1982 to a seminar of the Consiglio superiore della magistratura (Higher Council of the Magistracy).[10]

In their view, first-level crimes are mafia criminal activities that directly generate movements of money; second-level crimes are those related to the mafia search for profit and struggles between groups; and third-level crimes are those that seek to protect the mafia system, such as the murder of a politician or of a representative of institutions whose actions are regarded as dangerous.

As a result of media influence, the mafia organization has been seen as a three-storey building: on the ground floor are those who commit crimes, on the next one up those who give the orders, and at the top a sort of overarching political and financial group that dictates the general strategies, beginning with the major crimes.

Falcone always disputed this representation, citing criticisms and personal attacks that often verged on denigration, as if rejection of this view was equivalent to denying the existence of a relationship between the mafia and politics and hindering inquiries into this relationship.[11] In fact, Falcone was well aware of the implications of such a relationship. For example, the 1985 judgement decree of the Ufficio Istruzione (Investigating Office) for the *maxiprocesso* (maxi-trial), which was largely the result of his work, spoke of 'secret and worrying links' going beyond the proximity referred to in the prosecutor's report. Furthermore, Falcone made a decisive contribution to drawing up the legal definition of *concorso esterno* (complicity with the mafia), which seeks to target outside relationships – that is, the system of relationships that is the mafia's real strength.

The report in preparation for the *maxiprocesso* – which also referred to 'organic inter-penetration', with reference to documented cases such as those of the former mayor of Palermo Vito Ciancimino and the tax collectors Salvo – the examining order and the sentences handed down in the *maxiprocesso*, most of which were confirmed on appeal and then by the Court of Cassation, established some firm reference points. The verdict provided a summary profile of the institutional nature of Cosa Nostra as being simultaneously: *contropotere,* an alternative ruling authority because of its criminal nature; an authority rooted in its social background and able to adapt as conditions change over time; a legal order sharing the essential attributes of the state: a territory, a code of rules, a membership and a body of people who adjust to it; a pressure group (lobby) that plans and carries out projects to extend its territory and strengthen its power at national and international level.

Bearing in mind the limitations on and specific nature of a legal instrument, this appears to be a fairly accurate description of the various links between individuals engaged in politics and the mafia.

It seemed that the first steps had been taken on a new road. However, work through the courts virtually had to stop when the spotlight turned on the relationship between the mafia and politics, and almost all reactions provoked by proceedings against those in the forefront of political life, such as the many-time prime minister Giulio Andreotti, concentrated on attacking the magistrates engaged in those inquiries, who were accused of undue interference in political life.

Even information about the outcome of the Andreotti trial was distorted: the former prime minister and life senator was acquitted at his first trial, but found guilty on appeal of criminal association in the period prior to 1980, a crime that was time-barred, although he was acquitted as regards the subsequent period. That judgement was confirmed by the Court of Cassation. The press reported only the acquittal and ignored the seriously damaging findings of the judgement, at least with regard to a certain period: meetings with mafia leaders and other relationships that were established by the courts. The aim was to restrict the charge of criminal activity to the period before 1980, that is before approval of the antimafia law that criminalized mafia-type association, whereas before that law came into force the offence was only simple association. This may be regarded as a very serious transgression for a politician who played a leading role in Italian political life.

In fact, the relations between Andreotti and a person such as Salvo Lima – for many years mayor of Palermo, then a member of the Italian Parliament and subsequently of the European Parliament – whose links with mafiosi are documented in the proceedings of the parliamentary Antimafia Commission even though he was not found guilty by a court and who was killed on 12 March 1992, lasted until his death. Even if these are not regarded as matters of criminal concern, they have an ethical and political significance.

This is how in recent years a situation has arisen in Italy that could appear paradoxical but that in fact constitutes 'normality' there: magistrates have had their wings clipped and can only react to crimes and seek evidence that will stand up in court; there is no law governing complicity with the mafia; the political responsibility outlined in the Antimafia Committee's 1993 report, approved by a large majority on a wave of emotion generated by the massacres of those years, has remained a dead letter and the political forces have adopted no codes for self-regulation. People sentenced or on trial for mafia activities have stood for election and succeeded and some of them have attacked the magistrates, whose guilty verdicts attract opprobrium and their acquittals praise. In this context relations between the mafia and politics have become part of the Italian landscape.

## Culture, Subculture and Transculture

In common parlance, the term 'culture' is used to designate the possession of knowledge and instruments of knowledge, while in the language of anthropologists it simply means widespread or dominant codes and models of behaviour, on which no value judgement is made.

In the specific case of Sicily, we talk of 'Sicilian culture' or the 'nature of the Sicilians' as a fixed and unchangeable anthropological fact, frequently correlated with the mafia phenomenon and criminality in general.[12] This is an image of Sicilians handed down since at least the sixteenth century, which places the capacity to commit crimes alongside honour, sharpness and prudence in dealing with one's personal affairs and recklessness in the public sphere.

To define this culture we use expressions such as *sicilianismo, sicilianità* and even *sicilitudine*, the first drawn from the lexicon of the study of history and politics, the others from the language of literature and psychology. The image they give is of a closed and fossilized Sicilian culture: either a series of ideological tenets and a code of practice for living together in civil society or a way of being and feeling excessively influenced by the fact that Sicily is an island. The typical features of Sicilian culture are listed as: machismo, attachment to the family, the primacy of honour, a lack of respect for work, lack of public spirit and so on. The acceptance of these stereotypes induces a sort of depressive syndrome (which we could call *sicilianite*), a feeling of conviction of innate powerlessness and inevitable defeat, confirmed and made more acute by a belief that everything on the other side of the Strait of Messina is, and can only be, positive and normal, while everything on the Sicilian side is negative and distorted. This syndrome is supported by a deformation of memory in which even the most significant experiences are lost in the mists of obscurity.

As I have already noted, studies of the mafia have relied heavily on the concept of 'subculture', and criminologists have introduced the specific application of 'criminal subculture'. In anthropological terms, 'subculture' means 'a subset of cultural elements whether material or immaterial – values, knowledge, language, behaviour, lifestyles, working instruments – drawn up or used typically by a particular sector, segment or stratum of a society'.[13] Within the set of the dominant culture, this subset may be regarded as a differentiated or specialist variant or as a form of deviation or opposition. I have already stated that, in the first case, the concept of subculture is too vague – it would simply mean that the mafia, like any other actor in society, has its own code of behaviour, its own culture; in the second, it is misleading because it sees the mafia as something deviant and in opposition, ignoring all those aspects that derive from its interaction with the social and institutional background.

The misleading effects may be seen in the interpretation of the mafia as a subculture proposed by the German sociologist Henner Hess, who denied the existence of an organizing structure; he regarded this as a wrong idea, and saw the whole population of western Sicily as being implicated in the mafia subculture. Hess started from the theory that the mafia was a self-help group and ignored the attempts made by very many Sicilians to combat the mafia; he made a clear distinction between a state culture and a mafia subculture and ignored links between the mafia and the institutions.[14]

There is an abundance of literature on the criminal subculture and I have outlined the most important comments in the last chapter of *La violenza programmata*, where I proposed replacing the concept of subculture with that of 'transculture'. The analyses and theories about criminal subcultures may be summarized as follows: studies of delinquency, specifically juvenile delinquency, in Chicago, and those by American criminologist Edwin Sutherland on white-collar crime have been particularly revealing with regard to the mechanisms for learning and transmitting criminal behaviour; studies of juvenile delinquency by Albert Cohen and Robert Merton's theory of anomie have identified models of behaviour; Franco Ferracuti and Martin Wolfgang's integrated theory of subculture combines sociological and psychological aspects and the interdisciplinary approach of the most recent studies is seeking to generate a new paradigm.[15]

The Chicago School had the merit of linking the analysis of criminal phenomena with a study of social background and Sutherland paid particular attention to the crimes of the managing classes. He based his general theory of criminal behaviour on two hypotheses: differential association and social disorganization. Rejecting criminological theories based on economic conditioning and pathologies, Sutherland identified the element common to all forms of crime as learning – that is, the transmission of criminal behaviour by means of repeated links with the 'masters of crime' – and stressed the role of society which favoured illegal behaviour as distinct from formal law. He emphasized the business world in particular, a truly revolutionary concept compared with the stereotype that looked only at crime among the poor and marginalized. Indirectly, this made an important contribution to analysing the relationships between the mafia, economic activities and centres of power.

Cohen looked at subcultures as adaptation mechanisms and solutions to problems of status, in the sense of social position. Merton defined anomie as a result of the 'crisis of the cultural structure which occurs particularly when there is a discontinuity between cultural goals and the legitimate means available for reaching them'. The types or models of adaptation to the pressures resulting from combining cultural ends and institutional means are five in number: conformity, innovation, ritualism, retreatism and rebellion. He sees criminal behaviour as corresponding to the innovation model: adherence to cultural ends without respecting institutional means.

The criminologists Ferracuti and Wolfgang start from the position that the term 'subculture' as used by anthropologists and sociologists is highly ambiguous. They propose a composite, polymorphic model, specifically excluding a view of the modern mafia as a subcultural phenomenon. It 'has become a network of organized crime', making use of planned violence as 'the ultimate weapon of social and economic control, not unlike the death penalty in organized society', since it is used as 'a tool in order to obtain economic rewards'.

More recent studies favour an approach to criminal phenomena, particularly organized criminality, based on complex theoretical models. The concept of 'transculture' would allow us to grasp the complexity of the behaviour of mafiosi and those connected to them, through an across-the-board sweep embracing elements of several cultures, which enable various aspects to coexist with mutual benefits: the archaic (e.g. territorial dominance) and the far more modern (e.g. financial activities); the subcultural, derived from association codes, and other post-industrial facets.

From a cultural point of view, too, the mafia combines continuity and transformation, faithfulness to its roots and flexibility in its ability to adjust to changes in the world in which it operates. This enables it to maintain its base of family and relationship links while giving substantial scope to interests which may prevail over even the closest family ties (for example in the mafia war in the early 1980s Giovanni Bontate sided with the murderers of his brother Stefano). It uses inter-family forms of organization for trafficking, which goes beyond a restricted territorial area (originally cigarette smuggling, later drug trafficking). Similarly, as we have seen, formally the mafia organization is male-dominated but the involvement of women is attested by the daily press and talk of their role is growing steadily. Even what I have called the 'culture of subjection' underlying the social consensus which the mafia enjoys among large swathes of the population should not be seen as a static universe: it is disputed and brought into crisis by acts of individual rebellion linked, more or less successfully, with forms of action against the mafia.

Other elements of the mafia transculture (apprenticeship, initiation rites, the language, *omertà*, a hierarchical view of the organization and of society, acceptance of the social goals – such as enrichment, power, success – but not of the means, the role of aggression, the personalization of the conflict, a *sicilianista* and *meridionalista* ideology) should be seen as part of the dynamic that shapes the relationship between continuity and modernization within the mafia associations and in the social bloc linked to them. Virtually illiterate country people, such as Riina and Provenzano, have played a full part in international activities, such as drug trafficking and the laundering of illegal capital, because they have known how to use the work of technical specialists and consultants, thereby demonstrating surprising flexibility if we take into account their virtually non-existent cultural resources and their very limited direct experience. The concept of transculture, when used as described above, seeks to represent this coexistence of rural and modern models. If it had not been for this 'contamination', the world of the mafia would have been increasingly restricted to the villages and areas where it originated, and it would have resembled a species facing extinction on a reservation.

## Honour and Religiosity

Members of Cosa Nostra refer to themselves as 'men of honour', presenting themselves as people who respect moral principles and adhere to a code of values (sexual continence and the importance of the family, fidelity to promises, standing by commitments given, loyalty, courage, determination and so on); they therefore deserve esteem and respect. In reality their sense of honour consists of respect for the rules of the mafia organization, blind obedience to the leader and outward respectability, as in the case of sexual behaviour and family relationships. Even their courage manifests itself solely when they carry out crimes, especially murder, committed always in the context of an ambush and never face-to-face, even when the victims are defenceless or children.

The religious practices of which virtually all mafia leaders boast form part of the mask of respectability that serves to cover up their criminal activities. The use of holy pictures in the rite of initiation, of terminology taken from the vocabulary of religion, such as the word 'godfather', as used in Christian baptism, and references to saints in the Catholic calendar as protectors and founders of criminal organizations are all part of this formal religiosity, which is in line with that practised by the vast majority of the population and endorsed by the clergy. It is well known that during his long period on the run Bernardo Provenzano had a Bible in his hiding place and made good use of it for his *pizzini* (messages written on a slip of paper), in which he frequently included religious quotations and formulas; and the mafia leader Pietro Aglieri had set up in his place of refuge a chapel where a priest said mass for him. And yet both men had committed hundreds of crimes, which they regarded as obligations under the rules of the mafia organization, and had broken virtually all the commandments.

## The Social Consensus

The social consensus vis-à-vis the mafia changes as the social dynamics change: disapproval is strong and widespread when the degree of social mobilization is low; it is called into question and declines sharply when mobilization increases and there is some real prospect of renewal.

In large part this is the result of the advantages offered by mafia activities, both in economic terms and in opportunities for social mobility. For many people, to be part of the mafia, to enter into its network of relationships, means obtaining a slice of the cake generated by the revenue from these activities, securing contracts and subcontracts, enjoying the friendship and favour of administrators, politicians and representatives of institutions, being a member of the dominant class. These reasons, rather than fear, explain the behaviour of many individuals from a variety of social classes, from the highest to the lowest.

## A Mafia-Generating Society

The mafia is both the product of a society and its reflection. Elsewhere I have used the term *società mafiogena* (a mafia-generating society) to describe its distinguishing features.[16] These are:

1. A large part of the population gives moral acceptance to violence and illegality, which normally remain unpunished, regarding them as a means of survival and ways to acquire a social role which it would be impossible or difficult to secure otherwise.

2. The legal economy is too fragile to offer substantial and attractive opportunities.

3. The state and institutions in general are considered distant and alien, closed and inaccessible, except through the mediation of mafia members and their friends, who collude closely and have already demonstrated in previous struggles that the institutions and the mafia had united to ward off threats to the existing power structure.

4. The collective memory of earlier struggles against the mafia regards as common sense the view that defeat is inevitable, the mafia invincible and power unchangeable.

5. The network of civil society is too fragile and precarious (crises in the political parties, trade unions that are not really representative, the weakness of associations, etc.) to provide an effective antidote to the mafia organization and a space in which a new consciousness can develop.[17] While the argument that the regions of southern Italy lack a sense of civic consciousness for reasons dating back to the Middle Ages (as propounded by the American academic Robert Putnam) is unacceptable, the pattern of associative behaviour in the South outlined by recent research does not take account of the fact that many of the voluntary associations are too small and suffer from too many problems to be able to act effectively.[18]

6. The culture of distrust and fatalism feeds on all this and provides the best possible breeding ground for the mafia, an organization regarded as a natural phenomenon that has to be accepted and from which some advantage may be gained.

7. Daily life is characterized by aggression in even the simplest of relationships; the watchword is solidarity in illegality ('defend your own, right or wrong') and everything is seen in terms of advantage and self-interest.

Hence a series of elements operates at all levels to create a situation favourable to the mafia and widespread illegality. This picture is not unchangeable and, in particular, the history of Sicily, in the more or less recent past and even today, is full of attempts to achieve radical change.

The characteristics of which I have spoken were originally to be found in closed societies with limited horizons; in recent years at least some aspects of them can be observed in wider contexts and are becoming increasingly common throughout the world. We have moved from what might be defined as a 'mafia-generating village' to a world scene that generates criminality. To anticipate an argument to which we shall return later, we may say that global capitalism has the following characteristics:

1. Territorial imbalances and social disparities are tending to increase. One-fifth of the world's population consumes four-fifths of its resources and, instead of falling, inequality in the distribution of resources is tending to increase; in many areas of the globe (e.g. Africa, Latin America, the former communist countries of Eastern Europe) the only resource available, or the one most readily to hand, is the illegal accumulation of wealth.

2. In the name of neo-liberalism we are dismantling the welfare state and those who are weakest economically are becoming marginalized. Every day thousands of people flee from the countries mired in underdevelopment: this is an unstoppable flow, which is not discouraged by the current laws against clandestine immigration.

3. Unemployment is growing for structural reasons: the development model is introducing technologies that require decreasing amounts of labour and a single market assists the quest for labour at the lowest cost. The labour market is increasingly marked by flexibility and precariousness, unregistered and slave-type labour is taking an ever greater diversity of forms and the gains achieved by workers are coming under threat.

4. The opacity of the financial system, with its banking secrecy, tax havens and financial innovations, promotes the symbiosis between legal and illegal capital.

5. The contradiction between legality and reality produces results which fly in the face of expectations. The most important example is that banning drugs does not discourage consumption and hands over a highly profitable sector to a mafia monopoly.

6. The 'values' increasingly sought after are success at any price, personal enrichment and competition by any means, preferably those that are illegal, swiftest and most convenient.

These developments help extend and strengthen the illegal economy and encourage mafia-type criminal organizations. Unless these centres are tackled at their roots, measures to combat crime, beginning with those against the recycling of illegal capital, will have little effect.

## A Historical Process: Continuity and Transformation

Accepted ideas must be analysed when we consider the historical development of the mafia and the struggles against it; here too we come across stereotypes. There is talk of 'old mafia' and 'new mafia', of 'traditional mafia' and 'mafia-as-business', and as regards the struggles against the mafia attention focuses solely or primarily on the movements of recent years, which are considered an innovation.

The 'old mafia' and the 'traditional mafia' are seen as having a code of honour, being moderate in their use of violence and respectful of the values of a peasant society and of women and children, while the 'new mafia' is degenerate and the 'mafia-as-business' discovered the competition for wealth only in the 1970s.

These visions of a mafia that was originally idyllic and then degenerated was authoritatively confirmed by statements from mafiosi cooperating with the judicial authorities, particularly Tommaso Buscetta, who defended *his* mafia and attacked the mafia of his enemies, the Corleonesi, placing the blame for this change in nature on drug trafficking, of which he had been one of the pioneers.

In fact the mafia has always been a criminal organization, with a strong network of relationships habitually using violence both inside the organization and outside. The accumulation of wealth, by any means possible, has been a constant thread running throughout its history and, as we shall see, even through what we may call its proto-history.

Like all long-lasting phenomena, the mafia developed by combining continuity and transformation, aspects that are traditional with others that are innovative. In this way, archaic aspects, such as extortion, which was documented in Palermo at the end of the sixteenth century, coexist alongside new ones, such as drug trafficking; and when we look beyond the apparent contradictions, each may help the operation of the other. The mafia is neither a cultural fossil nor an out-of-control mutant. Formally, the mafia is rigid, merely waiting on orders from its leaders, but in fact it is flexible, as we see when we look at its activities past and present.

Individual phases may be identified, but only where one aspect predominates over the others and with due regard to changes in the social and territorial background, to which the mafia has always shown itself able to adapt.

The following picture of the historical development of the mafia may be sketched out: (1) a long incubation phase, from the sixteenth century to the early decades of the nineteenth century, when the term 'premafia phenomena' is more apt than talking about a real mafia as such; (2) an agrarian phase, covering the period from the unification of Italy to the 1950s; (3) an urban-entrepreneurial phase, in the 1960s; (4) a financial phase, from the 1970s to the present day. In recent years the phrase *mafia sommersa* has been used to designate a period with no headline-grabbing crimes.

An idea of this development may be obtained from the following brief comments. First, premafia phenomena may be broken down into two types: criminal activities that usually went unpunished because they were carried out by protected criminals, such as bandits in the service of barons in western Sicily, who established private armies and committed a variety of criminal acts that escaped justice; and certain forms of crime designed to accumulate wealth and that already entailed the exercise of territorial domination, such as extortion, kidnappings designed to secure ransoms and cattle rustling, normally planned and carried out with the complicity of the police at the time.

The unification of Italy resulted in the formation of a dominant bloc comprising the major industrialists of northern Italy and the landowners of the South. The economy was primarily agricultural and the class system of western Sicily had at the top the large landowners, in the middle those leasing large areas of land (*gabelloti*) and at the bottom the peasants. The mafia comprised principally leaseholders, whose role was in practice that of parasites but formally one of entrepreneurs based mainly on the exploitation of peasant labour. They were present also in the citrus plantations of the *Conca d'oro* ('golden basin': the fertile area round Palermo) and in the cities. The functions of the rural mafia were: the accumulation of capital, in competition with the landowners; the control and repression of the peasant movement, its main opponent, from the Fasci siciliani (1891–4) to the struggle for agrarian reform in the 1940s and 1950s; local government and mediation between the local community and the central institutions, thereby establishing one of the pillars of the client system through which the Mezzogiorno was integrated into the rest of Italy.

Beginning in the second half of the 1950s, the Italian economy became industrial-tertiary in nature and in the Mezzogiorno and in Sicily the tertiary sector was primarily parasitic, as employment in the public sector developed as a dumping ground and public expenditure continued to rise with the creation of the Region of Sicily as a special-statute region in 1946 and of the Cassa del Mezzogiorno in 1950. In this phase the mafia groups did not abandon the countryside but integrated themselves increasingly into the new reality, in particular profiting from the possibilities offered by building speculation connected with the expansion of the cities. The mafioso as entrepreneur was born primarily thanks to public money, contracts for public works and finance granted by credit institutions incorporated under public law. Hence the urban-entrepreneurial mafia is primarily a state bourgeoisie, meaning that the middle and upper strata evolve and assume a dominant role through their access to sources of public money and their links with sectors of the institutions. The mafia controls the markets for construction, food and credit and recruitment to local government bodies, and is becoming increasingly the dominant bourgeoisie at local level as it maintains and increases its sources of illegal accumulation of wealth (extortion, contraband cigarettes, involvement in international drug trafficking).

From the 1970s onwards, its ever-growing role in international drug trafficking, resulting in a considerable increase in the accumulation of illegal wealth, meant that the mafia could be considered financial in nature, that is a large factory for the accumulation of capital, with a corresponding increase in the role of the mafia groups in the market and in society. The demand for channels to recycle money and provide investment opportunities and for new areas to exercise power grew steadily, thereby rocking the hitherto stable boat, resulting in the emergence of bloody internal competition, which culminated in the mafia war of 1981–3, and triggering an external power struggle with the elimination of obstacles to the process of expansion. The victims include businessmen, magistrates, police officers and politicians, including those forming part of the government. The high point of this offensive was the murder of the president of the Region of Sicily, Mattarella (6 January 1980), of the regional secretary of the Communist

Party, La Torre (30 April 1982) and of General Prefect Dalla Chiesa
(3 September 1982). These crimes provoked a reaction from the state in
the form of approval of the antimafia law on 13 September 1982 and the
*maxiprocesso* resulting in the convictions of leaders and followers. Many
mafiosi who were being hunted by their enemies preferred to cooperate
with the judicial authorities. In 1992 and 1993 the Cosa Nostra
organization committed massacres (Capaci and Via D'Amelio, Rome,
Florence and Milan) in an attempt to put pressure on the state. This had
further boomerang effects: strict imprisonment and rewards for those
who cooperated.

For many of those who, explicitly or implicitly, buy into the
emergency stereotype, regarding the mafia as simply a crime factory,
the term 'hidden mafia' – used by the media in recent years, which
have seen no major crimes or massacres – means that the mafia has
been beaten, or at least gives no cause for concern. In fact, the mafia,
particularly in its criminal-military format, has suffered severe
blows, but these have only scratched the surface of its system of
relationships, and its decision to renounce the use of violence towards
the authorities is the result both of the blows it has suffered and of a
choice: controlling violence is a vital condition for continuing to play
a role in business and for renewing alliances, particularly with the
worlds of business and the institutions, through links with those now
holding the reins of power.

## Research

The research needed to verify these working hypotheses has been carried
out by the Centro Impastato, mainly using its own resources but in some
cases in cooperation with others. The following research has been
undertaken as part of the general project *Mafia e società*:

1.  Research into ideas about the mafia, theoretical models and the
    literature on the mafia and similar organized criminal phenomena,
    published in the works: *La mafia interpretata: Dilemmi, stereotipi,
    paradigm* and *Dalla mafia alle mafie: Scienze sociali e crimine
    organizzato.*[19] These review studies by sociologists, historians,
    economists, criminologists, psychologists and theologians and set
    out the main lines of the 'paradigm of complexity'.

2. Research into the origins of the mafia phenomenon, published in *La cosa e il nome: Materiali per lo studio dei fenomeni premafiosi.*[20] This sets out and analyses the documentation on the period when the mafia phenomenon was growing, with particular reference to unpunished criminality (e.g. bandits in the service of local lords) and to crimes designed to accumulate wealth and implying the first stages in the emergence of territorial domination (extortion, cattle rustling, kidnapping).

3. Research into murders and murder trials, published in: *La violenza programmata: Omicidi e guerre di mafia a Palermo e provincia dagli anni '60 ad oggi* and *Gabbie vuote. Processi per omicidio a Palermo dal 1983 al maxiprocesso.*[21] These examine crimes in the periods dominated by the mafia wars, the early 1960s and the early 1980s, and the murder investigations that often resulted in acquittals.

4. Research published in *L'impresa mafiosa: Dall'Italia agli Stati Uniti,*[22] which uses documentation produced to implement the 1982 antimafia law and official American sources to look at business activities managed, more or less overtly, by mafiosi, both in Italy and in the United States. These were chiefly intended to recycle illegal capital.

5. The research project on financial activities published in the essay 'The financial mafia. The illegal accumulation of wealth and the financial-industrial complex',[23] which looks at the ways in which dirty money is recycled and at the flow of capital at local, national and international level, and at the ways in which the world economy became increasingly speculative.

6. Research into international drug trafficking, undertaken with CISS (Cooperazione Internazionale Sud-Sud), a Palermo-based non-governmental organization (NGO), and in cooperation with NGOs in Europe, Asia and Latin America, published in four languages in *Behind Drugs: Survival Economies, Criminal Enterprises, Military Operations, Development Projects.*[24]

7. The research project into the mafia and politics, published in the pamphlet 'La mafia come soggetto politico', and documentation on that relationship collected in *L'alleanza e il compromesso: Mafia e politica dai tempi di Lima e Andreotti ai giorni nostri.*[25]

8. Research into the role of women in the mafia and the struggle against the mafia, using real-life stories, published in *La mafia in*

*casa mia*, the story of the life of Felicia Bartolotta, the mother of Peppino Impastato; *Sole contro la mafia*, the stories of Pietra Lo Verso and Michela Buscemi, ordinary women from Palermo who chose to take part in mafia trials; *Storie di donne*, the stories of Antonietta Renda, a communist leader in the postwar years, Giovanna Terranova, the widow of the magistrate Cesare Terranova, and Camilla Giaccone, the daughter of the university lecturer and police doctor Paolo Giaccone, the last two of whom were killed by the mafia, and a collection of essays and articles published in the volume *Donne, mafia e antimafia*.[26]

9.  Research into the struggles against the mafia, published in *La democrazia bloccata: La strage di Portella della Ginestra e l'emarginazione delle sinistre* and *Storia del movimento antimafia: Dalla lotta di classe all'impegno civile*.[27]

10. A collection of essays on the role of the churches, published in *Il Vangelo e la lupara* and other material; and a collection of essays published in *Mafie e globalizzazione*.[28]

11. The centre has paid particular attention to work in schools, with a number of publications, including *A scuola di antimafia, Oltre la legalità, l'Agenda dell'antimafia 2011*.[29]

# CHAPTER 2

# PREMAFIA PHENOMENA

The origins of the mafia are not lost in the mists of time, or to be sought in some obscure criminal propensity forming an integral part of human nature. Nor can they be found in myths that, while attractive, are improbable and clearly apologetic, such as those of the Beati Paoli or the non-existent Osso, Mastrosso and Carcagnosso, the supposed founders of the mafia, the 'ndrangheta and the camorra.

The term *mafiusi* appears for the first time in the title of the dialect play *I mafiusi di la Vicaria di Palermu*, written in 1863 by Giuseppe Rizzotto and Gaspare Mosca, while the word *maffia* is first used in an official document in a report of 25 April 1865 by the prefect of Palermo, Filippo Antonio Gualterio.

The mafia and all the implications of the organization manifested itself fully during the period leading to the unification of Italy. This does not mean that we cannot look further back in time, seeking out the *thing* that may have existed even before it acquired its *name*. My work *La cosa e il nome* makes use of an abundant if only partially explored documentation to reconstruct certain events that demonstrate that there was a long gestation period.[1] These may be referred to in various ways: as precursors of the mafia, premafia or protomafia. I prefer to talk of a 'premafia', manifesting itself in ways that may be grouped in two main categories: (1) criminal activities that remained regularly unpunished because those perpetrating them had links to people in power, either in practice or through an established structure; (2) types of criminality designed to accumulate wealth that may be seen as the exercise of territorial domination.

This means that all the activities in which private violence is used for enrichment and domination may be considered 'premafiosi'. They make quite a long list, the items of which have the following characteristics:

(1)  events and ways in which violence is exercised privately, that is outside the established structures, so not pursued through the official channels of justice and therefore remaining unpunished;
(2)  the habitual exercise of illegal violence, even by those holding power and by sections of the institutions;
(3)  eruptions of violence and illegality as recurrent behaviour and professional activities;
(4)  the existence of more or less structured or informal groups engaged in criminal activities in a particular area over which they exercise some form of control;
(5)  violent and illegal behaviour used to acquire wealth and secure genuine power, in practice not necessarily in opposition to the official power, normally remaining unpunished and given legitimacy through acceptance by the masses or their failure to respond.

Here we shall look at some typical cases: as regards those we may call 'protected criminals', we shall consider the bandits serving an overlord, the 'protomafiosi' of Palermo, the familiars of the Inquisition and the documentation about groups that may be regarded as forerunners of the mafia; in the case of crimes to amass wealth which imply territorial domination, including those where links with the institutions existing at that time are concerned, we shall look at extortion and cattle rustling. There follow a few reflections to outline the context in which the transition from feudalism to capitalism took place, with its specific characteristics, and some remarks on the development of the 'apologetic' myths which attempt to describe the mafia as something noble.

## Bandits Serving an Overlord

For centuries banditry has been endemic around the Mediterranean. It was largely a result of the living conditions of the lower social orders and attracted exemplary punishments, such as the dismembering of the bodies of those convicted. However, some groups enjoyed immunity, at least for long periods. These were the bandits employed by local lords, who formed private armies operating freely in certain areas in support of the domination exercised by their employers, who were engaged in their own disputes with each other and conflicts with the central power. As long ago as the reign of Federico II there are reports of *bravos*, whom the barons paid to terrorize the countryside; the landowners, who indulged in full-scale wars, later continued this practice. The most famous case is that of Sciacca where there occurred clashes, first in 1455 and later in 1529, between the Luna and the Perollo families, who had in their service armies made up of *facinorosi* (violent men).[2] As long as criminals and bandits served to support the power of the barons they remained unpunished, but anyone who threatened to make compromising revelations was eliminated. That was the fate of the bandit Rizzo di Saponara, who was poisoned in 1578 because of the fear that he might talk about his connections with those in power. The bandit Gaspare Pisciotta met the same fate in 1954 because he was threatening to reveal the links that the Giuliano band had with politicians and representatives of institutions.

## The Protomafiosi of Palermo and the Inquisition's Familiars

The presence in Palermo of thugs who killed in broad daylight, kidnapped women and lived by robbery through *composizione* (demands for money to return the property stolen) are documented in the sixteenth century.[3] One leader of such men was Girolamo Colloca, nicknamed 'the king of the Bocceria' (the *Vucciria*, or meat market, from the French *boucherie*). He was a friend of those in high places, revered and held in esteem by the nobles. In 1579 Viceroy Marco Antonio Colonna put an end to his operations by condemning him to death. The nobility and city officials intervened in his favour but the sentence was carried out, on a gallows higher than those used for his companions.

However, those who entered the service of the Inquisition, as its 'familiars', did enjoy impunity because they answered to a privileged court and could evade official justice. The Inquisition, founded to repress heretics who were regarded as public enemies, was in practice a politically repressive organization in the service of the Spanish government, which vaunted its Catholicism. The Inquisition's familiars included nobles, merchants and ordinary people and there was a waiting list to join (in the sixteenth century the familiars numbered some 30,000) because membership offered a degree of impunity.

In a letter dated 3 November 1577, Viceroy Colonna wrote that the ranks of the Inquisition's familiars included all the rich people, nobles and wealthy criminals. On the basis of substantial documentation, some scholars have regarded the Inquisition as a fully fledged mafia organization; this verdict may appear harsh but it cannot be denied that it resulted in criminals being protected and played a part in the development of the practice of impunity through the multiplicity of tribunals that it used to administer justice. It was what I have called the *polipolio della giustizia* (a multi-centred justice); some considerable time would elapse before the state acquired a monopoly of force, now considered an essential attribute of any modern state. In my view, we can speak of a genuine mafia when a claim is made, at least formally, to that monopoly: the mafia does not recognize it because, as we have seen, it has its own rules and its own justice, but nevertheless it enjoys impunity because the state fails to exercise its monopoly, since violence and illegality are essential tools in the maintenance and continuation of certain power bases.

## Economic Crimes and Territorial Domination

The practice of *pizzo* (extortion) in the Vucciria market is documented in the sixteenth century by Argisto Giuffredi, secretary to the Inquisition and author of *Avvertimenti cristiani*.[4] One day in the market, his companion, the city captain Fabio Bologna, arrested and beat a young man; when he was asked why, Bologna replied that the young man made the traders give him money and he had wanted to beat him in public to give him a lesson and to encourage the traders not to fear him (see box). With hindsight, we may consider that the lesson Bologna administered did not do much to prevent *pizzo* from becoming one of the main weapons in the mafia's armoury.

*Pizzo* is a crime designed both to accumulate wealth and assert territorial domination, since it is a form of criminal taxation, competing with that imposed by the state. Kidnappings for ransom are also widely documented, as are threatening letters demanding money. Another crime for which abundant documentation exists is rustling – the theft of animals. Herds and flocks amounting to several hundred animals cross wide swathes of territory and, if levies were not paid, they finished up in a clandestine slaughterhouse. To avoid such thefts, animals were marked as long ago as the twelfth century and there are countless legal instruments seeking to repress this form of crime. Rustling is a crime that links city and countryside, and so requires some organizational structure; it could not be perpetrated without a series of links, including the indispensable complicity and involvement of the *compagnie d'armi* (armed guards) that at that time acted as a police force.

---

### The *pizzo* in the Vucciria of Palermo

When I was with him [Fabio Bologna] one summer evening, I saw him meet near the square in Palermo they call the '*bucceria vecchia*' a young man whom he knew very well who, by fear, obtained money from the merchants in the Loggia, and similar things. He was walking late one afternoon with only his sword at his belt, he had him bound by the watch, took him to the Loggia which at that time is always thronged with merchants, insulted him, threatened him and treated him so badly that I was moved to compassion for him and begged don Fabio to release him for my sake, or at least to send him to prison: he whispered to me: 'you did right to ask me that because I did not wish to do to him more harm than I did'; and when I gestured for him to speak, said that when he was governor he did not go out in the evening. The prisoner begged me insistently and he released him; and when I said to the captain that he appeared to have been wrongly beaten, he said to me: 'never in my life have I done better justice; you should know that people in this Loggia feared him, and what he did could not be proved; with what I have done I have achieved three things: the first is that the merchants will not be so afraid of him; the second is that from now on he will not dare to do it again and the third is that his followers and friends, who have seen their leader dealt with in this way, will say: "if our leader was in such danger when he was not doing anything wrong, what will happen to us if we are caught committing some crime?"'

From Argisto Giuffredi, *Avvertimenti cristiani*, a sixteenth-century manuscript in L. Natoli (ed.), *Documenti per servire alla Storia della Sicilia*, IV/5, Palermo, 1896, pp. 59–60.

---

### Guards and Thieves: The Ancestor of the Gattopardo

The *compagnie d'armi* were established in 1543 and comprised a captain and ten men, often chosen from criminals and those awaiting trial.[5] Most frequently, instead of imposing order, carrying out police duties and seeking out bandits and criminals, these bands themselves behaved like criminal groups. In a document of 1563 we read:

> The Kingdom is much perturbed by these Captains at arms, who make their homes in and scour the countryside and who, established to seek out outlaws and criminals, commit robberies and perpetrate countless evils on the roads, and do anything other than carry out the duties given to them.

Often the roles of guards and thieves, police and criminals, were interchangeable. One captain of armed guards was Mario de Tomasi, founder of the family in which the writer Giuseppe Tomasi, prince of Lampedusa, was to be born.[6] Originally Tomasi had been enrolled among the foot-guards (the *provvisionati*), who were normally chosen from among the most desperate and dangerous. He then became a captain and grew rich thanks to a series of abuses, including extortion, misuse of public office, theft and even the killing of his victims. When he was rich he married a noblewoman, Francesca Caro, and founded the dynasty of the Gattopardi. In his bestselling novel, Tomasi di Lampedusa writes that the unification of Italy saw the jackals taking the place of the leopards (the bourgeoisie had replaced the aristocrats), but historical reality suggests that his own ancestor had more in common with jackals than with leopards.

## Unions, Brotherhoods, Sects, Parties and the Like

There is documentation on the existence of groups that may be regarded as precursors of mafia-type associations going back to the early nineteenth century. The document most often quoted is the report of 3 August 1838 from the chief prosecutor of the Trapani High Criminal Court, Pietro Calà Ulloa, to the Minister of Grace and Justice in the Bourbon government. He wrote:

> In many towns there are unions or brotherhoods, sects if you will, known as *parties*, with no political affiliation or purpose, which hold no meetings and have no links other than that they depend

on a leader, who may be a landowner or an archpriest. They have a common purse which may be used to secure the release of a member, or his defence, to protect one accused or to put blame on an innocent man. They are so many miniature Governments within the Government. The absence of a public force has increased the number of crimes! The ordinary people have come to a tacit understanding with the leaders. When thefts occur, mediators appear to offer arrangements for the recovery of the stolen property. There is no end to the number of these agreements. Many landowners have therefore thought it better to become oppressors rather than the oppressed, and have joined the *parties*. Many senior officials have hidden them under a cloak of complete secrecy; examples include *Scarlatto*, formerly crown prosecutor and later judge of the Palermo High Civil Court, *Siracusa* and not a few others. Sometimes the common purses cover several provinces so that thefts may be committed and stolen animals moved for sale from one province to another. Hence in one single night there occurred thefts of whole herds: scarcely a month ago 16 cattle were stolen from a single owner a few miles from Trapani and 200 sheep from another near to Caltanissetta! Nor do such thefts lack even today a *Scarlatti* or an *Artale* to cover them up.[7]

Calà Ulloa's text should be read with caution. It contains some contradictions: it says that it refers to informal organizations, but they have a common purse and their activities are ongoing and complex. And then his main concern is to protect the power of the Bourbons, and so he mixes together genuine criminals, their protectors and political opponents. We shall see this happen again later. Gualterio, the prefect of Palermo, would do the same in 1865.

In a report ten years earlier, on 16 October 1828, the prosecutor at Girgenti (now Agrigento) noted that there existed in Cattolica an organization comprising 100 members linked by an oath and having funds in common. He also reported mafia rituals, such as corpses with their tongues cut out.

In another report, of 27 October 1838, the Inspectorate of the Valle di Caltanissetta talks of a 'league of thieves', known as the *Sacra Unione*, which included two monks and was led by a priest. It was based at

Mazzarino and operated over a fairly wide area. The *Unione* was structured hierarchically into *omini* (men) and *scassapagghiara* (haystack breakers) and enjoyed the protection of both the authorities and landowners, the former taking a share of the income and the latter using the bandits to assert their power. A vast network of relatives gravitated around the group.

In a further report, dated 23 October 1841, Puoti, the deputy inspector at Termini (Palermo), speaks of groups of bandits and of sects structured in three levels: organizers, intermediaries and executives. The organizers were people of influence; the intermediaries appear to have provided technical support – having legal and administrative skills, they helped detainees and bribed public officials; the executives were the bandits, who, rather than being rebels, were criminals specializing in theft, kidnapping and murder. This 'integrated system' would lead to a subversive organization: the main thrust of his report was to secure intervention by the central government.[8]

It is clear that all the elements of the mafia phenomenon were in place: a secret association with an oath, a military-style organization, a base among family and relations, a criminal economy, territorial domination and interaction between criminals, the elements of society in the ascendant and the established authorities. We are no longer concerned with a premafia or protomafia but with the genuine article, the mafia, as we have known it in recent years.

## The Background:
## The Transition from Feudalism to Capitalism

The society of Sicily, particularly western Sicily, in the sixteenth to the nineteenth centuries was the background for the development of the premafia. Usually, Sicily is regarded as an island isolated from the rest of the world, the victim of subjugation by a series of dominant powers, as if oppression by foreign colonizers had been and had to continue to be the lot of Sicilians, who are in fact the result of a racial mixing caused by the island's central position in the Mediterranean, not its remoteness. Such a scenario would have condemned the Sicily of the period in question to a feudalism without end and irretrievable backwardness.

In fact this period saw a process of transition that contributes to the formation of what the historian Immanuel Wallerstein has called a 'one-world system'.[9] Naturally, this does not mean moving from the stereotype of insularity and backwardness to one of uniformity with no distinguishing features. The one-world system, whose formation began in the sixteenth century, leads to the establishment of the capitalist mode of production and of the nation state. The appropriation of the means of production by bourgeois entrepreneurs and the formation of strata of wage-earners goes along with the endorsement of absolute monarchies holding a monopoly of force.

The world system results in the formation of areas which communicate among themselves but remain quite distinct: central areas, semiperipheral areas and peripheral areas. In the first there is salary-dependent labour and a centralized state; in the second, share-cropping, a form of agricultural enterprise where the worker is often a small landowner and state authority is weaker; in the peripheral areas there is slave labour without any central power.

Karl Marx had already noted that the birth of the capitalist mode of production was linked to 'primitive accumulation', where the process of separating the producers from the means of production is characterized by the use of violence, exercised primarily by the state. However, this violence has both an 'economic' aspect, in that it helped shape the capitalist economy, and a 'political' aspect, in that it was implemented by the state through the forms that it was affording itself.

To acquire its monopoly of force, the state provided itself with bodies authorized to use force: at home; the police, and abroad; armies. At the same time, a bureaucracy was developing and a unified culture that accepted these arrangements was consolidating.

How and where does Sicily fit into this picture? Elsewhere I have suggested that Sicily could be defined as a *semiperiferia anomala* (anomalous semiperiphery). What does that mean? It means that in Sicily various forms of production, and in particular of cultivation of the land, existed side by side. There are the *latifondi*, the vast expanses of land where only cereals are grown, but there are also vineyards, olive groves and citrus plantations; there are *metatieri* (share-croppers), who work various parcels of land well outside towns and villages, and there are also labourers who work for wages. The bulk of the population, including landowners, live in the cities and rural towns; many landowners lease their land to tenants (*gabelloti*), whose concern is the maximum exploitation of peasant labour rather than agricultural innovation. Spanish rule did not succeed in securing a monopoly of force but had to coexist with other power centres: this led to a diarchy, with power being exercised jointly by the central state, represented by the viceroy, and the barons and the *polipolio della giustizia*, to which I have already referred.

As well as its criminal role, the mafia had a social and political role in this situation. Why only in western Sicily? There is no easy answer. At that time, eastern Sicily was subject to other factors. On the economic front there was the breaking down of large estates through emphyteusis, a long-term concession of land that allowed for improvements and innovations in cultivation. Politically, the views of leaders in Catania of the 1812 Constitution were opposed to those of the aristocrats in Palermo. In that year the Sicilian Parliament abolished feudalism, so unleashing a prolonged conflict between the central authority and local power centres. Social factors included the peasant uprisings in 1820 and 1860, which encouraged the wealthier classes in western Sicily to turn to the mafia, while culturally eastern Sicily had greater trust in the official authorities. All of these may have played a part, although even today further study is still required.

### The Creation of the Myth of Justification: the Beati Paoli

The Beati Paoli are said to be the descendants of a group of 'avengers', first reported in 1186, who operated mainly by night and whose leader was hanged by order of the King. In 1700 there were reports of Sicilian avengers who took justice into their own hands or who imposed justice on request. They were known as the Beati Paoli, and in his *Diari* the Marquis of Villabianca states that some of them were tried in the early years of the eighteenth century.

This is principally a legend that can be found throughout European literature; for example, in Germany, a sort of secret tribunal, *Fehmegerichte*, was referred to in a letter of 1836 by a Neapolitan official, Gabriele Quattromani. The myth reappeared in popular tales, such as those by Linares published in 1836, and a poetic version by Piola published in 1849.

In 1864, when the mafia was already an established phenomenon, Benedetto Naselli wrote a drama and in 1874 the Palermo council named a street and a piazza after the Beati Paoli because it was said to be where the secret group held its meetings to decide on the action to be taken. Luigi Natoli then wrote a popular novel that, published as a supplement to the *Giornale di Sicilia* in 1909 and 1910, gave the myth more substance.

Natoli's novel became a sort of bible for mafia members and even those who have cooperated with the authorities in recent years explain the origins of the mafia with reference to it, even if it is doubtful whether they have read the book.[10]

# CHAPTER 3

# MAFIA AND ANTIMAFIA IN AN AGRICULTURAL SOCIETY

The period from the 1860s to the 1950s is not one of unrelieved stagnation. It consisted of a number of phases that I suggest could be seen as follows: initial opposition to the government of the historical Right (but, as we shall see, the mafia had its feet in both camps, both government and opposition), followed by integration as power passed to the Left (here, too, generalizations should be avoided). The third phase is that of the fascist period, with the repression of the so-called *bassa mafia* and the integration of the *alta mafia*, and the fourth from the end of World War II to the 1950s. This period saw the relegitimation of the mafia, the violent repression of the peasant movement and the end of anti-fascist unity, as the parties of the Left were expelled from government, and the Christian Democrats, a party enjoying a relative majority, established as the sole holders of power with the 'mafia bourgeoisie' as part of the dominant bloc.

## Towards a Unitary State: The People's Bands and their Aristocratic-Bourgeois Opponents

As we have already seen, the mafia was well-established as far back as the 1830s: there was an organization, an ongoing series of activities, a network of relationships, a culture of illegality, impunity, interaction with institutions. The events of the Risorgimento and the formation of a unified Italy are important to our understanding of how mafia groups act in periods of transition and the role played by organized private violence alongside the official bodies in their opposition to the labouring classes in both the countryside and the cities.

The artisans of Palermo were organized in guilds or corporations and by 1735 the defence of the city walls had been entrusted to the 'watches' of the guilds; during the 1773 revolt against Viceroy Fogliani the corporations organized a people's police, which replaced the *compagnie d'armi* and the official police. During that period robberies, kidnappings and violence, often attributed to the police themselves, the 'cop criminals', ceased. This led to the song:

| | |
|---|---|
| *Evviva la mastranza* | Long live the people's police |
| *e cu la fici e fu* | and those who set them up |
| *chi la città è cuieta* | for now there is peace in the town |
| *e latri un ci nn'è cchiù.* | and no more thieves. |
| *E tutta sta sbirragghia* | And no more police |
| *chi java caminannu* | who roamed around |
| *e javanu arrubannu* | and stole |
| *e spiavano: cu fu?* | and asked 'Who did it?' |

The question is whether it was only the police who stole or whether the guild watches did so too. However, in 1774 the people's police was stood down, on the grounds that it was dangerous to leave force in the hands of the people.

During the 1820 revolt aristocrats and rich bourgeois formed the National Guard with the obvious intention of using it against the people's bands. The same thing happened in 1848: to protect their houses and goods, property owners even made use of armed heavies selected from among those awaiting trial. People's bands and their opponents also appeared at crucial moments such as 1860, when Garibaldi's Mille conquered Sicily, and 1866, when there was a revolt in Palermo against unification.

In 1860 the pickets of the people's bands stood alongside Garibaldi's men but the leaders of his army were not indifferent to the concerns of the property owners. The results were executions by firing squad to punish 'excesses' and the events at Bronte where, in August that year, Nino Bixio put down a revolt by the bourgeoisie and the peasants to secure expropriation of crown lands, which had already resulted in the deaths of some landowners, by imposing death sentences on its leaders, who had in fact sought to avoid the killings. In 1866 there was a further revolt in which the people's bands were once again in action, with the same leaders as had been involved before.

Historians have come to widely differing conclusions, most of them seeing the people's bands as merely another form of the mafia, and it is true that some of the most prominent leaders appear to have been assassins and brigands. However, others have noted the revolutionary nature of the bands, regarding them as a further stage in that striving for democracy which ran from the Sicilian Vespers in 1282 to the nineteenth century.

One thing that is certain is that the so-called 'people's mafia', in the form given it by the bands, was a dead end, being superseded by a mafia closer in form to their opponents, which took over to protect the interests of the property owners. This was intended to become a significant component of the dominant classes. More precisely: the violence of the lower classes was partly channelled into the popular and peasant movement and became increasingly integrated into the antimafia struggle, while part of it merged with the mafia phenomenon, a transclassist body regarded as a vehicle of operational mobility for joining the dominant classes. The democratic part was marginalized along with the Garibaldian opposition, and the other side won. The killing on 3 August 1863 of the Garibaldian General Giovanni Corrao is emblematic in this respect: Corrao, of lower-class origins, was regarded by his political opponents as an obstacle on an equal footing with the Bourbons, and as a mafia leader. He was killed because he had a large following, and not simply over a dispute concerning property in the Palermo countryside. Chronologically, this was the first politico-mafia crime.

## Public Order in Sicily: Violence and Political Struggle

An important document, which gives us an insight into the situation in Sicily immediately after the unification of Italy, is the report of 10 October 1861 by a Member of Parliament, Diomede Pantaleoni, to the Minister of the Interior, Bettino Ricasoli. The most serious matter was the lack of public safety: there were frequent killings, and crimes remained unpunished even though the perpetrators were usually well known. An example was the attack on an adviser to the Court of

Appeal, a supporter of Giuseppe Mazzini, in August that year. The *facinorosi* were linked to the Partito della Società Nazionale, the party in power. This means that there was already a 'political mafia' at work, carrying out murders and attacks as part of the struggle for power, and violence was used by the various political forces, although primarily by those in government, even though most of the accused belonged to the opposition.

In the view of an informer working for Prefect Gualterio, the *partito della Maffia* was part of the opposition and Corrao, as we have seen, was regarded as having links with the Bourbons and being the leader of the mafia. In fact in Sicily at that time the transition entailed a reshuffling of the cards, with the use of violence seen as a resource and a manifestation of the political struggle. Sicily might be in opposition to the governments of the historical Right but then, and later at times of change, the mafia had its feet in both camps. Violence was everywhere, even if the most notorious cases were ascribed to the opposition.

## The Castellammare Revolt and the Mafia as Mediator

These cases include the Castellammare revolt and the stabbings in Palermo, both of which took place in 1862.[1] Early in January, about a thousand people in the town of Castellammare del Golfo, in the province of Trapani, rose up in what was to become known as the revolt against the *cutrara* (the term means the bourgeoisie or gentlemen who had shared between them the *cutra*, or blanket – that is, had become rich by appropriating land – and were responsible for the administration of the municipality). Those taking part in the revolt, most of them peasants, were protesting against the compulsory levy and the tax burden but more generally against their miserable living conditions. They attacked the houses of the *cutrara* and the customs and municipal offices and killed five people. Their numbers included people who had taken part in the movements against the Bourbons and some could be seen as mafia leaders. One example is the members of the Ferrantelli family, who patrolled the town armed as if they were public officials and during the revolt carried out public order duties and mediated between the rebels and the authorities. Later one of them would turn to business and land speculation. In that way the members of the family succeeded in changing their social status, rising from being *bracciali* (agricultural labourers) to gentlemen and engaging in a variety of activities: money lending, cattle raising and land rental, combining legal activities with illegal practices, such as rustling. Marriage with women of a higher social class helped them to rise in society. One of them would be elected as a town councillor and was regarded as a 'friend of the mafia' but never convicted.

### The Palermo Stabbings: Use of the 'Strategy of Tension'

On the evening of 1 October 1862, 12 people were stabbed in Palermo, one of whom died a few days later. Using information given by one of the attackers arrested after the event, a trial was held, which resulted in several of the perpetrators being sentenced to death or prison terms. However, it proved impossible to determine who had given the orders; one of the names put forward was the Prince of Sant'Elia, Romualdo Trigona, the leader of the pro-government party and a senator in the national Parliament.

This event may be regarded as the first example of what has only recently, after the Piazza Fontana massacre in 1969, been called the 'strategy of tension' and was the outcome of the conflicts that had accompanied the birth of a united Italy. As in more recent times, justice was concerned only with the perpetrators and left unresolved the problem of who had given the orders.

Those who carried out the stabbings appear to have been hired felons drawn from the criminal underclass rather than members of a mafia organization; labourers for the mafia and hired hands, rather than genuine members of the mafia organization.

### 1863–5: The Thing Finds its Name

The popular play *I mafiusi di la Vicaria di Palermu* was staged for the first time in 1863 and the word *mafiusi* is used only in the title.[2] The text talks of *camorristi*, a term meaning the members of an association of prisoners (*sucività*) with a hierarchical structure, which operated a system of levies (*pizzo*) within the prison.

A key figure in the play is *L'Incognito* (a person unknown), identified as Francesco Crispi, one of the leaders of the Risorgimento, who worked on rescuing prisoners: in fact, the head of the camorra association will go on to join the workers' mutual support society, one of the first workers' organizations, and give up his life of crime.

Two years later came the report by Prefect Gualterio already mentioned, the first official document to use the word 'maffia'. The development of the so-called 'maffia', or criminal association, was ascribed to a misunderstanding between the country and the authorities; the *trista associazione* had had a role in all the movements, supporting the liberals in 1848, the Bourbons in the restoration of their power and the followers of Garibaldi in 1860. Now it was with the opposition: their leaders were first of all the Partito d'Azione, the Bourbons and Corrao, and then his successor, Badia. I have already noted that Gualterio used the same method as Calà Ulloa, building up a picture of the whole opposition as criminal, while the MP Pantaleoni explicitly referred to the links between the *facinorosi* and the governing party.

However, the word had now been baptized in a literary work, albeit a popular one, and confirmed by officialdom.

## From Opposition to Integration

Discussions of the early years of a united Italy, from 1860 to 1876, which saw power shift from the historical Right to the so-called Left, have seen the mafia as first in opposition and then as integrated into government. But was the mafia ever really in opposition? Sicily voted massively for the Left, which was in opposition, but in fact the mafia had its feet in both camps. We have considered the Corrao crime as politico-mafia and it was against a member of the opposition; the stabbers may have been following the orders of men in power, who were, however, unhappy with what they had achieved. The actions of the chief of police of Palermo, Giuseppe Albanese, and his clash with the prosecutor, Diego Tajani, are also significant.[3] Albanese took up a model formerly used by the Bourbon chief of police, Salvatore Maniscalco: he enrolled criminals in his force and in summer 1869 was stabbed. Tajani, who as a magistrate had tried to prosecute him for having engaged criminals to assassinate mafiosi (Albanese was acquitted), had become an opposition politician. In 1875 he made a speech to Parliament containing precise accusations: the police chief was knifed by a mafioso who had not accepted the deal of either joining the police or being sentenced to forced residence (being required to live in a different part of the country). And the Left constantly accused the governments of the Right of having established in Sicily an administration that colluded with criminals.

The Right lost power in March 1876 but first set up a parliamentary Commission of Inquiry on Sicily. This resulted in Romualdo Bonfadini's report describing the mafia as disorganized and reduced to 'an instinctive, brutal and self-interested solidarity, which unites against the state, the laws and legitimate bodies all those individuals and social classes that prefer to base their lives and comforts on violence, deceit and intimidation rather than on work'.[4]

In their private inquiry, which they carried out in 1875–6 alongside the official inquiry, the young Tuscan nobles Leopoldo Franchetti and Sidney Sonnino reached rather different conclusions. Franchetti had looked at the mafia, which he had seen in Sicily as being *facinorosi della classe media* (middle-class thugs) establishing an 'industry of violence' to gain wealth and power and becoming 'a class with its own industry and interests, a social force in its own right', whose existence and development depended on the dominant class. The state took a firm line against the working classes but was powerless against the mafia and the better off. He even identified firms run directly by mafia members. He too saw no centralized organization, but understood perfectly that the mafia, unlike other criminal groups that could be found more or less anywhere, was not only a criminal phenomenon but also a way of accumulating wealth and power.[5]

In 1876 the historical Left gained power and the historian Salvatore Francesco Romano has argued that the period saw the political legalization of the mafia, with the entry of its members into the institutions. The academic and politician Napoleone Colajanni has called the government 'the king of the mafia' and a first-rank historian and politician, Gaetano Salvemini, described Giovanni Giolitti, the Minister of the Treasury from 1889 and Prime Minister from 1892 and on several subsequent occasions, as the Ministro della malavita (Minister of Criminality).[6] The practices of *trasformismo* became generalized and the scandal of the Banca Romana among others demonstrates the extent to which political life had degenerated.

The first government of the Left, led by Agostino Depretis, had as its Minister of the Interior the former follower of Garibaldi, Giovanni Nicotera. Following the kidnapping of a British citizen, John Rose, by the bandit Leone, he appointed Antonio Malusardi as prefect of Palermo, who organized a military campaign against banditry using dubious methods. Landowners and mafiosi supported the campaign against the bandits, even though they had maintained and made use of them: this, too, is a sort of constant thread through the history of the mafia.

Malusardi also set out to uncover mafia-type groups. But who were the mafiosi? A list of 'maffiosi' in the areas of Cefalù and Termini, in the province of Palermo, updated in 1877, regards as such primarily those supporting bandits, including landowners, leading figures and professional people. There were also eight priests. In his July 1874 report, the prefect of Palermo, Gioacchino Rasponi, noted that the mafia was invading all classes of society: the rich, the middle classes – where it was particularly powerful, especially in the recruitment of lawyers – and the proletariat. He distinguished the criminal mafioso from the mafioso who does not reveal himself openly, and then defined a third sort, the *manutengoli,* who could be considered as associated with the mafia and who adopted that status either to participate in the illicit gains of the criminals or, through fear, to secure protection or to ensure the safety of their own lives and property. We may well wonder whether the information on which the list of mafiosi was based was not influenced by political interests. The measures applied to many of those listed were warnings and forced exile but many others accused of mafia activity would soon be brought to trial. However, it is significant that when Malusardi proposed attacking *manutengoli* and collaborators he attracted criticism from both the Right and Left and had to stop. Like Tajani before him, he would leave public administration for a career in politics; Cesare Mori would see exactly the same interruption of 'work in progress' in the 1920s.

The accusations of Gaspare Galati, a doctor in Palermo who was harassed by the guards of his citrus plot, are important documents showing how the mafia operated. Galati reveals that he had dismissed a guard who had been stealing from him; his replacement was killed. This happened in the early 1870s and the plot took place the village of Uditore (800 inhabitants), where 34 killings were reported in 1874: there was a war between the groups of the Badalamenti and the Amoroso. Galati was forced to leave Palermo but wrote down all that he had endured. The judicial authorities took no action and the Ministry of the Interior felt obliged to intervene. Ermanno Sangiorgi, whom we shall meet again later in this narrative, undertook the inquiry, which revealed protections even within the magistracy.

### Trials of Mafia Groups

In 1878 there took place in Palermo the trial of a group accused of being part of a mafia splinter group, the Stuppagghieri based in Monreale, near the city. This trial was the result of revelations by one of the first *pentiti*, Salvatore D'Amico, who was murdered one month before the trial. Twelve of the accused received sentences of five years in prison for criminal association while six others were acquitted. The verdict was overturned for procedural reasons and a new trial, held in Catanzaro, resulted in acquittals.[7]

Was this what we would today call a 'mafia-type' association or was it an invention? Even though the search for evidence and the conduct of the trial leave considerable room for doubt, and even though a large part of the reconstruction carried out by the local authorities and the police, which talks of a 'sort of internationalist, making war on people and property', was never proved, it is nevertheless true that a large number of crimes and a series of killings had been recorded in the Monreale area: 22 October 1874 saw the death of Felice Marchese, water keeper and so in charge of an essential resource for the cultivation of citrus fruits; 14 August 1876 marked the killing of landowner and National Guard captain Stefano Di Mitri, and 27 August that of Simone Cavallaro, who accused the Stuppagghieri before he died. And it was certainly no accident that the key witness D'Amico was killed before the trial. It is not possible to explain it all as merely the 'common interests' of individual operators – it has the characteristics of a strategy orchestrated within a more or less rigidly structured organization, able to work consistently and in depth at cultivating interests and undertaking criminal activities in pursuit of its aim of territorial domination.

By contrast, the trial in 1883 of the Amoroso brothers and others accused of involvement in the Porta Montalto band found that an association had indeed existed and passed nine death sentences on those found guilty of murder.

Sentences were also passed on those found guilty in the Fratellanza (Brotherhood) of Favara trial, which took place in Agrigento in 1885.[8] Charges of criminal association were brought against 168 people, of whom 107 were detained. The association extended over a number of municipalities and had some 500 members, under a leader and a statute that included initiation rites, an oath and recognition signs of Masonic origin (and talk of a 'universal republic'). The association had been formed in the prisons of Ustica and it included several subgroups, apparently intended for mutual assistance. Most of the members had worked in the sulphur mines, but there were also peasants, craftsmen and landowners. The prison sentences imposed ranged from two to four years.

---

## The Word 'Mafia'

Giuseppe Pitrè, the famous student of folk traditions, held that the word 'mafia' and its derivatives, particularly the adjective 'mafioso', were used in an area of Palermo, the Borgo, in the nineteenth century to mean 'beautiful, graceful, perfect, excellent of its kind'. Following the success of the play *I mafiusi di la Vicaria* ... it became 'synonymous with banditry, organized crime, criminality'. Pitrè's argument ties in with his view of the mafia, which always seeks to justify the organization.

The word 'mafia' could come from Arabic words such as *mahias* (boastful, aggressive), *maha* (a quarry also serving as a place of refuge) or *mu afah* (*mu* meaning salvation and *afah* to protect).

Others have proposed fantastical and baseless etymologies, clearly intended to cast the mafia in a favourable light, such as *Ma fia* (My daughter), the cry of the mother whose daughter was raped by a French soldier, the episode which precipitated the Sicilian Vespers in 1282, whence the acronym 'Morte Ai Francesi Italia Anela' (Italy desires the death of the French). Another version makes the founder of the mafia Giuseppe Mazzini, the word being an acronym of his terrorist and revolutionary programme: *Mazzini Autorizza Furti Incendi Avvelenamenti* (Mazzini authorizes thefts, fires and poisoning). The mafia as a secret criminal association may have incorporated rituals from other associations, such as the Carbonari and the Masons, but that does not mean it can be identified with Mazzini's movement.

Nor are there any grounds for deriving the word from the mythical group of dispensers of justice, the Beati Paoli, which was generally held to have defended the weak against abuses of power by the powerful.

---

## 1893: The Notarbartolo Murder and the Banking Scandals

Even though the 1875 parliamentary Commission of Inquiry had looked at the mafia, it could be said that Italy, and in particular public opinion, discovered the mafia after the Notarbartolo crime, since the trials were held in Milan, Bologna and Florence and the press followed them avidly.[9]

Emanuele Notarbartolo, mayor of Palermo from 1873 to 1875 and director of the Banco di Sicilia from 1876 to 1890, was conspicuous for his integrity as an administrator and for his steadfast opposition to the bank's speculative manoeuvres. He was killed on 1 February 1893, on a train bringing him back to Palermo.

Two men were charged with the killing at the first trial in Milan, but accusations by the dead man's son Leopoldo resulted in the arraignment of Raffaele Palizzolo, a Member of Parliament with close links to mafiosi and whom Notarbartolo had accused of receiving illicit favours from the bank. Palizzolo was found guilty at the trial in Bologna but the sentence was overturned for procedural reasons. At the trial in Florence he was acquitted due to lack of evidence.

Despite this final acquittal, the trials had shed light on the responsibilities of the magistracy in the conduct of the inquiry, the role of Palizzolo and his links with the criminal underworld. They also revealed the role of the 'Pro Sicily' committee set up to support Palizzolo, which marks the official birth of *sicilianismo*: the view that anybody who speaks of the mafia as a criminal association is guilty of insulting Sicily. The academic Giuseppe Pitrè, one of its founders, held that the mafia was merely a hypertrophied ego that had nothing to do with crime.[10] On the other side was Leopoldo Notarbartolo, who had done everything possible to identify those to blame, the first example of a family member who struggled to obtain justice and the truth. At the triumphal welcome that greeted the acquitted Palizzolo, he described Palermo as a 'cannibal city'.

The background to the Notarbartolo crime was not simply Sicilian: these were the years that saw the Banca Romana scandal involving the bank's governor, Bernardo Tanlongo, and politicians who received loans to finance their electoral campaigns. In the specific case of the Banco di Sicilia, there were links between speculators and notorious members of the mafia who engaged in crime to be able to continue their speculations.

## The Peasant Struggles:
## From the Fasci Siciliani to the Collective Leases

From 1891 to early in 1894 Sicily was the scene of a major mass movement which became known as the Fasci siciliani. The Fasci were a broad church. They were organizations halfway between trade unions and political parties (these were the years that saw the birth of the Socialist Party at national level), embracing peasants, craftsmen, sulphur miners, teachers and those working in the professions. Their demands were: labour contracts, increased pay, an eight-hour day, better conditions for share-croppers (peasants working on land belonging to landowners) and participation in the municipal administration.

There are at least three reasons why the Fasci may be regarded as the first movement to oppose the mafia:

1. In their plans to reform labour relations and renew local administrations, the Fasci came up against a power bloc in which the role of the mafia was far from being secondary.
2. The Fasci deliberately raised the problem of the mafia; partly to rebut the accusation of being associations of criminals, their rules excluded mafiosi and criminals and they accepted only minor offenders whom they believed they could reintegrate into society.
3. The Fasci movement was put down in blood by the institutions and the mafia: there is documentary evidence that both the forces of law and order and the mafia shot down demonstrators.

These points do not apply to all the Fasci but are true of the bulk of them, who saw themselves as socialists and, more or less coherently, based their actions on socialist principles. Alongside them were Fasci that arose primarily from local quarrels and interests and in two cases turned out to be organizations of mafiosi, who later even sought to align themselves with the popular protest.

The Fasci movement was born in a situation dominated by economic crisis and in which the 'agrarian question' was attracting the attention of the international workers' movement, which had a very different point of view. While for some the question was how to bring peasants of all kinds (the real workers as narrowly defined, the small peasants and those with medium-sized holdings) to embrace socialism, others saw this as possible only for the first group, the agricultural labourers.

In Sicily the Fasci marked the moment when the lower classes transformed their mutual assistance societies, operating under the protection of the more favourably inclined employers, into an autonomous organization. That is why the Fasci were interested in the theoreticians and leaders of the workers' movement both in Italy and elsewhere in Europe: including Friedrich Engels, who alongside Marx was the main socialist ideologist, Antonio Labriola, the main Italian socialist thinker, and Filippo Turati, the national secretary of the Socialist Party.

The Fasci rose and fell in a few years. The first were born in 1891 and 1892, and on 21 and 22 May 1893 the regional congress resulting in a leadership committee was held in Palermo; from August to November that year there was an agricultural strike to secure implementation of the Corleone Pacts, which reformed agricultural contracts, and in October there was the miners' congress. The year 1893 opened and closed in blood: on 20 January there was a massacre in Caltavuturo (Palermo), where the Fascio had not yet been established: the forces of law and order shot at demonstrators demanding the allocation of state land usurped by the middle classes, leaving 13 dead and many wounded. In December 1893 and early in January 1894 agitation against taxes degenerated into the traditional peasant revolts, but the response was disproportionate and over 90 died. On 3 January, Prime Minister Francesco Crispi ordered the dissolution of the Fasci, and the leaders and most active members were put on trial.

The Fasci had an extensive organizational network that exerted a form of territorial control, were self-financing and totalled between 300,000 and 400,000 members. Women played a significant role; indeed in some centres, for example at Piana dei Greci (Palermo), Fasci consisting only of women were established. Alongside their political work, they were extremely active on the cultural front, teaching reading and writing (the illiteracy rate was extremely high, reaching almost 100 per cent among women), organizing theatrical productions and forming musical bands. The national government, led by Giovanni Giolitti from Piedmont, sought to criminalize the movement by sending in the chief of police, Giuseppe Sensales, who drew up reports recording only minor criminal infringements (mostly involving contravention of public safety rules arising from action by pickets to prevent blacklegging during strikes), arrested many leaders but avoided using force. The new prime minister, Crispi, linked with the landowners who were increasingly concerned by the growth and success of the movement, decided to put it down with bloodshed, promising measures to help the peasants, which were not adopted.

The trials demonstrated the character of the leaders of the Fasci, who gained the esteem and admiration even of the military advocates they were assigned, and resulted in heavy sentences, although an amnesty was granted after a few years. In the years that followed, about one million people left Sicily. They were essentially young people: an exodus that would be repeated after subsequent phases of the peasant struggles.

The peasant movement reawoke in the early years of the twentieth century with a number of initiatives. The most notable include collective leases and the formation of alternative credit institutions. Co-operatives that sought to lease land, through the practice known as 'collective leasing', were formed to remove the management of the land from the mafia lessors: this was a strategic choice aimed at destroying the mafia's social and business role. Cooperatives were also founded by both socialists and Catholics engaged in social activities, as prescribed by Pope Leo XIII's encyclical *Rerum novarum*. Collective leases flourished in four regions: Sicily, Emilia, Piedmont and Lombardy. Sicily was in the lead with 56 leases in 1906 covering 39,800 hectares of farmland and a membership of 15,900. Although the cooperative offered better conditions, the landowners regarded collective leases with suspicion since they increased the role of the peasant movement; they preferred the mafia lessors who ensured exploitation of the peasant labour force. World War I dealt a fatal blow to this experiment.

To counter the problem of usury, which the landowners used to fleece the peasants, the *casse rurali* (rural savings banks) offering small-scale credit were founded, primarily by Catholics. They grew swiftly and spread throughout Italy in only a few years; Sicily, which had 145, was in fifth place behind the Veneto, Lombardy, Piedmont and Emilia. Palermo, with 40 banks, was the leading province in Sicily.

---

### The role of Women in the Fasci Siciliani

*The journalist Adolfo Rossi meets some women in Piana dei Greci:*

'What do you hope for from the Fasci?'
A married peasant woman, beautiful with gleaming white teeth and wide eyes sparkling with intelligence:
'We want everybody to work as we do. For there to be no more rich or poor. For everybody to have bread for themselves and their children. We should all be equal. I've got five children and only one small room, where we have to eat, sleep and do everything while lots of rich people have ten or twelve rooms, large houses all to themselves.'
'So you would like to share out land and houses?'
'No, we should just own them in common and share out fairly what they yield.'
'Aren't you afraid that, even if we managed to achieve collective ownership, some trickster, some arch-deceiver might not emerge?'
'No, because brotherhood should prevail and anybody who failed in that respect would be punished.'

'What are your relations with your priests?'

'Jesus was a true socialist and wanted exactly what the Fasci are asking for, but the priests don't represent him accurately, particularly when they lend money. When the *Fascio* was set up our priests opposed it and in the confessional they said that the socialists were excommunicated. But we said they were wrong and in June, to protest against their attacks on the *Fascio*, none of us went to the Corpus Christi procession. That was the first time anything like that had happened.'

An old lady (who stood up and spoke in the middle of the circle so that I could hear her clearly): 'Originally, the rich were not religious and now we have the *Fascio* they have joined up with the priests and insult us socialist women as if we had been dishonoured. The least they say is that we are all the chairman's trollops.'

From Adolfo Rossi, *L'agitazione in Sicilia. Inchiesta sui Fasci dei lavoratori*, Palermo: la Zisa, 1988, pp. 68–9 (1st edn 1894).

## 1898–1900: The Reports by Police Chief Sangiorgi

Between 1898 and 1900 the Palermo police chief, Ermanno Sangiorgi, drew up a series of reports containing a detailed picture of the mafia in that city. In his report of 8 November 1898, Sangiorgi wrote:

The countryside of Palermo, like other parts of this and neighbouring provinces, is sadly in thrall to a vast association of criminals, organized into sections and divided into groups: each group is governed by a leader, called *capo-rione* (ward-boss), and, depending on the number of members and the extent of the territory in which he is required to work, the ward-boss is assisted by a *sottocapo* (underboss), who is empowered to replace him if he is absent or otherwise unable to act. And over all this company of criminals is set a supreme leader. The ward-bosses are chosen by the members and the supreme leader by the ward-bosses in a meeting, normally held in the countryside. The aim of the association is to secure a dominant position, and hence to impose on the landowners, the stewards, the keepers and the labourers, the tolls and prices for the sale of fruit and other products of the earth: anyone who prefers to avoid problems and harm accepts these levies: anyone who wishes to enjoy the peace of staying in the countryside in other ways must make a financial contribution, which is normally requested by means of threatening letters.[11]

It is plain that this is the organizational structure of Cosa Nostra as it was to be revealed by Tommaso Buscetta and other mafiosi who cooperated with the authorities in the 1980s.

Using confidential sources, Sangiorgi succeeded in reconstructing a series of crimes. The murders included that of a girl, Emanuela Sansone, the daughter of the inn-keeper Giuseppa Di Sano, who had been the target of a failed attack by mafiosi who suspected her of having reported them because she had discovered that they were forging coins. Di Sano resisted intimidation and accused the mafiosi of being responsible for the crime. In the trial held in Palermo in 1901, of the 51 defendants, there were 32 convictions and 19 acquittals.

After the trial, Sangiorgi's reports were consigned to oblivion and there grew the idea of a mafia without form or structure, the word being understood merely as a description of how Sicilians behaved and operated. It took almost a century for a view of the mafia based on the existence and relationship of a hierarchically ordered organizational structure, like the one that Sangiorgi had outlined in his reports, to re-emerge.

## The Slaughter of Militants and Leaders: Panepinto, Verro, Alongi and Orcel

In the early years of the twentieth century, mafia violence claimed further victims among those active in the peasant movement and its leaders. In 1905 the agricultural labourer Luciano Nicoletti was killed in Corleone; the following year saw the death there of the doctor Andrea Orlando, who had supported the peasants in their requests for collective leases. The socialist leader Lorenzo Panepinto was killed in Santo Stefano Quisquina (Agrigento) in 1911 and in 1915, again in Corleone, it was the turn of Bernardino Verro, a leader of the peasant movement since the days of the Fasci siciliani and the socialist mayor.

Following the end of World War I, the peasant struggles resumed with the occupation of land. During the war, there had been promises to redistribute land and 1919 saw the promulgation of the Visocchi and Falcioni decrees on the redistribution of land which was badly cultivated or not cultivated at all. The socialists and the Catholics in the Partito popolare were now joined by soldiers' and veterans' associations.

Repression by the mafia and the institutions also resumed. In 1919 Giovanni Zangara was killed in Corleone, Giuseppe Rumore in Prizzi

(Palermo) and Alfonso Canzio in Barrafranca (Enna). In that year, the police in Riesi (Caltanissetta), acting on the orders of Inspector Messana, whom we shall meet again in the 1940s, fired on peasants at a demonstration, killing 15 and wounding 50. On 27 July 1920 there was a massacre in Randazzo (Catania), again by the police, which left nine people dead. The following day six people died and some 40 were wounded in Catania during a meeting organized by the socialist leaders Maria Giudice and Giuseppe Sapienza.

The peasant leader Nicolò Alongi was killed on 29 February 1920 in Prizzi, the socialist trade unionist Paolo Mirmina on 3 October in Noto (Siracusa) and the secretary of the metal workers' union Giovanni Orcel on 14 October in Palermo. Alongi and Orcel were working to unite the struggles of the peasants and workers, the urban and the rural campaigns, something that had already been an aim in the time of the Fasci. None of these crimes were ever punished.

## Mafia and Antimafia before and during Fascism

The years 1919 and 1920 have gone down in history as the *biennio rosso* (red two years) because of the struggles by workers that led to the occupation of factories throughout Italy. In Palermo, too, thanks to Orcel and the FIOM (the metal workers' union), the shipyard, the biggest factory in the city, was occupied and self-management implemented with the construction of ships, including one named after Alongi, the peasant leader killed at the end of February 1920. The unity of intent, which was also marked by the dispatch of foodstuffs from the countryside, should be noted.

Before the arrival of Fascism in Sicily the struggles against the mafia and for democracy coincided: where the mafia was present, in western Sicily, attacks on working people were directed by mafiosi, while in eastern Sicily groups of *squadristi* (fascist squads) were formed resembling those elsewhere in Italy. Violence marked the years 1921 and 1922. In January 1921 in Vittoria (Ragusa), where the town council was socialist, veterans adopting nationalist positions, fascists and the local mafia group of goat herds wrecked the socialist club and shot at members: the town councillor Giuseppe Compagna was killed. On 9 April in Ragusa fascist *squadristi* attacked a demonstration, leaving four dead and over 60 wounded. At the end of May in Modica

(Ragusa) nationalists and fascists, supported by police officers, shot at workers returning from a demonstration, killing six. There were further deaths in other towns and the violence of the *squadristi* was tolerated and encouraged by the authorities.

In western Sicily the mafia and the fascists were active. On 28 April 1921 Vito Stassi, the president of the Lega Contadina, was murdered in Piana dei Greci. On the night of 30 April/1 May the offices of the metal workers' federation in Palermo were gutted. On 8 May in Castelvetrano (Trapani) fascists shot on those attending a socialist meeting: in the exchange of gunfire that followed three socialists and two fascists were killed.

During 1922 the socialists Domenico, Mario and Pietro Paolo Spatola and Antonino Scuderi were killed in Paceco (Trapani), the young communist Orazio Sortino died in Vittoria and the socialist mayor of Monte San Giuliano (the modern-day Erice, Trapani), Sebastiano Bonfiglio, was murdered. Fascism was on the way to power; following the 'march on Rome' in October 1922 Mussolini became leader of the government. In the wake of the landowners who had supported his accession to power, there were mafia groups within the Fascist Party and the new regime. On 11 January 1923 the transfer of the large estates to peasant cooperatives was abrogated and subsequently non-fascist parties and organizations were banned, and trade union and political leaders and activists were sent to prison or into forced residence.

There are differing opinions on the measures taken by Fascism against the mafia. The regime's supporters argue that Fascism routed the mafia, but in the view of its opponents it merely attacked its lower echelons while coopting the higher ones. One thing that is certain is that the work being carried out by Prefect Cesare Mori was abruptly interrupted just when he was beginning to attack some highly placed people who were integrated into the new power system.

Cesare Mori had already been in Sicily, in the Trapani district, as police commissioner from 1904 to 1914; he returned there in 1916 and later, from 1924 to 1925, was prefect of Trapani. In October 1925 he was appointed prefect of Palermo with the specific task of undertaking the battle against the mafia to achieve 'the Fascist purification of the island'. He stayed in Sicily until June 1929, when he was retired at just 57 years of age. It is said that Mussolini decided to engage in this battle following a visit to Sicily during which the mafia leader and mayor of Piana dei

Greci, Ciccio Cuccia, told him that he did not need his police bodyguard because the Duce was his guest.

Mori made use of the special powers he had been granted to capture a large number of real and presumed bandits and mafiosi, laying siege to places such as Gangi in the Madonie, and made 11,000 arrests. These resulted in massive trials with sentences and acquittals. He targeted principally the mafia land lessors in order to free landowners from the burden they imposed, but he very quickly realized that many of them were deeply involved in and supported Fascism. He secured the arrest of the fascist leader Alfredo Cucco and attempted to aim as high as General Antonino Di Giorgio; at this point he was sidelined. Fascism's operations against the mafia must be regarded as ambiguous: it attacked the emerging middle classes and brought into the regime the landowners, who appeared in the trials as prosecution witnesses rather than accomplices and supporters.

In political and social terms, the elimination of the peasant movement removed from the scene the mafia's traditional opponent, and the redistribution of the large estates remained virtually a dead letter. The basic features of the situation that had given rise to the mafia remained unchanged, however. Several mafia groups were eliminated and their members imprisoned, but they would re-emerge immediately after World War II and the fall of the dictatorship.

## After World War II: The Mafia and Separatism

The war in Sicily finished in August 1943, a few weeks after the Allies had landed on 10 July. What part did the mafia play in the landing? For many years its role was considered important, if not decisive, but more recent studies have radically reassessed this. The military operations required a large number of men and resources and almost all the mafia leaders were in prison or had emigrated. The mafia certainly played a major role in the period after the landings and in the social control of the island, which, for seven months until February 1944, was subject to government by the victors: the AMGOT (Allied Military Government of Occupied Territories).

Because the mafiosi were regarded as having been persecuted by Fascism, they were appointed as mayors and landowners, and mafiosi were to be found at the head of the separatist movement, which aimed to separate Sicily from Italy and make it one of the United States of America. It also established its own army, including bandits such as Salvatore Giuliano, who led one of the many bands formed at that time.

In fact the difficult restoration of democracy, the formation of political parties and the organization of trade unions, plus the renewed mobilization of the peasants, led to fears that Sicily too would feel the effects of the so-called 'wind from the North', and landowners and conservatives prepared to deal with the situation: they threatened separatism but endeavoured to defeat the parties of the Left and secure regional autonomy under their own control. The national government from 1944 to 1947 was an anti-fascist coalition comprising the Christian Democrats, the Socialist Party, the Communist Party and the Partito d'Azione (Party of Action), while from 25 April 1945 the Allies and partisan groups fought the Nazis and fascists in central and northern Italy.

In October 1944 the anti-fascist government issued the Gullo decrees, named after the Minister of Agriculture, the communist Fausto Gullo. The two most important of these laid down that yields should be shared, with 60 per cent going to the labourers and 40 per cent to the landowners, and that land that remained uncultivated or badly cultivated should be allocated to peasant cooperatives. These provisions gave rise to a unprecedented movement: up to the mid-1950s more than half a million people would be involved, first in the implementation of the Gullo decrees and then in agricultural reform.

## The Peasant Struggles in 1945 and 1946

The peasant struggles in the period after World War II fall into three phases: (1) from 1944 to 1945, the fight for people's granaries and for implementation of the Gullo decree on the division of the yield; (2) from 1945 to 1949, the fight for the allocation of uncultivated or badly cultivated land; (3) from 1949 to the early 1950s, the struggle for agricultural reform.

The people's granaries provided for the compulsory procurement of wheat to meet food needs; they were openly boycotted by separatist landowners and in some provinces remained almost empty. The police were particularly harsh with small- and medium-sized producers but very gentle on the major producers. Agitation for implementation led to the first clash with landowners and the mafia. On 12 August 1944 Andrea Raia, a member of a committee overseeing the granaries, was killed in Casteldaccia, in the province of Palermo. On 27 May the secretary of the provincial communist federation, Santi Milisenna, was killed during a separatist demonstration in Regalbuto, in the province of Enna, and on 16 September the regional communist leader, Girolamo Li Causi, was attacked in Villalba (Caltanissetta), the stronghold of the mafia leader Calogero Vizzini, who supported simultaneously the Separatist Party and the Christian Democrats. When Li Causi began to talk about the mafia, shots were fired and the town mayor, Beniamino Farina, Vizzini's nephew, threw a bomb which wounded Li Causi. Vizzini was sentenced in 1949 but lived in hiding while still continuing to carry out his activities.

The struggles in the countryside continued and in the towns there were demonstrations against the rising cost of living. In Palermo, on 19 October, officers ordered soldiers to fire on a crowd of demonstrators, leaving 19 dead and 108 wounded, according to the official figures. The Comitato di liberazione counted 30 dead and 150 wounded – children and some women were among the fatalities.

In summer 1945 the grain harvests sparked battles over the allocation of the crops, led by share-croppers in villages in the provinces of Agrigento, Caltanissetta, Enna and Palermo. These were villages where the Fasci had been strong and were now led by the Socialist and Communist Parties. Their demand was for the implementation of a national law, but the landowners, large land lessors, gamekeepers and police claimed to have no knowledge of the law – it did not exist. In this way a struggle for the rule of law turned into an illegal struggle for a law that did not exist. In 1945 more trade unionists died: Agostino D'Alessandria on 11 September in Ficarazzi (Palermo) and Giuseppe Scalia on 25 November in Cattolica Eraclea (Agrigento). These deaths continued in 1946: the socialist mayor Gaetano Guarino died on 16 May in Favara (Agrigento); the socialist mayor Pino Camilleri died on 28 June in Naro (Agrigento); on 22 September a bomb was thrown into a house where a meeting was being held in Alia (Palermo), killing the peasants Giovanni Castiglione and Girolamo Scaccia; on 22 October a share-cropper, Giuseppe Biondo, died in Santa Ninfa (Trapani); on 2 November the peasants Giovanni, Vincenzo and Giuseppe Santangelo were killed in Belmonte Mezzagno (Palermo); and on 23 December

Nicolò Azoti died in Baucina (Palermo). The aim was to decapitate and terrorize the peasant movement by striking at its leaders and most active members.

## The Portella Massacre and the 1947 Crisis

The year 1947 began with the murder, on 4 January, of Accursio Miraglia, the secretary of the Sciacca (Agrigento) Camera del lavoro (Trades Council) and a communist leader. This was yet another death that had been foretold: Miraglia had received threats but nothing had been done to protect him. The judicial process followed its usual course: the murderers confessed but the Palermo Court of Appeal acquitted them because they had withdrawn their confessions on the grounds that they had been tortured. The police officers accused of ill-treatment were acquitted because 'the facts did not stand up', but the investigation into who had carried out and planned the murders was not reopened.

On 17 January the communist activist Pietro Macchiarella was killed in Ficarazzi (Palermo) and on the same day at the Palermo shipyard a number of mafiosi, led by the local boss of the Acquasanta area, Nicola D'Alessandro, fired on workers protesting against the presence of the mafia and demanding the dismissal of the head of the canteen, Emilio Ducci, a fascist sent to Palermo by the Piaggio company, which was managing the shipyard. Of the workers, Francesco Paolo Di Fiore and Antonino Lo Surdo were wounded.

On 7 March, during a demonstration against the high cost of living in Messina, *carabinieri* shouted 'Avanti Savoia' ('Up with Savoy'), the former royal house of Italy (the Republic had already been established in Italy in 1946), and fired into the crowd, killing the demonstrators Biagio Pellegrino and Giuseppe Maiorana.

On 20 April the first regional elections were held and, in a break with the former elections, the parties of the Left won. In the referendum on the monarchy held on 2 June 1946, the monarchists had won in Sicily with 1,219,100 votes against 705,949 for the republicans, and in the elections for the Constituent Assembly the Christian Democrats had won 643,355 votes (33.62 per cent), the Socialist Party 234,318 (12.25 per cent) and the Communist Party 151,734 (7.91 per cent) – together, the Socialists and Communists had fallen well short of the Christian Democrat vote. Now the parties of the Left, grouped in the Blocco del

Popolo (People's Bloc), won with 567,392 votes (29.13 per cent) while the Christian Democrats had 399,860 (20.52 per cent). The main centres of support for the parties of the Left were in country areas and they won because they were at the forefront of the peasant struggles. Their proposal was to form a unified government, similar to the anti-fascist coalition then governing Italy.

Ten days later, on 1 May, the Portella della Ginestra massacre took place: bandits from the Giuliano band shot at participants in a demonstration to celebrate Labour Day and the victory of the People's Bloc. Official sources put casualties at 11 dead and 30 wounded but the real figures were much higher. That month too the parties of the Left were forced out of the national government and in Palermo a regional government was formed without them. The Christian Democrats entered into an alliance with the parties of the Right, whom it was suggested had ordered the Portella massacre. Li Causi talked of 'political banditry', directed by Inspector Messana, under the protection of the Minister of the Interior, the Sicilian Mario Scelba, who could not have been unaware of the career of the person who had perpetrated the Riesi massacre.

What explanation can be given for the crisis in May 1947, caused by the expulsion of the parties of the left from both the national and the Sicilian governments? What were the relative weights of local and national interests, and international interests stemming from the Yalta agreements, which had divided the world into two major spheres of influence: one under the control of the United States and the other dominated by the Soviet Union? The most convincing explanation is one that links the various levels: the interests of landowners in the South and in Sicily, those of the industrialists in the North and those of the Vatican in its battle against communism coincided perfectly with the geopolitical interests of the world's great powers. Contrary to what Scelba claimed, the massacre was not an isolated act for which bandits could be blamed but was the reply by the landowners, the mafiosi, the conservative parties, the secret services and the neo-fascists to the gains of the peasant movement, which had resulted in the victory of the Left. There followed a dramatic phase in the life of Italy, which culminated in the elections of 18 April 1948, won by the Christian Democrats who would go on to govern Italy for half a century.

The situation became increasingly unfavourable for the peasant struggles and there were more murders during 1947: on 22 June the

Giuliano band and the mafia carried out a series of attacks, killing the activists Giuseppe Casarrubea and Vincenzo Lo Jacono in Partinico (Palermo); on 22 October Giuseppe Maniaci, the secretary of the Confederterra, was killed in Terrasini (Palermo), followed by the death in Marsala (Trapani) on 8 November of Vito Pipitone, another leader of the Confederterra; on 21 December the police killed three demonstrators in Canicattì (Agrigento) during a strike.

On 12 January 1948 there was a major demonstration in Palermo under the slogan: 'Faremo il '48' ('Let's do '48 again'), recalling the centenary of the revolt there in 1848. It was criticized by national Communist Party leaders, who were alarmed by the political framework it represented, but the demonstration was perfectly peaceful and saw the birth of the Costituente siciliana per la terra. An outline project for agricultural reform was also presented. On 2 March 1948 the socialist and peasant leader, Epifanio Li Puma, was killed in Petralia Soprana (Palermo); on 10 March the socialist and secretary of the Camera del lavoro, Placido Rizzotto, died in Corleone; and on 2 April the socialist and secretary of Confederterra, Calogero Cangelosi, was killed in Camporeale (Palermo).

Both the political parties and the country became increasingly divided and, after the elections of 18 April, the divisions grew deeper: on 14 July an attempt was made on the life of the Italian Communist Party leader, Palmiro Togliatti, and during the general strike the trade unions, which had previously been united in the CGIL (Confederazione Generale Sindacati dei Lavoratori), split, with the formation of a union linked to the Christian Democrats, the CISL (Confederazione Italiana Sindacati dei Lavoratori).

## The Struggles for Agricultural Reform

The year 1949 was one of struggles in the Mezzogiorno and clashes with the Celere, the police force set up by Scelba, the Minister of the Interior: on 29 October at Melissa in Calabria the police opened fire on demonstrators who were occupying land, leaving three dead. The president of the Council of Ministers, Alcide De Gasperi, went to Calabria and undertook to give land to the peasants.

In Sicily new tactics were tried in the struggle, with the occupation of land and work-ins involving ploughing and sowing. One of these occasions, 10 March 1950, saw the arrest of the communist leader Pio La Torre, who was to remain in prison until August 1951; in this period thousands of demonstrators were arrested. Figures published by a regional committee for democratic solidarity put the number at over 3,000.

At national level two laws offering partial agricultural reform were adopted during 1950: the Legge Sila No. 230 of 12 May and the Legge stralcio (an 'extract' from the agrarian law) for the South and the islands No. 841, also of 12 May. In Sicily, Regional Law No. 104 of 27 December 1950 was dubbed by the opposition the 'agricultural counter-reform'. The figures speak for themselves and transcend any interpretations offered: implementation of the Gullo decree on uncultivated and badly cultivated land gave the cooperatives concessions covering over 86,000 hectares, run by 50,000 peasants. The regional law assigned by individual ballot (which was a clear invitation to dissolve the cooperatives) gave 99,049 hectares in 17,157 parcels. Only 11 per cent of the 154,000 applicants received a minute piece of land. Prior to implementation of the law, the landowners circumvented it by selling at inflated prices – 193,785 hectares – which fetched between 30 and 60 billion lire, most of which ended up in the pockets of mafia intermediaries.

These struggles continued in the years to come, which saw more deaths: on 7 August 1952 the peasant Filippo Intili was killed in Caccamo (Palermo), on 16 May 1955 the socialist and trade unionist Salvatore Carnevale died in Sciara (Palermo) and on 13 August that year the communist mayor Giuseppe Spagnolo died in Cattolica Eraclea. On 18 March 1958 the trade unionist Vincenzo Di Salvo died in Licata (Agrigento).

During the second half of that decade there began a major migratory flow which over 20 years resulted in more than a million and a half people leaving Sicily. This was the last stage of the movement of Sicilian peasants which, for many years, had been one of the largest social movements in Europe.

## Milazzismo, Mafia and Antimafia

At the end of the 1950s, Sicily became a focus of national attention thanks to the phenomenon of 'milazzismo', named after Silvio Milazzo, who was elected president of the Region of Sicily in 1958 and who, following a dispute with his party, the Christian Democrats, founded a new party: the Unione Siciliana Cristiano Sociale.

Within the Christian Democrats, the party leaders, hitherto comprising well-known veterans, now consisted of ambitious young men who included elements from the right-wing parties, more or less linked to the mafia. The mafiosi of Camporeale in the province of Palermo, led by Vanni Sacco, were eager to join the DC (Democrazia Cristiana); the young Christian Democrat mayor Pasquale Almerico sought to oppose this and was isolated by the party leaders; he was killed on 25 March 1957. Sacco was tried and acquitted for lack of evidence. The DC was successful in the 1958 municipal elections.

Milazzo formed regional governments with men from the Right, supported from the Left by parties that saw his work as undermining the power of the Christian Democrats. Milazzismo was in fact a motley coalition embracing mafia supporters and antimafia provisions, such as the attempt to drive the mafiosi out of the consortia engaged in land improvement. In 1960 the experiment met an inglorious end: an attempt to bribe a deputy to ensure a majority resulted in the briber falling into a trap prepared by the Christian Democrats, who returned to power, heralding a period of centre-left government including the socialists.

At the end of the 1950s and during the early 1960s antimafia activity grew in the building sites of Palermo and in its shipyard. A trade union organization managed to take root on the building sites, against the wishes of the foremen. In the shipyard, located in the Acquasanta area, which was dominated by the mafia, action was taken against the mafiosi who ran the canteen and organized the recruitment of workers by the subcontracting firms. In the mid-1960s a law forbidding the subcontracting of labour was passed.

## The Role of Women

Women played a significant role in all stages of the peasant struggles that followed World War II, either as participants in the occupation of land or as leaders of and activists in political groupings.

The peasants were engaged with their whole families and women died in Portella because they were taking an active part in the demonstrations. As in the time of the Fasci, women often acted as a protective buffer between the demonstrators and the forces of law and order, with whom they sought dialogue and by whom they were arrested and sentenced. Some of them were 'professional revolutionaries' and played leading roles.

A women's movement also began to develop and the first congress of Sicilian women took place on 8 March 1953 in Palermo, accompanied by a large demonstration.

One of the most influential women was Francesca Serio, first abandoned by her husband and then widowed, the mother of the trade unionist and socialist leader Salvatore Carnevale, who was killed by the mafia in 1955. Francesca gave evidence in the trial and sought justice; the mafiosi accused were found guilty at first instance but acquitted on appeal. The future President of the Republic, Sandro Pertini, stood by her side; the defenders of the mafiosi included Giovanni Leone, another future president.

She continued her battle for many years, accusing mafiosi and telling her story throughout Italy, though she died, forgotten, in her little house in Sciara on 18 July 1992.

---

### The Mother of Salvatore Carnevale

*The writer Carlo Levi dedicated to Francesca Serio some of the finest pages of his book* Words are Stones:

She spoke of the death and of the life of her son as though she were resuming a discourse that had been interrupted for a moment by our entrance. She talked, she recounted episodes, she reasoned and discussed and accused, with extreme rapidity and precision, alternating dialect with Italian and detailed narration with the logic of interpretation; and she was simply and completely absorbed in this continuous, endless discourse, the whole of her, without reserve her life as a peasant, her past as a woman deserted and then widowed, the work she had done for years, and the death of her son, and her loneliness, and her house, and Sciara, and Sicily, and the whole of life; all these were contained in that violent yet orderly flow of words. Nothing exists in her, nothing exists for her, except this trial over which she presides and which she carries through all by herself, sitting on her chair beside the bed: the trial of the feudal system, of the servile state of the peasants, the trial of the Mafia and of the government. She identifies herself absolutely with her trial and herself has all its qualities: she is sharp, watchful, suspicious, astute, skilful, imperious, implacable. That is what this woman has made of herself, in one day: tears are no longer tears but words, and words are stones. She speaks with the hardness and precision of a judicial inquiry, with a profound and absolute assurance, like one who has suddenly reached a firm point on which to take a stand, a certainty: and this certainty, which dries her tears and makes her ruthless, is justice itself. True justice, that is; justice as the realization of its own action, as a decision taken once and for all and from which there is no turning back: not the justice of judges, not official justice. That kind of justice Francesca mistrusts and despises: that kind of justice is a part of the injustice that there is in things.

'After my son was dead,' began Francesca, 'the magistrate came to make his report, and he seemed angry. "Don't take any notice of all those workmen looking at you," I said. "All you have to do is your ordinary legal duty; we won't say you're doing it out of affection because he was human flesh and blood like you. You feel yourself to be an exalted kind of person, and this person here didn't seem of any importance to you at all." Then he gave a contemptuous shake of his head, and said: "Ah, it wasn't the moment to do it!" When I heard him talking like that, I turned round and said to him: "Oh you coward, you're quite right to say it wasn't the moment, because you're thinking of the elections and you're losing ground. When you're in power, then, are you going to come in here and kill me? Is that the sort of discipline you bring with you? Why do you make this report just in order to deceive us? Why don't you go home? Certainly, it wasn't the moment."'

And so, face to face with the injustice that there is in things, stands injustice, which is a certainty. But Francesca's reply is not the anarchic, individualist reply that puts arms into the hand of the brigand and thrusts him forth to exile and ostracism and the woods: it is a political reply, bound up with the idea of a common law that is a power upon which one can rely, a power that is the enemy of power: the Party. The law which gives Francesca certainty is not authority or its instruments: these belong by nature to the enemy world.

From Carlo Levi, *Words are Stones*, translated from the Italian by Angus Davidson, New York: Farrar, Straus & Cudahy, 1958, pp. 189–92.

## The Role of the Catholic Church

Throughout the various stages of the peasant struggles, the main feature of the role played by the Catholic Church was its virtually exclusive focus on opposition to socialism and communism. And, since the leaders of the peasant struggles were socialists and communists, the Church, despite some examples of engagement in support of the demands of the weakest strata of society, took a position opposing them.

During the period of the Fasci siciliani only a few members of the lower clergy took the side of the demonstrators and only the Bishop of Caltanissetta, Giovanni Guttadauro, wrote a pastoral letter acknowledging the reasons for discontent. But he, too, like all his colleagues, later took a firm stance against those who, 'with ill intentions', were stirring up people 'destined to be disappointed'. The Archbishop of Palermo, Cardinal Celesia, condemned 'anarchist and socialist agitators' and General Morra di Lavriano, who had directed suppression of the Fasci, visited him in his palace to thank him.

Later, Catholic associations and institutions were founded with the aim of alleviating the poverty of the people and Don Luigi Sturzo, the founder of the Partito popolare, was instrumental in setting up co-operatives to manage some collective leases and savings banks to combat usury. There were also 'social priests' who fell victim to mafia violence. These included Costantino Stella, killed in Resuttano (Caltanissetta) in July 1919, and Stefano Caronia, killed in Gibellina (Trapani) in November 1920. But there were also churchmen who formed part of mafia families, such as the two bishops and three priests in the family of the *capomafia* Calogero Vizzini and the archpriest of Castel di Lucio (Messina), Gian Battista Stimolo, who was killed in 1925 as a result of disputes within the mafia groups.

In the 1940s and 1950s the position of the Church was firmly opposed to the peasant movement led by the parties of the Left, and the Archbishop of Palermo, Cardinal Ernesto Ruffini, even when faced with the Portella della Ginestra massacre, wrote that, while he condemned all acts of violence, this was a reaction to the 'arrogance' of the communists. Following the elections of 18 April, he asked for the Communist Party to be banned and for the Christian Democrats to form a common front with the parties of the Right. In the 1960s, particularly following the Ciaculli massacre in June 1963, Cardinal Ruffini was again one of the leading figures in the attacks on the communists, who had 'invented' the mafia and denigrated Sicily. In his view, even the accusations levelled against the friars based in Mazzarino, in the province of Caltanissetta, were inventions by communists. In the late 1950s and early 1960s some of the friars were tried and convicted for their connections with mafia members, whom they were assisting with extortion rackets.

# CHAPTER 4

# MAFIA AND ANTIMAFIA IN THE 1960s AND 1970s

The 1960s and 1970s may be considered as a transitional period as regards the changes affecting society, the mafia and the struggle against it. The role of agriculture in the Sicilian economy steadily gave way to service industries, as can be seen from the following figures: between 1951 and 1971 the numbers working in agriculture fell sharply, from 760,000 (56 per cent) to 399,000 (29 per cent), while those working in industry rose from 338,000 (25 per cent) to 463,000 (34 per cent) and those engaged in the service (tertiary) sector rose from 255,000 (18 per cent) to 512,000 (37 per cent). While emigration emptied the countryside, the cities grew in response to the needs of industry, chiefly construction, and a tertiary sector comprising principally the public services.

The history of the mafia entered a new, 'urban-entrepreneurial', phase. As explained above, this was not a wholesale move from the countryside to the cities (the mafia continued to be present in rural areas and was already established in the cities) but a shift in its centre of interests. These now focused on building speculation, the channelling of the public funds provided by the Region of Sicily and the Cassa del Mezzogiorno, set up in 1950, and international trafficking, first in cigarettes and then in drugs. These were the areas where the mafia groups squared up to each other, formed their alliances and engaged in bloody battles.

Once the peasant movement had collapsed, the struggle against the mafia was no longer a mass movement. It was the struggle of minorities, carried out at the institutional level by the opposition, which secured the establishment of a parliamentary commission following the Ciaculli massacre, and at the social level through the work of groups and individuals such as Danilo Dolci and Giuseppe Impastato.

## The Mafia War in the Early 1960s

The activities of the mafia in urban areas and in business include: managing business activities, particularly in construction, often acting as an intermediary between landowners and outside firms (the so-called 'sack of Palermo', which began as long ago as the 1950s, was headed by firms from outside Sicily such as Immobiliare using Vatican capital and cooperatives from Emilia that had a monopoly of social housing); control of the food markets; control of recruitment to local government and control of credit. Thanks to these links with institutions the 'mafia bourgeoisie' became increasingly dominant. The sources for the illegal accumulation of wealth were both traditional (extortion), and new (cigarette smuggling, in cooperation with operators in Corsica and Marseilles, and heroin, marketed for consumption primarily in the United States). In October 1957 there was a summit meeting in Palermo between the Sicilian and American branches, which set up a working party concerned with drug trafficking. These activities were managed on an international scale by a single inter-family unit.

The role of the various families would be traced by judicial inquiries, particularly that headed by Cesare Terranova who, using confidential information, documented the formation of a central body: the provincial committee, comprising the heads of the various families. These inquiries followed the many crimes that resulted from the mafia war in the early 1960s but they would be accepted only in part at the largest trial, in 1968, when 114 people appeared before the Catanzaro Assize Court; there were a few convictions and many acquittals. Once again, the organizational structure, which had been revealed by the Sangiorgi reports and again by the Terranova inquiries, was buried and would be disinterred only in the 1980s with the revelations by Buscetta and others who cooperated with the authorities.

The origins of the mafia war fought between 1960 and 1963 lay in the internal power struggle that ranged the traditional families, such as the Greco, against newly emerging figures such as the brothers Angelo and

Salvatore La Barbera. Besides murders carried out using traditional shotguns, cars packed with explosives were also used. On 26 April 1963 an Alfa Romeo packed with dynamite killed the mafia leader Cesare Manzella, the uncle of Peppino Impastato. The greatest slaughter was on 30 June that year when nine people were killed, seven of them at Ciaculli outside Palermo where soldiers inspecting another carload of explosives aimed at local mafiosi detonated an explosion.

The Ciaculli massacre set off alarm bells at national level and the mafia was 'rediscovered' yet again. The parliamentary Antimafia Commission, which had been fruitlessly called for since the 1940s, finally began its work.

In the late 1950s and early 1960s war broke out at Corleone, where Luciano Liggio wiped out his rivals, beginning his blood-spattered career with the murder of the doctor and mafia leader Michele Navarra in August 1958.

## The Role of the Opposition and the Antimafia Commission

At the height of the mafia war that was drenching the streets of Palermo with blood, on 30 March 1962, the Sicilian Regional Assembly approved a motion requesting the establishment of a parliamentary Commission of Inquiry. The Senate approved the law setting up the commission on 11 April and the Chamber gave its final approval on 12 December. However, it did not begin work until after the Ciaculli massacre.

The pace of the commission's work declined steadily from 1963 to 1976 and initial expectations were very soon dashed. It established 12 investigating groups, interrogated national and local authorities and many witnesses, and collected legal and other documents. The chairman, the Christian Democrat Donato Pafundi, described the commission's archive as a 'powder-keg' but its work during the fourth legislature, which ended in 1968, resulted in the publication of three sparse pages. Meanwhile the trial in Lecce of those accused of the murder of the police chief, Cataldo Tandoy, in Agrigento on 30 March 1960 demonstrated his involvement with the local mafia. In July 1966 Agrigento also witnessed the disastrous landslide that was provoked by building speculation in which both the mafia and local government were involved.

Work began again in the fifth legislature under the chairmanship of the Christian Democrat Francesco Cattanei and reports on the mafia and bandits, the wholesale markets and some individual mafia members were approved and published, but the early dissolution of the legislature meant that no final report could be issued.

In July 1972, with the sixth legislature, the chair passed to the Christian Democrat Luigi Carraro. One of the members of the commission was Giovanni Matta, a former Christian Democrat portfolio holder in Palermo, who had been interviewed in that capacity by the previous commission during the course of its inquiries into the city government. The communist members sought and failed to secure the dismissal of Matta, and resigned along with all the other members apart from those belonging to the MSI-Destra nazionale (Italian Social Movement-National Right). In February 1973 the commission was re-established, again under the chairmanship of Luigi Carraro. In 1976 a majority final report was presented, along with two minority reports, one from the PCI (Italian Communist Party), whose signatories included Pio La Torre and Cesare Terranova, and one from the MSI.[1]

The commission's work had been marked by two opposing currents: many members argued that the mafia no longer existed, having become merely a set of urban gangsters with no social foundation (this view was also supported by certain academics), while others acknowledged that the mafia phenomenon had changed and stressed the links between the mafia and institutional and political structures.

The majority report saw the mafia as a feature of the governing classes in earlier periods and embraced the argument that there was no organizational structure, which had been revived in a successful book by the German sociologist Henner Hess. It also spoke of political links but limited them to Vito Ciancimino, a former portfolio holder in the city councils led by Mayor Salvo Lima.

The communist report saw the mafia as still a phenomenon of the governing classes, highlighted the political responsibilities for the Portella della Ginestra massacre and extended the links with politics to the Christian Democrat group in power, headed by Salvo Lima. The MSI report also dealt with links to politics by reporting the history of Luciano Liggio; its final pages were devoted to Salvo Lima.

The commission's work achieved nothing in operational terms but the years following saw the publication of many volumes of documents, which form a valuable archive for reconstructing the story of the mafia at that time.

## Studies on the Mafia

As the commission was carrying out its work, a number of studies were published, principally by sociologists and historians. I have already mentioned the German academic Henner Hess, who defined the mafia as a type of behaviour resulting from a 'subculture' that existed among the population of eastern Sicily, and considered the argument that there was any sort of organization to be wrong.

At the request of the commission, the sociologist Franco Ferrarotti carried out an inquiry into a number of Sicilian municipalities and concluded that the mafia was no longer a local phenomenon but what he described as a basic problem in national development, which also had an international dimension.[2]

Turning also to historical studies, the commission requested Francesco Brancato look into how public opinion reacted to the problem of the mafia and to analyse the relationships between the government and the private and public inquiries. In 1963 Salvatore Francesco Romano published his *Storia della mafia*, the first full treatment of the subject from its origins to World War II and one that also dealt with the American mafia. Romano saw the mafia as the product of a society developing from feudalism into capitalism and regarded the mafia of his day as a power group being used by political, economic and social forces, and that had now spread beyond Sicily. That period also saw the publication of books by Michele Pantaleone, who drew attention to the mafia's links with politics and documented its role in drug trafficking.[3]

## Cardinal Ruffini and the Reverend Panascia

Immediately after the Ciaculli massacre, the Waldensian minister Pietro Valdo Panascia had pasted up on walls in Palermo a poster expressing solidarity with the relatives of the victims and demanding that the authorities shoulder their responsibilities in the name of respect for life. This document attracted the interest of the Vatican, and the Under-Secretariat of State wrote to Cardinal Ruffini asking whether it would not be opportune to promote measures to distinguish the so-called 'mafia' mentality from the religious mentality and encourage more consistent observance of Christian principles.

Ruffini's reply was stern and acerbic; there were no links between the mafia mentality and religion and Panascia's initiative was merely a *ridiculous* attempt by Protestants to exploit the situation. In his view, the socialists and communists talked about the mafia and its links with the Christian Democrats in order to defend their interests in competition with the mafia organizers or those considered as such. Ruffini regarded the mafia as mere criminals like those who could be found anywhere and believed that the Catholic Church had nothing to apologize for – it was at work every day while Panascia's action was a one-off.

On Palm Sunday 1964, Ruffini published a pastoral letter on *Il vero volto della Sicilia* (*The true face of Sicily*) in which he argued that Sicily had been denigrated by, among other things, the novel *Il Gattopardo* (*The Leopard*, by Giuseppe Tomasi di Lampedusa) and the work of Danilo Dolci.[4] The mafia constituted a tiny minority and Sicily had so many monuments and natural attractions, the Sicilians were not superstitious but genuinely Christian and the Cardinal hoped that progress would continue so that 'the lives of individuals, families and society in general could become shining examples of our holy religion'.

The Reverend Panascia wrote to 'His Eminence', explaining that to talk about the mafia and the evils of Sicily was not to denigrate the island and asking the Cardinal to look at living conditions and unemployment in certain areas of Palermo. Ruffini replied, starting his letter 'Dear Sir' and restating his certainties: there was crime everywhere and the Catholic Church worked hard to help the poorest people. That was the end of the exchange of letters and it would not be until the 1980s that an Archbishop of Palermo would adopt a different tone.

## Opposition to the Sack of Palermo

One of the subjects considered by the Antimafia Commission was building speculation in Palermo. In November 1963 the Region of Sicily asked Prefect Tommaso Bevivino to carry out an inspection of the municipality of Palermo, which resulted in a report documenting the so-called 'sack of Palermo'. A significant figure: of the 4,205 building licences granted between November 1959 and November 1963, 80 per cent went to five frontmen: a bricklayer, a coal merchant and three other people who proved not to be builders. The city plan had remained merely a paper exercise and the planning committee had ceased to exist when its mandate ran out.

The parties opposing the Christian Democrat councils had attacked speculation and demanded and secured the resignation of Ciancimino when he was elected mayor in October 1970 and the mafioso, Giuseppe Trapani, was sitting on the executive.

## Danilo Dolci and Non-Violent Action

Following his experience with Don Zeno Saltini at the Nomadelfia centre for children mutilated in the war, Danilo Dolci, who was born in the province of Trieste, moved to Sicily in 1952 and began to implement his personal reinterpretation of non-violence. He supported the fishermen of Trappeto (Palermo), organized 'strikes in reverse', set up study groups and centres, held a fast at Cortile Cascino, a developing area in the centre of Palermo, published works that became famous at national and international level and tackled a justice system which, as it had done in the years of the peasant struggles, regarded the occupation of land and popular uprisings as crimes. He was supported by well-known intellectuals such as Piero Calamandrei, Norberto Bobbio and Bertrand Russell.

In his struggle against the mafia he collected documentation on people such as the minister, Bernardo Mattarella, who pursued him and secured his conviction for libel. Despite splits in his group, Dolci continued his work after the earthquake in 1968. On 25 March 1970 the Centro studi e iniziative in Partinico, founded by Dolci, began broadcasting on the Radio dei poveri cristi; on the following day hundreds of police stormed the building and confiscated the broadcasting equipment.

Dolci's work is a rare example of a synthesis of analysis, publicity, planning, organization and mobilization. In the years immediately prior to his death in 1997 he was particularly concerned with training for world citizenship through educational activities, without ever abandoning his writing of poetry, for which he was awarded the Viareggio prize.

## Rebel Women: Serafina Battaglia and Franca Viola

During the 1960s two unusual women stood out on the Sicilian stage. The first was Serafina Battaglia, the partner of a mafioso, Stefano Leale, who was killed in 1960. She encouraged her adopted son to avenge his father's death but he too was killed in 1962. Serafina broke with the mafia tradition of silence and accused those who had murdered her partner and her son. She told Cesare Terranova, the judge who took her deposition: 'If the wives of the men who have been killed decided to speak out, not to exact revenge but because they demand justice, the mafia would have been dead long ago.' But her testimony was not enough to secure convictions against the mafiosi. She relapsed into silence and died, forgotten, in 2004.

The other woman, 17-year-old Franca Viola, was abducted and raped by a mafioso in Alcamo, in the province of Trapani. Normally, rape is followed by marriage to cancel out the offence and the Italian penal code, which viewed sexual violence as an offence against public morality rather than against the person, saw the wedding as extinguishing the crime. Franca rebelled against this, stating that she did not wish to marry the rapist and had him and his associates arrested. This hit the press and Franca became the icon of a cultural shift. She later married a man she loved.

## The New Left and Giuseppe Impastato

The protests by young people which swept across Europe and the United States in 1968 also affected Palermo and Sicily and gave rise to a movement that had some unusual characteristics.[5] The student movement grew up in secondary schools and university faculties where, in addition to addressing the basic topics of the fight against authoritarianism and student power, certain elements also considered the specific problem of the mafia. This was thanks to the work of a local organization, the Lenin Circle in Palermo, directed by the politician and economist Mario Mineo. In 1970 the Circle joined the national Manifesto group, publishing a document arguing that the mafia was not just a criminal organization but a social phenomenon, which in recent years had formed a 'capitalist-mafia bourgeoisie' holding a dominant position within the privileged bloc. On the basis of this analysis, the Manifesto group in Palermo organized a campaign for the expropriation of mafia property which remained merely declaratory. It would require a further 12 years before the 1982 antimafia law provided for the confiscation of mafia assets.

The analyses and proposals of the Palermo group provoked criticisms and confusion even within the Manifesto group in Sicily. At national level, they were harshly criticized by communist leaders, who stuck to the line of the *patto autonomistico* (the Sicilian version of the 'historic compromise' between Christian Democrats and the Communist Party) with the productive sectors on the island and regarded them as a way of ascribing criminal motives to all and sundry.

Giuseppe 'Peppino' Impastato had been active in new Left groups from a very early age.[6] Born in Cinisi (Palermo), son of a mafia family, he first manifested his cultural and political commitment by breaking with his father and relatives, including his uncle, the mafia leader Cesare Manzella, who was killed by a car bomb in 1963. As his mother, Felicia Bartolotta, describes in the story of her life published in *La mafia in casa mia* (*The mafia in my home*), that event was of crucial importance in helping the young Peppino come to maturity. Very soon after, he began his antimafia work with a duplicated periodical *L'idea socialista*. He then engaged in student demonstrations and became active in left-wing groups ranging from the PSIUP (Italian Socialist Party of Proletarian Unity) to Lotta continua. He was active on many fronts, from cinema discussions to theatre and musical shows, including public information activities using leaflets and photographic exhibitions and, in his last years, the independent radio station 'Radio Aut'. Peppino and his companions used radio to monitor mafia activity, report on links with the local administration and, by using satire in the well-loved broadcast *Onda pazza* (*Crazy Wave*), destroy the myth of the mafia, starting with the leader Gaetano Badalamenti.

Peppino was killed, in a manner that was intended to brand him as a terrorist who had committed suicide, on the night of 8–9 May 1978. Some of his friends, his mother and brother, and the Centro siciliano di documentazione, established in Palermo in 1977 and subsequently named after him, worked hard to keep his memory untarnished and secure justice. The instigators, Gaetano Badalamenti and Vito Palazzolo, were not sentenced until more than 20 years after the murder and in 2000 the parliamentary Antimafia Commission adopted a report that stated clearly that the representatives of the police and the judiciary had impeded the inquiries and concealed those responsible. The film *I cento passi* (*The Hundred Steps*) also helped to secure for Peppino Impastato the position of one of the most important figures in the struggle against the mafia.

## The Work of the Centro Impastato

In 1977, on the initiative of the author and others active in the New Left groups, the Centro siciliano di documentazione began work in Palermo,[7] with a national conference titled 'Portella della Ginestra: una strage per il centrismo' ('Portella della Ginestra: a massacre for the centre-right'). In an atmosphere dominated by the 'historic compromise' – the political strategy of promoting links between the Communist Party and the Christian Democrats, which saw the massacre of 1 May 1947 as a distant bloody event requiring only ritualistic commemoration – the conference sought to analyse the slaughter at Portella della Ginestra in the light of the events leading up to the end of unity against Fascism and the exclusion from national and regional government of the parties of the Left, despite the victory of the popular bloc in the Sicilian regional elections. Discussions linked local and national history with the international situation created by the Yalta agreements, stressing the convergence of interests between the mafia, landowners, the conservative parties, Italian capitalism and the world powers.

The next year saw the Impastato killing and the Centro took a leading role: on the morning of 11 May it was represented at a meeting in the university and, along with other groups, presented a paper to the public prosecutor. At Cinisi, in the afternoon, Umberto Santino led the meeting which Peppino should have chaired at the end of the local election campaign and, at the suggestion of his friends, cited the mafia and Badalamenti as responsible. On 16 May Peppino's family, breaking with their mafia relatives, presented a report accusing Badalamenti of responsibility for the crime. This was the start of a long period of cooperation which was, after a considerable amount of time, to prove fruitful. In 1979, on the first anniversary of the killing, the Centro organized a national demonstration against the mafia, the first ever in Italy, attended by some 2,000 people, which argued that the mafia was a national issue.

The Centro, named after Giuseppe Impastato in 1980, has carried out a variety of work during its 38-year life: research, with scores of books and hundreds of articles, work in schools, which it began in the early 1980s, and support for social battles, ranging from the quest for peace in the early 1980s to the fight for housing. The Centro is self-financing because it has asked the Region of Sicily to pass a law laying down the criteria for obtaining public money, a request that has not yet been granted.

---

### Peppino Impastato's Mother

*On 7 December 2004 Felicia Bartolotta, the mother of Peppino Impastato, died. She had broken away from her mafia relatives and had become a key protagonist in antimafia activity. Below is a brief extract from the story of her life, as told to Anna Puglisi and Umberto Santino.*

*Umberto*: 'At a certain point Peppino was thrown out of the house?'

*Felicia*: 'Precisely because he was speaking against the mafia.'

*U*: 'Was it your husband who threw him out?'

*F*: 'Yes, it was. He said: "Get out and don't set foot in here again."'

*U*: 'So there were constant battles between Giuseppe and his father?'

*F*: 'There were flare-ups from time to time. When elections were due, he called him: "Hey Giuseppe, now there are elections coming up, be careful, don't talk about the mafia. If you'd got your degree, my friends would. . ." "Your friends? What do I want with a job? I'd sooner die of hunger than work for your friends." Then: "Get out."'

Felicia Bartolotta Impastato, *La mafia in casa mia*, Palermo: La Luna, 1986–2003, pp. 33–4.

# CHAPTER 5

# MAFIA AND ANTIMAFIA FROM THE 1980s TO THE PRESENT DAY

## The Major Crimes of the Early 1980s

As noted, Peppino Impastato was killed in May 1978, and 1979 saw subsequent murders committed in Palermo. The bloody sequence of killings included: on 11 January, police lieutenant Filadelfo Aparo; on 26 January, the journalist Mario Francese; on 9 March, Michele Reina, the provincial secretary of the Christian Democrats; on 29 July, Deputy Chief of Police Boris Giuliano; and on 25 September, the magistrate Cesare Terranova and police officer Lenin Mancuso.

This is described as a 'turning point'. Previous assassinations had included Chief Prosecutor Pietro Scaglione, killed in Palermo on 5 May 1971 along with his driver Antonino Lo Russo, and ex-colonel Giuseppe Russo, killed along with the teacher Filippo Costa at Ficuzza near Corleone on 20 August 1977; as long ago as 12 March 1909 the mafia had killed the Italian-American agent Joe Petrosino. Since such cases were rare, the belief had grown that the mafiosi did not kill members of the police or magistrates. Even the killing in Milan on 11 July 1979 of Giorgio Ambrosoli, who was liquidating Banca Privata, which had belonged to Michele Sindona, a financier with mafia connections, could be seen as a sign of change.

The murders went on unabated throughout 1980: on 6 January in Palermo the Christian Democrat president of the Region of Sicily, Piersanti Mattarella; on 4 May in Monreale the *carabinieri* captain Emanuele Basile; and on 6 August in Palermo, Chief Prosecutor Gaetano

Costa. Blood continued to be shed on the streets of Palermo in 1982 with the killings, on 30 April, of the regional secretary of the Communist Party, Pio La Torre, and his co-worker Rosario Di Salvo; on 11 August of the police doctor Paolo Giaccone; on 3 September of the prefect, General Carlo Alberto Dalla Chiesa, his wife Emanuela Setti Carraro and his bodyguard Domenico Russo; and on 14 November of the police officer Calogero Zucchetto. On 29 July 1983 the chief investigating magistrate, Rocco Chinnici, was killed along with his escort, Salvatore Bartolotta and Mario Trapassi, and the doorman of his building, Stefano Li Sacchi, by a car loaded with dynamite and parked in front of his house. On 28 July 1985 Police Chief Beppe Montana was killed, followed on 6 August by the head of the flying squad, Ninni Cassarà, and a police officer, Roberto Antiochia.

Mafia killings were not confined to Palermo: Valderice, in the province of Trapani, saw the death on 25 January 1983 of Deputy Prosecutor Giangiacomo Ciaccio Montalto; and on 2 April 1985 near Trapani, Barbara Rizzo Asta and her twin boys, Giuseppe and Salvatore, died in an attack on the magistrate Carlo Palermo. On 5 January 1984 the writer and journalist Giuseppe Fava died in Catania. Other journalists had died at the hands of the mafia: Cosimo Cristina, found dead on 5 May 1960; Mauro De Mauro, disappeared on 16 September 1970; Giovanni Spampinato, murdered in Ragusa on 28 October 1972; Mario Francese, murdered on 26 January 1979; and, later, Beppe Alfano was killed on 8 January 1993. Peppino Impastato and Mauro Rostagno, who was killed on 26 September 1988, were also working as journalists.

## The Mafia War 1981–3: The Siege of the Corleonesi

In the early 1980s, alongside the violence it was unleashing on the outside world, the mafia was also engaged in its bloodiest ever internal power struggle. It began spectacularly in Palermo on 23 April 1981 when Stefano Bontate, the young heir to a mafia dynasty, was killed. Then, on 11 May, another mafia leader, Salvatore Inzerillo, was killed; the violence was to continue until 1983. The number of deaths is put at 1,000, including the *lupare bianche* (where the victims are not found), which are difficult to count. Research by the Centro Impastato into murders in the city and province of Palermo from 1978 to 1984 has found that 332 were instigated by the mafia, of which 203 concerned people close to it.

Initially it was quite hard to understand what was happening. Then statements from reliable witnesses began to provide some clues: there was an attack on mafiosi from Corleone who had made agreements with mafiosi in the city and province and were trying to assert their power through the physical elimination of opponents, the leaders of the traditional mafia families, such as the Bontate, the Inzerillo and the Badalamenti, and their supporters. The aim of the fighting was, as always, a struggle for power within the organization, going as far as persuading members of the traditional families to turn traitor, and for the control of business activities, starting with the ever-expanding trafficking of drugs, where the Corleonesi were the poor relations. The winner was the side that was better armed and used violence first. In the outside world, the mafia attacked police, magistrates and politicians who had opposed their requests and interests, which had grown with an increase in the amount of wealth accumulated illegally.

The standoff resulted in a victory for the Corleonesi, led by Totò Riina, who imposed a sort of dictatorial command structure on an organization that had traditionally been of a confederal nature, but this proved a Pyrrhic victory. The large-scale crimes in the outside world, particularly the murder of Dalla Chiesa, rebounded on them, provoking an institutional reaction that resulted in the adoption of the antimafia law, arrests, trials and convictions. Inside the mafia, the war had been bloody enough to persuade several on the losing side to cooperate with the judicial authorities. These were not truly *pentiti*, even though they were given that name, but people seeking a sort of revenge through legal channels. This was the start of a long process, to be regulated only later with the introduction of the laws on rewards. It would generate a positive spin-off through the reconstruction of organization charts and the attribution of individual responsibility for an endless series of crimes. The price to be paid was the reduced penalties imposed on those who had cooperated.

The chief of these was a mafioso from Palermo whose activities and experience were international in scope, Tommaso Buscetta. He was accompanied by Badalamenti and others on the losing side. It was Buscetta who revealed that the association was called Cosa Nostra, that it was based on families, that its organizational structure was pyramid-like, with a command centre, the provincial commission or 'dome', that there was a regional commission and that the head of the Palermo committee was supreme. As we have seen, this is more or less the structure that Sangiorgi had described, as confirmed by Terranova's inquiries.

## Collaborators and State Witnesses

Contrary to popular opinion, the law of *omertà* is frequently ignored even by the mafiosi themselves. Many of them have given information to the police and magistrates and their revelations provided the basis for the Sangiorgi reports and guided the investigations by Judge Terranova. We know the names of some mafiosi who have cooperated with the judicial authorities, such as Salvatore D'Amico, whose revelations led to the trial of the Stuppagghieri of Monreale, but was killed before he could testify. In 1916 the doctor Melchiorre Allegra revealed information about the mafia of his time.

More recently, in March 1973 Leonardo Vitale confessed his role in several murders to the Palermo police and described the work, organization and complicity of the Altarello family of which he was part. He is perhaps the only *pentito* whose motives were ethical and religious. Only his confessions of crimes he himself had committed were believed; Vitale was convicted, sent to a criminal asylum and then into exile. This long and painful path was to lead to his death: on 2 December 1984 he was attacked when leaving church with no protection and died five days later.

From the 1980s onwards many mafiosi cooperated with the authorities: rather than repentance, this could better be described as a choice dictated by the dangers of the mafia war then in progress. However, they made a substantial contribution to our knowledge of the mafia organization and to understanding a large number of crimes.

The mafiosi who cooperated received reduced sentences and state protection but it was only after the massacres in Capaci and Via D'Amelio that Law No. 306/92 was passed to regulate the rewards granted, which were later made subject to conditions, such as the obligation to make the revelations within a certain time (six months from the start of cooperation). These conditions were introduced because in some cases those cooperating had used the protection provided to continue their criminal activities; there were also concerns about statements that were beginning to touch on connections between the mafia and politicians.

In June 1996 those cooperating numbered 1,177: 430 from the Sicilian mafia, 224 from the camorra, 158 from the 'ndrangheta, 102 from the Sacra Corona Unita in Apulia and 264 from other mafia-type organizations. Subsequently the number has fallen.

State witnesses are citizens who have witnessed crimes and cooperated with the judicial authorities as a civic duty. One of the first cases was that of the bar owner Giuseppa Di Sano, who denounced the murderers of her 17-year-old daughter Emanuela Sansone, killed in Palermo in 1896.

The most famous cases include Piera Aiello, the widow of the mafioso Nicola Atria killed in 1991; the commercial traveller Piero Nava, who witnessed the killing of the magistrate Rosario Livatino; and the businessmen from Gela (Caltanissetta) and Calabria, Nino Miceli and Pino Masciari respectively, who reported extortionists. All these had to change their names, abandon their homes and jobs and live elsewhere.

For years the legislation (Law No. 82 of 15 March 1991) drew no distinction between state witnesses and mafiosi cooperating with justice, so that witnesses were obliged to live in exile, suffering great difficulties. Typical is the case of Rita Atria, who was sent far from her village to live in a flat in Rome and killed herself through despair following the killing of Paolo Borsellino. Law No. 44 of 23 February 1999 introduced measures to protect businessmen who reported extortionists and Law No. 45 of 13 February 2001 separated witnesses from those cooperating and introduced different arrangements for the two groups. In February 2008 the parliamentary Antimafia Commission approved a report allowing for further measures to assist witnesses, who numbered 71 in 2007.[1]

## The Antimafia Law and Subsequent Legislation

On 13 September 1982, ten days after the killing of Dalla Chiesa, parliament passed Law No. 646, the so-called 'antimafia law', which made the mafia a criminal activity in itself and defined the mafia-type criminal association referred to earlier. One of the main innovations of the law was the introduction of the sequestration and confiscation of the property of mafiosi.

This law was more than a century overdue and was designed to deal with the mafia of the 1950s and 1960s, the so-called 'business mafia' or 'urban-entrepreneurial mafia', rather than its financial and political manifestations. Attempts were made to deal with these by subsequent legislation on the laundering of dirty money (Laws No. 197 and 413 of 1991) and repression of the so-called 'political-mafia electoral trade-off': an offence introduced by Law No. 356 of 1992 on the buying of votes for money, a reductive formulation that bore little resemblance to reality. The relationship between the mafia and politics is much wider and more complex and it is difficult to present in this form, even if votes are traded for a series of 'favours' granted to those mafiosi who support candidates for election.

The magistrates sought to close this legislative gap through an offence of judicial origin based on behaviour, 'complicity with the mafia', a charge brought against a number of people, with some convictions but many acquittals.

In the early years of the 1982 law, sequestrations and confiscations were quite limited so, as a result of a petition by the association Libera, in 1996 Law No. 109 legislated on the social use of the goods confiscated, which were to be distributed to associations, bodies and cooperatives.

## The Antimafia Pool and the Maxi-trial

In the early 1980s the chief investigating magistrate, Rocco Chinnici, introduced into the Palermo court a practice that was to prove highly successful in judicial terms: instead of allocating the investigation of individual crimes to individual magistrates, a group of magistrates (the 'antimafia pool') was set up to deal with all crimes committed by the mafia, which would be considered as a single entity. This meant that proper attention could be paid to crimes such as the laundering of dirty money, through an investigation carried out by the examining magistrate, Giovanni Falcone. Despite lack of cooperation from banking institutions, including those in Switzerland, he managed to reconstruct a great deal of the journey undertaken by illegal capital to make it 'clean' and hence usable for investment. The decision was reached on 6 June 1983.

At the same time the Palermo antimafia pool carried out a major investigation that resulted in the so-called 'maxi-trial' (*maxiprocesso*). The 1983 attack that killed Rocco Chinnici was the mafia's reply to the work of the prosecutor who had launched the work of the antimafia pool and had begun to turn the spotlight on powerful men such as the cousins Nino and Ignazio Salvo, who held the monopoly for tax collection in Sicily. He was replaced by Antonino Caponnetto, from Florence, who formally established the antimafia pool.

The inquiry was greatly helped by those mafiosi who were cooperating with the judicial authorities and who now confirmed their accusations under cross-examination. The maxi-trial, which took place at first instance in 1986 and 1987 in the specially constructed bunker courtroom, concerned 475 bosses and followers and concluded with heavy sentences: 19 life sentences and thousands of years in prison. On appeal and in the Court of Cassation many of these sentences were confirmed (the number of life sentences was reduced to 12).

## The End of the Antimafia Pool, the Gela War and the Massacres of 1992 and 1993

Contrary to expectations, instead of being strengthened and its future work facilitated, the pool was dissolved. Clearly concerns had been raised by references in the establishing decree to its investigation, if a page were really to be turned, of politico-mafiosi crimes. On 21 June 1989 Giovanni Falcone was the victim of an unsuccessful attack at his summer residence, after having been severely humiliated. He had not been made chief investigating magistrate when Caponnetto resigned – the veteran Antonino Meli, who halted the inquiries into the mafia, was appointed instead. Falcone was transferred to the Ministry of Justice in Rome where, as Director-General for Penal Affairs, he drew up a national strategy to fight the mafia based on the establishment of two new bodies: the DNA (Direzione Nazionale Antimafia: National Antimafia Directorate) and the DIA (Direzione Investigativa Antimafia: Antimafia Investigative Directorate).

During the first stage of the maxi-trial the mafia suspended its use of violence but resumed in 1988 with the killing of the former mayor of Palermo, Giuseppe Insalaco (12 January), police officer Natale Mondo (14 January) and the businessmen Donato Boscia (9 March) and Luigi Ranieri (14 December). On 25 September the judge, Antonino Saetta, a candidate for the presidency of the Court of Appeal for the maxi-trial, and his son Stefano were killed. In 1989 the police officer Antonino Agostino and his pregnant wife Ida Castelluccio were murdered, a crime believed to be linked with the failed attempt on Judge Falcone.

Between 1987, when the mafia boss Francesco Madonia was killed, and 1991 the city of Gela saw a real war between Cosa Nostra and the Stidda for the control of public contracts. This reached its peak in November 1990 with a massacre in a gaming hall that left eight dead and 13 wounded. November 1992 saw the death of Gaetano Giordano, a businessman who had refused to pay extortion. Another businessman, Antonino Miceli, was driven out of the city. The Stidda killed the magistrate Rosario Livatino on 21 September 1990.

Between the ruling of the Court of Appeal and the judgement of the Court of Cassation, on 9 August 1991 the magistrate Antonino Scopelliti, who had been appointed prosecutor for the maxi-trial, was killed in Calabria. Confirmation by the Court of Cassation of the accusations based on Cosa Nostra acting as a single body and its responsibility for a series of crimes committed by its command group, the commission or 'dome', unleashed mafia violence in 1992 with massacres at Capaci on 23 May, which killed Falcone, his wife and three men of his escort, and in Via D'Amelio on 19 July, which killed Paolo Borsellino and five police officers in his escort. Falcone was preparing to take over as national prosecutor in the DNA he had set up, and Borsellino would probably have succeeded him. In Rome on 26 July the 17-year-old daughter of a mafia family, Rita Atria, who, together with her sister-in-law Piera Aiello, had cooperated with the judicial authorities, committed suicide. The mafia also settled accounts with people such as Salvo Lima, killed on 12 March, and the tax collector Ignazio Salvo, killed on 17 September. On 28 September, the former naval captain Paolo Ficalora was killed at Castellammare del Golfo. Unaware of his guest's identity, he had accommodated in his tourist complex Totuccio Contorno, another person who had cooperated with the judicial authorities. On 21 April of that year, the businessman Paolo Borsellino, who had prevented mafiosi from entering his reinforced concrete plant, was killed in Lucca Sicula (Agrigento), followed, on 17 December, by his father Giuseppe, who had cooperated in the inquiry into his son's murder.

In 1993 violence moved on to the national stage, with an attack in Rome on 14 May (the target was the television presenter Maurizio Costanzo, who had made several programmes about the mafia), and massacres that left five dead in both Florence (27 May) and Milan (27 July). Also on 27 July two bombs exploded in Rome, in front of the basilica of St John Lateran and in front of the church of St Giorgio in Velabro. Monuments that were now targets included the Uffizi Gallery in Florence, the Contemporary Art Pavilion in Milan and churches in Rome. On Sunday 31 October there was a failed attempt to massacre spectators in the Olympic Stadium in Rome.

The massacres and murders in 1992 and 1993 provoked a fresh response from the state, with laws providing for severe prison conditions for mafiosi (No. 41bis, cutting off any contacts with the outside world) and establishing rewards for mafiosi who cooperated. This response was once again conceived as a reaction to an emergency, as was the anti-racketeering law passed immediately after the murder in Palermo on 29 August 1991 of the businessman Libero Grassi, who had publicly stated that he would not pay 'protection money' and had been shunned by other businessmen (the only meeting to support him, attended by the writer, attracted no more than 30 people).

On 15 January 1993, after 23 years of evading justice, the head of the Corleone mafia, Totò Riina, was arrested. The villa where he had taken refuge was cleaned up as if to remove all traces of something dangerous. There was talk of a *papello*, a document containing the demands of the mafia to be met for an end to violence: abolition of the severe prison conditions and reviews of the trials and of the antimafia legislation providing for the confiscation of goods.

The trials ensuing from the massacres in the early 1990s resulted in sentences for mafia bosses and suggested that other individuals (businessmen, politicians and Freemasons) were responsible; this was not, however, confirmed.

### Powerful Men on Trial: From Andreotti to Dell'Utri

At the end of the 1980s and in the early 1990s, the fall of the Soviet Union had a global impact. In Italy the investigation into corruption known as 'Tangentopoli' resulted in the disappearance of the Christian Democrats and the Socialist Party. The Communist Party furled the red flag and changed its name. The mafia was no longer a bulwark against communism and it would seek to establish dialogue with those now in power. First there came the attempt to establish a Lega Meridionale (Southern League), like the Lega Nord which was threatening the secession of the so-called Padania area, but then it decided to align itself with the new national political formations.

In 1994 Silvio Berlusconi founded Forza Italia (Come on, Italy!) and then Popolo della libertà (People of the Freedom) which, with the exception of a few years of centre-left government, was to govern Italy in conjunction with the Alleanza Nazionale and the Lega Nord.

This is the background to trials of men from both the old and the new power structures. The politicians on trial included Andreotti, whom I have already mentioned, the president of the province of Palermo, Francesco Musotto, and the former minister, Calogero Mannino, who were all charged with complicity with the mafia. Musotto was acquitted; Mannino was acquitted at first instance and convicted on appeal; the Court of Cassation then annulled the sentence and ordered a retrial, which ended in acquittal. Marcello Dell'Utri, one of the founders of Forza Italia, received a nine-year sentence for complicity at the first trial; on appeal this was reduced to seven years. In March 2012 the Court of Cassation quashed the guilty verdict. A new trial will be held.

Other trials concerned members of the forces of law and order, such as Bruno Contrada, originally of the Palermo flying squad and later director of the secret services, who was also convicted of complicity.

## The Catholic Church Discovers the Mafia

At the requiem mass for Piersanti Mattarella in January 1980, the Archbishop of Palermo, Cardinal Salvatore Pappalardo, preached a sermon in which he described the mafia as a cradle of crime and referred to other hidden forces outside Sicily. On 31 October 1981 he celebrated a mass for all the victims of the mafia (the antimafia mass).[2] In December that year Pope John Paul II urged the bishops to commit themselves to combat the evils in Sicily, and the mafia in particular. At the funeral of Dalla Chiesa and his wife Setti Carraro, Cardinal Pappalardo preached the so-called 'Sagunto sermon', based on a Latin quotation (*dum Romae consulitur Saguntum expugnatur*: While Rome debates, Saguntum is conquered), to describe the dramatic situation in Palermo. In November 1982 the Pope was in Palermo but did not mention the mafia in his speech and, following some attacks, Pappalardo said that he had been misunderstood, rejecting the label of 'antimafia cardinal'.

Meanwhile some priests had adopted a clear antimafia stance and in Palermo the S. Saverio social centre in the Albergheria area was beginning restoration work in one of the poorest parts of the historic centre of the city. The term that was beginning to be adopted, although unwelcome for the hierarchy, was 'pastorale antimafia', action intended to promote an ongoing commitment on the part of priests and the faithful but also open to non-believers. However, the real problem was the relationship between the mafia and those in authority, and in particular with the Christian Democrats, who were at the centre of power, both locally and nationally.

In 1991 the Italian bishops' conference published *Educare alla legalità* (Education for Legality) addressing the problem of the mafia, which it saw as a symptom of the decline in lawfulness. Following the 1992 massacres, the Pope returned to Sicily in May of the following year. In Agrigento he pronounced an anathema against mafiosi who committed murder, but ignored a letter sent to him about the Archbishop of Monreale, Salvatore Cassisa, who was under investigation for corruption. On 27 July 1993 there were bomb attacks on churches in Rome and on 15 September Father Pino Puglisi, the parish priest of the Brancaccio area of Palermo, a stronghold of the mafia, was killed. He had sought to prevent young people from being recruited into the mafia and had initiated a dialogue with mafiosi. The Pope returned to Palermo in November 1995 for the national congress of Italian churches and again spoke of the mafia.

Theologians who have considered the subject and the Pope himself have spoken of the mafia in terms of 'structural sin' and 'social sin', but there has not yet been an adequate development of these ideas that could result in changes of behaviour. Meanwhile some bishops and priests, not solely in Sicily, have continued their work. On 19 March 1994 the parish priest Don Giuseppe Diana was killed in Casal di Principe (Caserta), a stronghold of the camorra, and in some dioceses of southern Italy the bishops have shown great commitment. Examples include Bishops Tonino Bello (Molfetta, Bari), Raffaele Nogaro (Caserta) and Giancarlo Bregantini (Locri, Reggio Calabria), who organized social cooperatives and was then transferred. By contrast, there have been cases of clerics involved in mafia activities such as Agostino Coppola, who ceased to be a priest after his conviction, or charged with assisting the mafia, such as the Carmelite, Mario Frittitta, a parish priest in Palermo who visited the fugitive mafia boss Pietro Aglieri. He was initially convicted but then cleared.

### The Mafia's Victims Include Children

In November 1993, 11-year-old Giuseppe Di Matteo, whose father Santo had cooperated with the judicial authorities, disappeared. He was held hostage until January 1996, strangled and his body dissolved in acid. The crime, which was intended to make his father recant, was committed by Giovanni Brusca, who confessed, and other mafia members.

In October 1986, 11-year-old Claudio Domino was killed in Palermo because he might have witnessed the activities of certain drug dealers. This was at the time of the maxi-trial and one of the accused, Giovanni Bontate, the brother of Stefano, the mafia boss killed in 1981, made a statement distancing himself from such a loathsome crime. Bontate was killed along with his wife, Francesca Citarda, in September 1988.

These were not the first children to die as a result of mafia violence, either as targets themselves or as the victims of shoot-outs in public places, which refutes the mafia claim that it respects women and children. A short and incomplete list includes: in 1911, during the fighting between mafia groups in Monreale, a 12-year-old in the

Sciortino family was killed; the victims of the Portella della Ginestra massacre on 1 May 1947 included Vincenzina La Fata, aged eight, Giovanni Grifò, 12, Giuseppe Di Maggio, 13, Serafino Lascari, 15 and Margherita Clesceri, the mother of six children and expecting a seventh; in Corleone in 1948, Giuseppe Letizia, a child who had witnessed the kidnapping of the trade unionist Placido Rizzotto, died from an injection administered by the doctor and mafia boss Michele Navarra; in Palermo in 1959, Anna Prestigiacomo and Giuseppina Savoca were killed, the first for vendetta and the second in the course of a shoot-out; in the same year at Godrano (Palermo), a battle between mafia families killed Antonino Pecoraro, aged 10, and his brother Vincenzo; in 1961 in Palermo, a long-standing feud between mafia families caused the death of 13-year-old Paolino Riccobono; and in 1976 in Catania, four children – Giovanni La Greca, Riccardo Cristaldi, Lorenzo Pace and Benedetto Zuccaro – who had unwittingly snatched a bag belonging to the mother of the mafia boss Nitto Santapaola, were killed. I have already noted the deaths of the twins Giuseppe and Salvatore Asta, who were killed with their mother near Trapani, in the course of the attack on the magistrate, Carlo Palermo, on 2 April 1985. Other child victims include Salvatore Cutroneo and Rosario Montalto, killed while playing in the street at Niscemi (Caltanissetta) on 27 August 1987 during a fight between mafia groups; and Andrea Savoca, aged four, killed in Palermo on 26 July 1991 along with her father, a relative of mafiosi.

## The Antimafia in the 1980s and 1990s:
### Women, Schools, the Use of Confiscated Goods and the Anti-Racketeering Movement

The 1980s and 1990s saw demonstrations against the major crimes and massacres, and a number of committees and associations in civil society worked ceaselessly against the mafia. In 1981 a committee of women comprising relatives of victims, such as Giovanna Giaconia, the widow of the magistrate Cesare Terranova, and Rita Bartoli, the widow of the prosecutor Gaetano Costa, and women engaged in political and social activities, began work.[3] In 1984 the committee became the Associazione delle donne siciliane per la lotta contro la mafia (Association of Women in Sicily Against the Mafia) and engaged in a range of activities. With the Centro Impastato, it supported working-class women in Palermo, such as Michela Buscemi and Vita Rugnetta, who had become parties to the maxi-trial and so been cut off not only from their relatives but also from the antimafia associations following the decision not to allow them access to the funds collected for the legal expenses of such parties, which were available only to relatives of those employed by the state. The Centro Impastato and the women's association stressed the importance of the gesture made by the two women in breaking with the culture of subjection to the mafia and collected money that was given to the women, since the lawyers had provided their services free of charge. These events are recorded in the book *Sole contro la mafia*.

In 1984 the Centro Impastato proposed the formation of an antimafia coordinating committee; this took decisions collectively for a while before becoming an autonomous association.

In August 1987 the Christian Democrat Leoluca Orlando became mayor of Palermo at the head of a council supported by the Left. This was the start of the so-called 'Palermo spring' in the city's local government, which saw the council's ruling group become increasingly open to the Left and to civil society. The mayor spoke openly of combating the mafia and established a close relationship with the antimafia coordinating committee, while other groups, including the Centro Impastato and the Centro Sociale S. Saverio, urged a move away from a policy focusing on image to one of concrete choices, such as a break with Salvo Lima, whose men sat on the ruling groups in the council. In the 1990 local elections, Orlando headed the Christian Democrat list, with a man linked to Lima in second place and, partly thanks to votes from a traditionally left-leaning electorate, led the DC to a historic victory, while parties and groups on the Left lost ground heavily. Orlando was not re-elected mayor and left the party, founding a new group, La Rete (the Net), which for several years secured support throughout Italy for its policy of concentrating on fighting the mafia.

There were a number of initiatives at national level and groups and associations were set up to extend the work of combating the mafia, which had become increasingly widespread and was now considered a countrywide problem, particularly with regard to drug trafficking. In 1995 the umbrella group Libera was formed, with the aim of recovering historical memories, working in schools and using confiscated goods. Since 1996, 21 March has been a day of remembrance, dedicated to honouring the memory of mafia victims, and that year too, following the collection of a million signatures by Libera, Law No. 109 on the use of confiscated goods for social purposes was passed. Subsequent years saw the formation of cooperatives to manage confiscated land, and the products of that land were distributed nationally. In recent years, in response to the struggle for housing in Palermo, houses confiscated from mafiosi have been allocated to the homeless.

Schools in Sicily have begun to take steps against the mafia following Regional Law No. 51 of 4 June 1980, passed following the murder of Mattarella.[4] After the massacres of the early 1990s and the circular of 25 October 1993 on teaching lawfulness from the Ministry of Education, initiatives in schools spread throughout the country. These were often exercises in box-ticking and implemented only from time to time, because of a view that saw the mafia as a criminal emergency and legality as respect for laws divorced from their content (the racial laws from the fascist period were formally in force, as were those passed by centre-right governments to protect private interests and to ensure automatic acquittal should those in the highest positions of power, such as the Premier, be brought to trial).

The late 1980s and early 1990s saw the growth and spread of extortion, and shopkeepers and businessmen began to take action.[5] The first group started in December 1990 at Capo d'Orlando, in the province of Messina, where criminals had become mafiosi only recently and those active in the economy were not subordinate to it or complicit in it. Palermo took longer to establish an anti-racketeering movement, despite attempts to follow the example of Libero Grassi. It is only in recent years that shopkeepers have joined the anti-racketeering campaign and have reported extortionists to the police. This development is partly due to a group of young people who make up the Comitato Addiopizzo (Goodbye Extortion Committee), and who have taken action against extortion and in favour of critical (i.e. ethical) consumer practices. Employers' organizations at Sicilian and national level have announced that they will expel members who pay 'protection money' and do not cooperate with the judicial authorities, and in November 2007 the Liberofuturo association was founded in Palermo; its name is a reference to Libero Grassi.

## The Hidden Mafia

After the arrests and convictions following the massacres of the early 1990s the mafia suspended its use of violence. There was talk of an 'invisible', 'sunken' or 'hidden' mafia, and the end of the crime emergency saw a slackening off in antimafia legislation, beginning with restrictions on the cooperation offered by the so-called turncoats. The magistrates talked of blunted weapons and a great lack of resources: there was no petrol for cars or paper for the photocopiers. And the turncoats were found to have become unreliable since they had begun to talk about links between the mafia and politicians.

The strategist of the mafia's 'new approach' was Bernardo Provenzano. In fact, Provenzano is a man for all seasons: in his youth he was a killer with Luciano Liggio, then one of Riina's hit men; now that the effects of the massacres have rebounded upon him, he is dusting off his former practice of acting as a mediator based on the control of violence, particularly that aimed at high places, which has provoked a reaction from the institutions. As long as violence was directed against struggling peasants or left-wing militants and leaders and helped perpetuate a power base, it remained unpunished; as soon as it was turned against members of the institutions it was repressed. Provenzano learned the lesson and set about restoring a consensus and building new links. He knew that this meant renouncing weapons, even if a few crimes to sever a branch of the organization were carried out and he had to take a firm line with the Stidda. But politicians, magistrates or members of the forces of law and order should not be attacked, and with businessmen and shopkeepers a practical approach was needed: pay little, pay everybody.

Provenzano continued to be a boss even when he was in hiding, using folded scraps of paper (*pizzini*) to give orders, recommend people, provide advice and dispense blessings in the name of God and his saints. After 43 years on the run, he was captured on 11 April 2006, a few kilometres from his home in Corleone, which he had left only to have an operation in a clinic near Marseilles.

Like Riina, Provenzano had completed the second stage of elementary school and had limited experience of life. However, he was believed to control vital sectors such as contracts and health to an extent made possible only, or primarily, through a system of relationships with those working in these sectors: professional people, businessmen, administrators and politicians whom he maintained and supported.

In recent years the Sicilian health system has become a business: public health provision has been dismantled in favour of the private sector through agreements with the Region, resulting in a sharp increase in costs. The prime example is the Santa Teresa clinic in Bagheria (Palermo) managed by the businessman Michele Aiello, who is linked to Provenzano. Treatment for prostate cancer cost the Region €136,000; after confiscation and with controlled administration it costs just over €8,000. In the tradition we have already seen documented, doctors are still involved, being either close to the mafia or themselves bosses or associates.

## Where Now? Mafia and Antimafia in the Years to Come

The Sicilian mafia, most of which forms part of the Cosa Nostra organization, now has some 6,000–7,000 members out of a population of 5,021,000; its annual turnover is about €30 billion.

On 5 November 2007, in a country house near Giardinello, half an hour away from Palermo, the mafia boss Salvatore Lo Piccolo, who had been on the run for 25 years, his son Sandro, on the run for ten years, and two other fugitives, Andrea Adamo, head of the Brancaccio group, and Gaspare Pulizzi, of the Carini mafia family, were all arrested. Lo Piccolo was one of those seeking to take Provenzano's place and had rebuilt connections with the 'escapees', those on the losing side in the mafia wars of the early 1980s who had taken refuge in the United States. Investigators and the press spoke of a power vacuum in Cosa Nostra: almost all the mafia bosses were arrested and convicted; the only one still free was Matteo Messina Denaro, the young scion of a Trapani mafia dynasty, who had been on the run since 1993. But the network of relationships does not seem to have unravelled too much. Recent legal proceedings include the conviction at first instance of the president of the Region of Sicily, Salvatore Cuffaro: on 18 January 2008 he was sentenced in Palermo to five years for favouritism, but unaggravated by having favoured the mafia, even though the people 'favoured' included the doctor and mafia boss Guttadauro. Initially, Cuffaro remained in office but on 26 January, following protests from various parties, he resigned. In January 2010 he was sentenced to seven years on appeal, with the aggravation. In January 2011, following confirmation of his sentence by the Court of Cassation, Cuffaro was sent to prison.

The evidence found in the villa where the Lo Piccolos were arrested included a sort of master register with some 500 names of shopkeepers and businessmen who paid 'protection money', but there were also professional people and those seeking employment and favours. The picture that emerged was one of a local baron working through a recognized and accepted network.

Even today accusations by a handful of shopkeepers and businessmen, the positions taken by Confindustria (Associazione degli imprenditori: businessmen's association) and the work of Addiopizzo, still constitute a rebellion by the few rather than the orchestrated uprising against the mafia dictatorship that is needed, although it is true that the work of the investigators has continued and resulted in the arrest of virtually all the bosses, or at least the best known. Recently, the number of anti-racketeering associations has grown (from 42 in 1997 to 115 in 2012). Most of these are in Sicily and southern Italy.

The use of confiscated goods by cooperatives and now the homeless is the only example of a social antimafia movement involving unemployed young people and ordinary citizens, who have traditionally been subservient to the mafia, but just a few hundred people are involved. Other forms of protest could be described as the 'antimafia in civil society'.

Work in schools has continued, focusing on education in legality, but with the limitations described. The most significant initiatives are those concerned with territory and the recovery of historical memory, such as those undertaken by schools following the educational approach within the 'Memorial laboratory for the struggle against the mafia', proposed by the Centro Impastato.

What is still lacking is anything resembling, even in embryonic form, a comprehensive project able to take on the mafia in all its aspects and forms, to break down the system of relationships and construct a concrete alternative. On the legislative front, we are still waiting for a codification and updating of the existing rules that would take account of how the mafia has developed.

An antimafia code was approved in September 2011; it can only be described as incomplete and inadequate. The new code has been criticized for the following reasons: it does not govern complicity with the mafia; it does not cover the crime of exchanges between politicians and mafia members, hitherto limited to trading votes for cash (it should also include trading votes for contracts and other services); and it does not introduce rules to govern ineligibility for and removal from public office of those accused or found guilty of mafia activities.

On the judicial front, structural problems resulting in intolerable delays in proceedings combine with the lack of staff and resources to impede the work of the investigating magistrates. Investigations suffer from the same problems, although there have been undeniable successes such as the capture of bosses and followers.

In economic terms, predatory parasitism, represented chiefly by the forced levy of extortion, combines with the accumulation of wealth, principally from international trafficking, to generate a vast quantity of money which, recycled in various ways, is funnelled back into the legal economy and forms the basis for a web of alliances and for complicity. This is the foundation on which the social bloc and the mafia bourgeoisie have grown and prospered, bound together by shared interests and joint adherence to a cultural viewpoint that sees illegality as a resource and a channel of social mobility and access to power.

Politically, the self-regulatory codes and efforts to combat the mafia are demonstrations of good intentions rather than effective choices to break links with people and places connected with the mafia. In April 2007 the parliamentary Antimafia Commission proposed that anybody indicted for mafia and other serious crimes should not be eligible to stand for election to town and provincial councils, but in the 170 municipalities dissolved because of infiltration by the mafia, no fewer than 130 councillors were re-elected, and even politicians who had been convicted or were on trial were elected with a large number of votes. Some of these stated that they respected the work of the magistrates and would defend themselves at the trial, while others explicitly attacked the magistrates as politically motivated and claimed to be persecuted by the judicial authorities. The elections of 13 and 14 April 2008 saw the renewal of a by now familiar spectacle, although with a significant new twist: Marcello Dell'Utri who, as we have seen, had been convicted at first and second instance for complicity with the mafia, described Vittorio Mangano, a mafioso with many convictions, as a 'hero' because he had respected the law of *omertà* by refusing to talk about his relationship with Berlusconi, at whose villa in Arcore he had been a 'stable boy'. That represented a new departure.

Recent revelations suggest that Marcello Dell'Utri had replaced the mafia politician Vito Ciancimino in negotiations between mafia bosses and representatives of the institutions in putting an end to the massacres of the 1990s, on the basis of the so-called *papello*. In May 2013 in Palermo began the trial on the *trattativa* Mafia-State, against the bosses Riina and Provenzano, some *carabinieri* generals and former ministers.

Culturally, research work depends on the interests of individual scholars; alongside the few publications with more or less adequate documentation there are many of little scientific value, while, with very few exceptions, cinema and television continue to propagate stereotypes, often presenting mafia bosses as charismatic heroes, even if they are negative figures destined to be finally trapped by the law.[6]

# Mafia today in Palermo

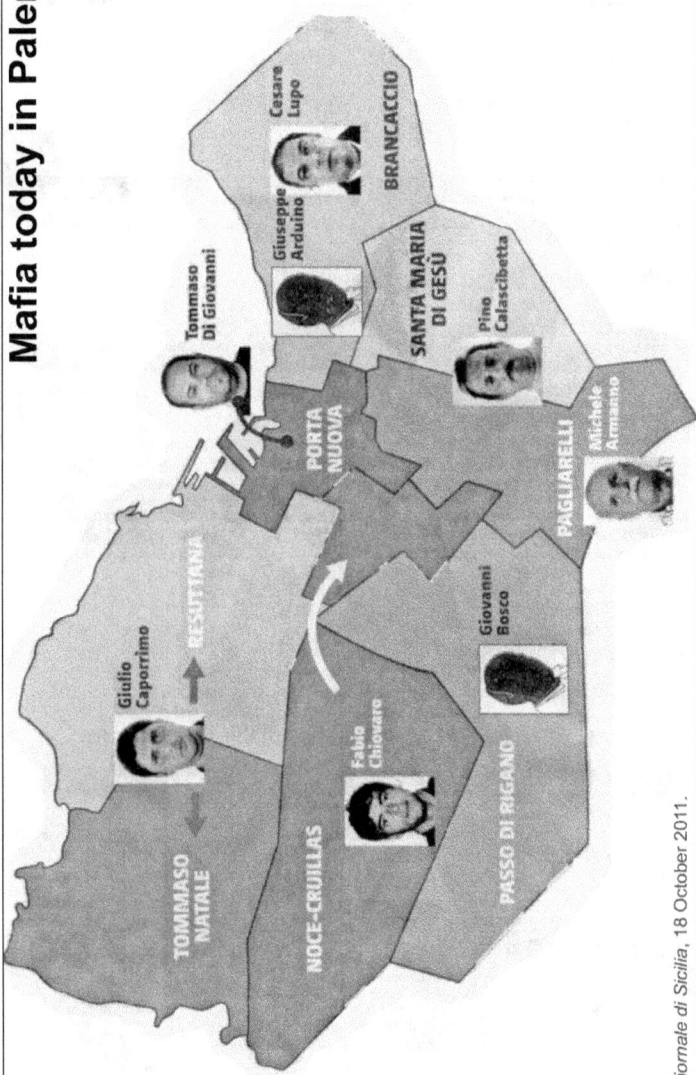

Source: *Giornale di Sicilia*, 18 October 2011.

# MANDAMENTI IN PALERMO

## 1. Tommaso Natale

Capo mandamento: Giulio Caporrino

Families:
San Lorenzo
Tommaso Natale - Cardillo
Partanna Mondello
Pallavicino

## 2. Resuttana

Capo mandamento: Giulio Caporrino

Families:
Acquasanta
Arenella - Vergine Maria

## 3. Passo di Rigano

Capo mandamento: Giovanni Bosco

Families:
Passo di Rigano
Uditore
Boccadifalco

## 4. Pagliarelli

Capo mandamento: Michele Armanno

Families:
Pagliarelli
Borgo Molara
Corso Calatafimi (Filippo Annatelli)

## 5. Noce

Capo mandamento: Fabio Chiovaro

Families
Noce
Cruillas
Altarello

## 6. Porta nuova

Capo mandamento: Tommaso Di Giovanni

Families:
Porta nuova
Palermo Centro
Borgo Vecchio

## 7. Santa Maria di Gesù

Capo mandamento: Pino Calascibetta

Families:
Santa Maria di Gesù
Villagrazia
Guadagna

## 8. Brancaccio

Capo mandamento: Giuseppe Arduino

Families:
Brancaccio
Ciaculli
Corso dei Mille
Roccella

# MANDAMENTI IN PROVINCE OF PALERMO

| Bagheria | Misilmeri | San Giuseppe Jato | Termini |
|---|---|---|---|
| Families: | Families: | Families: | Families: |
| Bagheria | Misilmeri | San Giuseppe Jato | Termini Imerese |
| Villabate | Baucina | Monreale | Trabia |
| Ficarazzi | Ciminna | Altofonte | Caccamo |
| Casteldaccia | Bolognetta | Piana degli Albanesi | Montemaggiore |
| | Marineo | Camporeale | Cerda |

| Corleone | Partinico | San Mauro Castelverde |
|---|---|---|
| Families: | Families: | Families: |
| Corleone | Partinico | San Mauro Castelverde |
| Cefala Diana | Balestrate | Collesano |
| Prizzi | Borgetto | Gangi |
| | Cinisi - Terrasini | Polizzi Generosa |
| | | Finale di Pollina |

# PROVINCE OF PALERMO

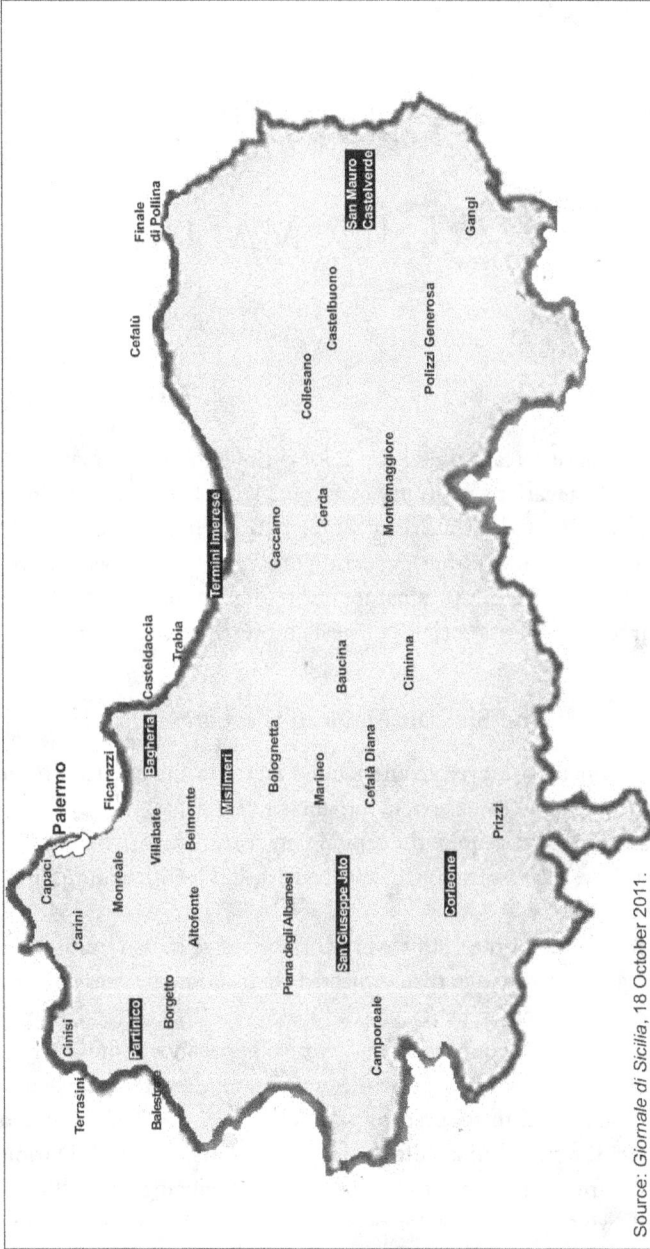

Source: *Giornale di Sicilia*, 18 October 2011.

# CHAPTER 6

# OTHER MAFIAS

As we have already seen, for a long time the term 'mafia' has been used for a variety of forms of criminal behaviour, corruption, client relationships and favouritism. Properly used, it would cover only those forms of organized crime (appearing of course in a number of guises) that demonstrate the complex nature of the Sicilian mafia through its ability to interact with its social, political and institutional surroundings.

## The Sicilian Mafia in the United States

Sicilian mafiosi moved to the United States in the nineteenth century.[1] Once there, to some extent organized crime has enabled immigrant ethnic groups to acquire the capital they require to play a substantial role in society. That is just as true for the Irish and Jewish communities as for the Italians.

By the end of the 1800s every US city where Italian immigrants were living also had gangs that subjected their fellow Italians to blackmail; they were known in general as the *Mano Nera* (Black Hand). Early in the next century, Italo-American criminals began to move into more profitable areas such as prostitution, gaming, labour rackets and drugs.

Prohibition, introduced by the Volstead Act in 1920 and abolished in 1933, resulted in a shift in the nature of its activities. During those years various criminal groups got rich by producing and selling alcohol (beer, wine and whisky) for popular use, consumption of which was not reduced by prohibition. Their increased illegal wealth meant that criminal groups could establish relationships with politicians and administrators in centres such as New York and Chicago and invest in the legal economy. This was the start of the mafioso as businessman and the respectable gangster, who enjoyed prestige both within his community and in the wider world. Investments ranged from clothing to the food industry, public services and contracts for public works. Criminal groups played a particularly important role in putting down labour unrest and running unions in key sectors, such as that of road transport (Teamsters), but they continued to be engaged in illegal activities, often with the protection and complicity of a corrupt police force and a political machine that was open to manipulation. In the years immediately before and after World War II they began to lay the foundations for the world market in drugs, through connections with Europe and the Middle East. Leaders in this area included characters such as Lucky Luciano and Frank Coppola, both Sicilian in origin. At the Palermo summit in 1957, the American and Sicilian mafias reached agreement on controlling drug trafficking. In 1963, the mafioso Joe Valachi revealed to the McClellan Committee of the Senate the existence of an organization called Cosa Nostra, although it was only the Buscetta revelations in the early 1980s that revealed that this name was also used by the Sicilian mafia. It was then that the organizational structure and the names of the bosses and leaders became known.

A 1988 Senate report described how the Italo-American mafia was set up.[2] There were five families operating in New York: the Bonannos, with 109 members; the Colombos, with 102; the Gambinos, with 203; the Luccheses, with 113; and the Genoveses, with 193. There were other families operating in New Jersey, Philadelphia, Chicago, Tampa, New Orleans, Pittsburgh, Kansas City, Detroit, Los Angeles, Boston and Miami. The 'Pizza Connection' trial in the 1980s centred on drug trafficking, which was dominated by the two Cosa Nostra organizations under the direction of Gaetano Badalamenti, the Cinisi mafia boss who was sentenced to 45 years in prison and then in 2002 to life imprisonment in Italy for the murder of Peppino Impastato.

In recent years Cosa Nostra in the United States has been hit by official measures that have led to the arrest and imprisonment of many of its bosses and associates. Competition from new organizations, run by Hispanics, Chinese and others, has curtailed its activities, beginning with the loss of its monopoly on trafficking in narcotics.

There has been talk of a 'Twilight of the Godfathers' but the problem of global terrorism, which emerged with the attack on the

Twin Towers in New York on 11 September 2001, has reduced the attention paid to organized crime. Recent years have seen traditional mafia families build a strong presence in gambling, usury, extortion, the manufacture of counterfeit goods and building, including works related to the 11 September attack, such as removing the debris of the World Trade Center.

Arrests in February 2008 contradicted, at least in part, the argument that Cosa Nostra in the United States was finished. Operation 'Old Bridge' resulted in the arrests of 54 American bosses and 23 mafiosi from Sicily, almost all of them well-known figures. The list included the Inzerillo, the so-called 'escapees', those who had fled to America during the mafia wars of the early 1980s, Filippo Casamento, 82 years old, who was expelled from the United States in 2005 and other men from the Gambino family. One new name was Frank Calì, born in New York to Sicilian parents, married to an Inzerillo and arrested in his lover's house. The 'bridge' – which was many years old and which had been rebuilt mainly at the behest of Lo Piccolo – was designed to help the 'escapees' to return as a precondition for re-establishing links with the American families and stood on traditional foundations: drug trafficking, extortion and firms engaged in food distribution and construction. A 'Pizza Connection' that was thought to have been buried had resurfaced.

The United States is home to an impressive array of analyses and studies of the mafia carried out by institutions, such as Senate committees, and individual academics. Their views may be broadly divided into two: the first sees the mafia as an 'alien conspiracy', of which American society is a victim; the second regards crime as part of the 'American way of life', the way society in the United States is. They view crime as a pathway to integration for the various immigrant ethnic groups who are enabled to accumulate the wealth they require for social mobility, so that the disadvantaged can climb the ladder of social progress. At the same time, in 1970 legislative activity resulted in the Organized Crime Control Act (OCCA) and the Racketeer Influenced and Corrupt Organizations (RICO) statute, which is mainly concerned with the economic activities of criminal organizations. Central to these laws is the concept of 'conspiracy', an offence similar to that of mafia association introduced by the 1982 Italian antimafia laws.

Contrasting with this analytical work has been the vast array of novels, films and television screenplays presenting the mafia in a good light. These range from the three *The Godfather* movies, based on the novel by Mario Puzo and directed by Francis Ford Coppola, to TV's *The Sopranos*, whose success can be explained by the force of suggestion that enables stereotypes to imbue the mafia with a romantic image even today.

## The Sicilian Mafia in Canada

Mafia families originating in Sicily also operate in Canada.[3] The best known is the Caruana-Cuntrera family from Siculiana in the province of Agrigento, which is one of the most active in international drug trafficking and money laundering. The Caruana-Cuntrera clan acts like a real holding company, with branches in Venezuela, Brazil, several European countries and Asia, but it has retained close ties with Sicily.

During the 1980s it was found that the Sicilian-Canadian clans had close ties with Vito Ciancimino, the former mayor of Palermo, and recent press reports have alleged that the Canadian clans are interested in building the bridge over the Strait of Messina.

## The 'ndrangheta in Calabria

The roots of the 'ndrangheta lie in the world of farming and animal husbandry, where it played a role similar to the Sicilian *gabelloto*, the *industriante*, who managed the estates and used armed guards to control the land and intimidate the peasants.[4]

The term *'ndrangheta* or *'ndranghita* is probably derived from a Grecanica word meaning a brave man: an etymology clearly intended to impart a favourable gloss. A second hypothesis derives the term from verses that used to accompany some steps of the tarantella – *e'ndrangheta e 'ndrà* – and has a negative connotation: ballet dancer, fool and so on. Originally this criminal organization in Calabria was referred to by the judicial authorities as 'picciotteria'; they then used 'camorra' and more recently adopted the expression "ndrangheta', which is now in common use.

The basic organizations are the *'ndrine*, which mainly correspond to blood families; the family link is more important than in the Sicilian mafia. The organizational structure as reconstructed thanks to those cooperating with the authorities, is: (1) *corpo di società*, with a head and 24 men, constituted in cities where courts are located; (2) *'ndrina generale,* which groups a number of *'ndrine* and is subdivided into *maggiore* (greater), comprising *camorristi,* and *minore* (lesser), comprising *picciotti.* At the head of each *'ndrina* is the *sergio (saggio:* wise) *capo,* also known as the *crimine,* assisted by the *contabile,* the *mastro di giornata* and the *puntaiolo.* The *camorristi* are further divided hierarchically: *camorristi semplici, di società, di fibbia, formati* and *di sgarro,* who may be *di sangue* and *definitivo.* A number of *'ndrine* make up a *locale* corresponding to a village or area of a town. The headship passes from father to son.

Written texts comprising the statutes, acceptance rituals (baptism) and oaths have been found. Tradition refers to the three mythical founders of the mafia, 'ndrangheta and camorra: Osso, Mastrosso and Carcagnosso, legendary figures intended to provide the founding myth with an aura of nobility. Religious symbols abound, and each task has its own patron saint: Santa Liberata for the *picciotti,* Santa Nunzia for the *camorristi,* Saint Elizabeth for the *sgarrista di sangue* and Archangel Gabriel as protector of the *locale.* The cult is centred on the Sanctuary of the Madonna of Polsi, deep in the Aspromonte, where the 'ndrangheta holds its summit meetings.

A *Santa* is a complex organizational structure whose job is to liaise with public institutions and the police to enhance the power of the organization and conclude deals; and a *Vangelo* is a sort of criminal union that controls operations in a social context. The names used are those of historical figures (Garibaldi, Mazzini, Charlemagne), once again intended to paint criminal activities and criminals in a favourable light. Both older and modern sources document the role of women.

Traditionally the structure has been horizontal in nature, spread over a large area with inevitable fragmentation. There is no supreme head but recently there have been attempts at coordination. For example, three commands were set up in the province of Reggio Calabria: Ionian, Central and Tyrrhenian, along with a provincial commission.

The conflicts between the various families, and the rules on vendettas that had gone on for generations, plunged Calabria into a bloodbath with a series of feuds lasting decades. The 30 years from 1950 to 1980 saw 2,100 killings.

The activities of the 'ndrangheta included extortion and, for a long time, kidnappings, which between 1963 and 1983 involved 200 people. These continued over the following years and it is estimated that over a

20-year period about 400 billion lire was paid in ransoms, almost all of which was laundered.

During the 1970s the 'ndrangheta became increasingly involved in business and evolved into a prominent player in drug trafficking. Its network extended into northern Italy and the rest of Europe and it established itself in several countries, including the United States and Australia.

In the mid-1970s, disputes between the various families led to a first mafia war, resulting in 93 deaths in 1975 and 101 the following year. The war broke out again between 1985 and 1991, leaving some 600 people dead.

Little attention was paid to its activities because few crimes hit the headlines, the exceptions being the killings of the politician and businessman Ludovico Ligato in summer 1989 and, on 9 August 1991, of the Court of Cassation prosecutor Antonino Scopelliti, who was to have participated in the Cosa Nostra maxi-trial: this was done as a favour to the Sicilian mafia. Furthermore, few people cooperated with the authorities, with the result that the Calabrian mafia was able to increase its influence until it became the richest and most widespread organization in Italy. This was certainly assisted by its links with the Masonic lodges, which have a strong active presence in the region. Internationally, the Calabrians dominate cocaine trafficking, which has been estimated to total some 400 tonnes per year.

Recently, the 'ndrangheta has struck again, with the murder on 16 October 2005 of Dr Francesco Fortugno, vice-president of the regional council, and the massacre in Duisburg, Germany, on 14–15 August 2007 of six people in what was the next episode of a feud that had originated in the village of S. Luca (Reggio Calabria). The latest investigations have revealed that the 'ndrangheta is involved in health, along with workers in the sector and politicians. The situation is a deadly mixture of the old and modern, of feuds and the internet: the Calabrian mafia is the one that makes most use of the web.

Recent figures put the 'ndrangheta at 132 groups with some 10,000 members out of a regional population of 2,077,000. Its annual turnover is around €35 billion, the highest for organized crime in Italy. Between 1991 and November 2012, 64 town councils, including 38 in the province of Reggio Calabria, were dissolved because of mafia infiltration. In the same period in Sicily 58 town councils were dissolved.

## The Antimafia in Calabria

After both World Wars I and II, Calabria saw peasant struggles to recover the land taken over by the great noble families and to secure agricultural reform. Land ownership was mainly in the hands of a few families while smallholdings were fragmented. The Gullo decrees of 1944 saw the formation of peasant cooperatives and land occupation. A neo-fascist-type response was violence. Between September 1943 and March 1945, 13 peasants and trade unionists died in the province of Reggio Calabria. Following the arrest of the son of the communist mayor, Pasquale Cavallaro, in Caulonia, an autonomous republic was declared for five days, 5–9 March 1945, with a people's court to try and sentence landowners and fascists. In that period the 'ndrangheta may be regarded as divided into two arms: the more popular part, linked to the peasantry, went with the Communist Party, and some leaders and activists broke their links while others were less decisive; the other arm stuck firmly to the Christian Democrats and other right-wing parties. Many people were sent into internal exile, often for political reasons, to help the conservative parties.

The peasant struggles continued in the years to come, with the formation of land committees and reverse strikes. Women played a significant role. On 28 November 1946 in the province of Crotone a gamekeeper killed Giuditta Levato, a 31-year-old mother of two children and expecting a third, who was a leading figure in the peasant struggle. Repression was principally the task of the police: on 13 April 1947 at Petilia Policastro, in the province of Catanzaro, the *carabinieri* opened fire on peasants, killing Isabella Carvelli, aged 25, and Francesco Mascaro. On 29 October 1949 in Melissa (Catanzaro) a detachment of the Celere fired on peasants who were occupying land. Three died: Francesco Nigro, 29, Giovanni Zito, 15, and a woman, Angelina Mauro, and 15 were wounded, all shot in the back. The Prime Minister, Alcide De Gasperi, went to Calabria and promised to meet the peasants' requests. May 1950 saw the Sila Law, which initiated a partial and inadequate agricultural reform with the expropriation of marginal and poor land for which the landowning nobles were paid substantial compensation. That year also saw the foundation of the Cassa del Mezzogiorno, which was to prove a gravy train for well-connected individuals but would not solve the problem of the divide between North and South. A mass exodus began from both Sicily and Calabria: between 1951 and 1961, 342,600 people left Calabria for the Americas and northern Italy.

In recent years, partly as a reaction to mafia violence – which has hit those active on the Left, such as the communists Rocco Gatto, killed in Gioiosa Jonica (Reggio Calabria) on 12 March 1977, Giuseppe Valarioti (Rosarno, Reggio Calabria, 11 June 1980) and Giovanni Losardo (Cetraro, Cosenza, 21 June 1980); businessmen such as Gennaro Musella (3 May 1982); landowners such as Antonino Cordopatri, who refused to sell land to 'ndrangheta bosses and was killed on 10 July 1991; magistrates such as Scopelliti and politicians such as Fortugno – committees, associations and social cooperatives for the use of confiscated goods have sprung up, in some measure thanks to the efforts of certain clerics, such as the Bishop of Locri, Giancarlo Bregantini. The 'ndrangheta has responded with attacks and intimidation. In recent years demonstrations have been held to relaunch antimafia activity in Calabria and the Mezzogiorno, and immigrant workers have organized demonstrations against racism, the 'ndrangheta and exploitation.

## The Camorra in Campania

The origins of the camorra are said to reach back to the Guarduna, a fifteenth-century confraternity which existed in Spain from 1417.[5] Originally, the term referred both to the organization and the use of extortion as practised mainly in prisons, and could derive from the Spanish – either a short jacket, as referred to by Giovan Battista Basile in the *Pentamerone*, or to be disputatious: *hacer camorra* means to seek a quarrel – but the most careful academics note that, like the mafia, it is a southern Italian, not Spanish, phenomenon. What is certain is that the camorra grew up in prisons and an urban context, particularly among the poorest in society. Later it became more middle class and acquired other meanings: the word *guapparia* is used for common delinquency and *camorra amministrativa* for misbehaviour by those in power and, more recently, the terms *camorra massa* and *camorra impresa* have been used.

The history of the camorra has been marked by gaps and by fragmentation in its organization. It was only in the 1970s that bloody fighting broke out between two coalitions: Raffaele Cutolo's Nuova Camorra Organizzata and his opponents' Nuova Famiglia. This was followed by disintegration and permanent war between the various groups. In the Caserta area, at Casal di Principe where one of the richest and most aggressive groups operates, the clans have a structure similar to that of the Sicilian mafia and some members of the camorra are linked to Cosa nostra.

Its activities range from extortion to cigarette smuggling and drug trafficking, from firms in the clothing sector with the production of fake designer goods to refuse collection and the misappropriation of public money, particularly in connection with reconstruction after the 1980 earthquake.

In recent years this may be regarded as an all-encompassing and general 'system' shaken by tensions between the clans operating in cities such as Naples and in the provinces. This ongoing state of war creates problems for the population in general: many crimes involve shoot-outs, causing casualties among passers-by, and there are frequent internal feuds involving the relatives of bosses and followers. Campania has the highest murder rate in Italy, accounting for 21.06 per cent of the total. There are strong and pervasive links with politicians and institutions, with the largest number of municipal councils dissolved because of mafia connections. The problem of waste disposal in Campania has created a very serious situation, with images of streets clogged by uncollected rubbish published throughout the world.

The camorra also takes advantage of a 'culture', widespread among the most marginalized and in the ghetto areas, that is built on songs, plays and films, both television and cinema, which present its members as popular heroes who succeed in rising above their excluded and lowly situations and who offer a way out, especially for those young people in a similar situation or worse due to declining industries and the lack of jobs. Recent sources put camorra membership at 6,700 out of a population in Campania of 5,788,000 and its annual turnover at €28 billion. The region with the largest number of local councils dissolved because of mafia infiltration was Campania with 91; 48 of these were in the province of Naples.

Activity against the camorra has been carried out by study centres and associations that commemorate the victims of its violence, such as the mayor of Pagani (Salerno), Marcello Torre, killed on 11 December 1980; the journalist Giancarlo Siani, killed in Naples on 23 September 1985; the priest Giuseppe Diana, killed in Casal di Principe on 19 March

1994; and the mayor of Pollica (Salerno), Angelo Vassallo, killed on 5 September 2010.

Recent years have seen the development of anti-racketeering associations, partly thanks to the work of Tano Grasso, a founder of one such association in Capo d'Orlando and a consultant to the Naples municipal administration. Immigrant workers have organized demonstrations against racism and the camorra.

## The Mafia in Apulia

The mafia in Apulia is known as the 'fourth mafia' and is the product both of the presence in the area of the three traditional criminal organizations and the social background, with widespread corruption in its administration, abuses of power, a crisis in agriculture, de-industrialization, and the opportunities offered by illegal activities, exacerbated by the collapse of 'real socialism' and the opening of relations with Albania and the other countries of the Adriatic.[6]

The result was the formation of a variety of criminal groups, with pride of place going to the Sacra Corona Unita which, while imitating other organizations, camouflages itself by using mystic, religious and Masonic symbols. It is questionable whether this is really a mafia-type association or just an attempt to be one, but its organizational structure, the complexity of its activities and its network of relationships show that it has made considerable progress down that road, despite the testimony of turncoats leading to the arrest of bosses and members and so dealing it some significant blows. The Sacra Corona Unita has 2,000 members out of Apulia's total population of 4,077,000.

In Apulia, too, the period after World War II saw peasant struggles for land reform and the democratic management of the placing of labour, traditionally in the hands of the *caporali*. A repressive response was not lacking: on 29 November 1949 at Torreggiano, in the province of Foggia, the police opened fire on peasants and killed Communist Party activists Antonio La Vacca and Giuseppe Lamedica.

Currently antimafia operations are being led by committees and associations dedicated to figures such as Renata Fonte, a municipal councillor killed at Nardò (Lecce) on 31 March 1984; Gianni Carnicella, the mayor of Molfetta, killed on 7 July 1992; and Francesco Marcone, director of the Registry, killed at Foggia on 31 March 1995. The Bishop of Molfetta, Tonino Bello, who died prematurely in 1993, played a significant role in initiatives against the mafia and to promote peace.

## In Basilicata: The Basilischi

The criminal groups operating in the Basilicata, which were investigated by the parliamentary Antimafia Commission in its 1992 report, are also referred to as mafia.[7] In the province of Matera, both on the Ionian coastal strip and inland, there are family-based groups that behave like mafia criminal groups, carrying out a variety of activities: extortion, receiving stolen goods, kidnapping, possession of weapons and drug trafficking; its members have been charged with and sentenced for mafia-type association. As in mafia areas, there have been battles for the control of territory resulting in murders and legal activities have been infiltrated, particularly after the earthquake in 1980.

The organization known as I Basilischi was set up in Potenza in the early 1990s and spread throughout the region. Initially it was an offshoot of the 'ndrangheta, later becoming organizationally and operationally autonomous. Police investigations have identified and wiped out its management.

Basilicata also had a strong peasant movement and on 14 December 1949 at Montescaglioso, in the province of Matera, during a demonstration supporting the reallocation of land held by the large landowners, a policeman killed Giuseppe Novello, a labourer.

## Mafia Activity in Northern Italy

There is documentary evidence from the 1960s that the Sicilian mafia was present in other regions thanks to the law on forced residence and the links that various mafia members formed in those areas. What is happening in Lazio is significant. There, encounters with other groups and local criminals have resulted in worrying developments such as the Banda della Magliana, which has become a nucleus for criminal and political trafficking and interaction, and the growth of substantial business activities, including those headed by Enrico Nicoletti, who built the second university at Tor Vergata.

The region that has seen the greatest development in mafia-related activities is Lombardy, where a number of inquiries launched following a rise in the murder rate have demonstrated the presence of mafia members. The number of confiscations of goods places the region in fifth place on the national scale, behind Sicily, Campania, Calabria and Apulia.

The laundering of dirty money accumulated by various mafias through the casinos at Saint Vincent, Sanremo, Campione d'Italia and elsewhere in the world, from Nice to St Maarten and Las Vegas, is well known.

As long ago as the 1960s the 'ndrangheta was active alongside the Sicilian mafia in Piedmont in the arrangement and placing of labour, particularly in the construction sector. A typical example is that of Bardonecchia (Turin), whose municipal council was dissolved because of its mafia associations. There is a substantial Calabrian presence in Emilia-Romagna and Lombardy, where their interests range from small-scale building works to major projects such as the high-speed rail network and the 2015 Milan Expo.

The camorra, particularly the group from Casal di Principe, is represented in various regions, especially Liguria, Emilia, Lombardy and the Veneto.

I have already mentioned the Sicilian-American and Sicilian-Canadian mafias but the other Italian mafias also operate on an international scale and there is documentary evidence of their activities in several European countries, the United States, Canada and Australia.

The so-called 'Brenta mafia' has operated in the Veneto for some years and various criminal groups from different countries, such as the clans from Corsica and Marseilles, the Albanian and Russian mafias, the Chinese Triads, and Italian groups operating in close cooperation with other groups (e.g. the Colombian cartels) have been and are still active in Italy.

## The Clans from Corsica and Marseilles

The criminal groups originating in Corsica and operating in Marseilles from the 1940s to the early 1970s dominated cigarette smuggling and heroin trafficking,[8] both because of the presence of Corsicans in several countries from Asia to Africa and the Americas and because of their connections with politicians. One of the strongest clans was the Guerini, who took control of civic life in Marseilles, in alliance with city officials, and had links with the secret services, starting with the CIA (Central

Intelligence Agency) in its battle with communism. The Guerini brothers were provided with money and weapons to put down port workers and trade unionists. During the 1947 strikes in which 80,000 workers took part, both criminals and police fired into the crowd, killing several people. Marseilles later became a key centre for heroin trafficking: the Corsicans, the so-called French Connection, imported morphine from Turkey and produced heroin that was sent to Canada, the Caribbean and the United States, the main consumer market. The Marseilles clans ceased to dominate international drug trafficking in the 1970s, as the Sicilian mafia took over, using the Marseilles clans as technicians. The magistrate Pierre Michel, who was provided with no protection, was investigating this link when he was assassinated in Marseilles on 21 October 1981.

Later the most important Corsican criminal organization was the Brise de mer, named after a bar in Bastia that was a criminal haunt. It was organized in concentric circles: 'soldiers', associates and outside protectors; it was present throughout the island, had links with nationalist groups and criminal organizations in various countries, and used French and Swiss banks to launder its dirty money. Its activities included kidnapping, extortion, the management of casinos, bars, restaurants, discotheques and commercial centres, and investments in property.

## The Mafias of the East and Former Socialist Countries

For many years the Turkish clans played a strategic role in drug trafficking, exploiting the position of their country as a transit zone from the Middle East to the West. They imported opium from the areas of production, the Golden Crescent (Iran, Afghanistan, Pakistan) and the Golden Triangle (Burma-Myanmar, Laos, Thailand), processed it into morphine-base and handed it on to the Corsicans in Marseilles.

Following the establishment of large Turkish communities in many European countries, the criminal clans managed drug trafficking on their own account and also bought and sold weapons. For many years the best-known group was the Mussululu, with links to the Sicilian mafia and money-laundering professionals in Switzerland. They also had strong links with politicians and the institutions. Turkey was regarded as a 'mafia state' because of the role played by its government, which had on its payroll men from the Grey Wolves, the politico-criminal band with secret service connections, one of whose members was Alì Agca, who attempted to assassinate Pope John Paul II in 1981.

After the fall of the communist regime in Russia a number of criminal groups emerged, practising extortion, drug trafficking and weapons trading, and investing large amounts of capital in the property markets of other countries.[9] Official sources put the number of these groups in the early 1990s at about 5,700, with around 100,000 members. Some of them derive from the so-called 'thieves in law' who were active from the 1920s: this was a secret society formed by professional thieves who did not recognize the abolition of private property, which also acted as a political opposition. Within the USSR the so-called 'Soviet mafia' operated. This expression had two meanings: the use of criminal practices (corruption, extortion, sometimes even murder) by the Communist Party in power, and its links with purely criminal circles. The breakdown of the communist state and especially of the secret service, the KGB, resulted in the appearance and growth of criminal organizations that perpetrated enormous financial frauds and managed the dismantling of the military stockpile. Following the fall of the Berlin Wall, Sicilian mafiosi too acquired property, hotels and factories that had closed, or were being shut down. Contracts for privatization were awarded to mafia groups. Instead of bringing efficient businesses into being, this handed criminals a great bargain, so that in practice they became the 'nouveaux riches', a real 'mafia bourgeoisie'. Lodged in the very heart of the institutions, the Russian mafia turned into a sort of 'criminocracy'. Because the raw materials (cannabis for the production of hashish and marijuana, opium for heroin) are produced on its territory, and because of the size of its domestic market and the extent of its international links, the Russian mafia has taken on the leading role in global drug trafficking.

Other former socialist countries are involved in criminal activities and have witnessed the proliferation of local groups and the involvement of foreign ones. In some cases, these may be considered 'mafia States'.[10]

Following the armed conflicts in the former Yugoslavia the heroin routes moved further north, away from the traditional route across the Balkans (from Istanbul through Belgrade) and into Bulgaria, Romania and Hungary. Romania became an international crossroads for cocaine. This traffic also involved high-ranking police officers with links to the 'ndrangheta in Calabria. Criminal groups in Romania also control rackets concerning the adoption of children and prostitution.

In Bulgaria the cultivation of cannabis and opium poppies has increased in recent years and pharmaceutical firms are producing psychotropic drugs and amphetamines. Poland, too, is producing amphetamines: 20 per cent of these substances seized in Scandinavian countries come from Polish laboratories. The former socialist countries offer plentiful opportunities for laundering dirty money through the purchase of property and the management of hotels and casinos. For example, Sicilian mafiosi and *camorristi* from Campania have done excellent business in Prague. It is said that the war in the former Yugoslavia was financed with the proceeds of drug trafficking.

Albania produces marijuana and is a transit area for heroin en route to the Italian mafia, transported in powerful cars, and production laboratories have been established. The clans in Albania run cigarette smuggling, trafficking in drugs and weapons, illegal emigration and prostitution, in cooperation with mafia groups based in Apulia.

## The Chinese Triads

Chinese immigration into Italy began in the 1980s, the largest communities being in Milan, Rome, Florence and Prato. They are also established in other cities, including Palermo, and are particularly active in restaurants, low-cost clothing and trade. The crimes carried out by the Chinese in Italy include extortion, criminal conspiracy, smuggling, gaming, prostitution and trafficking illegal immigrants. The most important trial took place in Florence, with a judgement in May 1999 that compared the role of the Chinese operating in the area with mafia associations, because of their roots within the community and their widespread use of extortion, which could be regarded as the first way of exercising territorial sovereignty.

The Chinese Triads are secret societies that emerged in the seventeenth and eighteenth centuries as a means of protection and mutual assistance.[11] They played a part in the history of China, and in the battle between the Communist Party and the Kuomintang, the grouping of conservative forces, they backed the latter. After it was defeated they moved to neighbouring countries and turned increasingly to illegal activities. Their presence is greatest in Hong Kong, where they control rackets, the building sector, gaming, prostitution, private police forces and drugs. The most important Triads are said to be the Wo Shing Wo, the 14K, founded in the 1940s by the Kuomintang; the Sun Yee On, the Lung Ying Shea and the Triad of the Great Circle, which is reputed to be made up of ex-Red Guardsmen who fled China after the Cultural Revolution. A Triad usually numbers from 100 to several thousand members. The biggest Triad has been the Sun Yee On, with 38,000 members.

In Europe there are Triads in Great Britain, particularly in London, Manchester and Glasgow, and also in the Netherlands, especially in Amsterdam. Their main activity is drug trafficking, the profits from which are then recycled in Chinese restaurants, gambling houses and video shops. They have their bases in the Chinatowns of Europe and the United States.

---

## The Opium Wars, Prohibition and Drug Trafficking

China was the scene of the Opium Wars launched by the United Kingdom, the first from 1839 to 1842 and the second from 1856 to 1860. China was seeking to prevent the opium trade on its territory, while the United Kingdom wanted it to continue because of the profits it yielded. China lost both wars and had to accept legalization of the opium trade.

Later a movement for prohibition gathered momentum, particularly in the United States, its first result being the International Opium Convention, signed in The Hague in 1912, which contained measures to control the international trade in opium.

During and after its prohibition of alcohol (1920–33), the United States led campaigns to ban narcotics. In 1925 the Geneva Conference resulted in two conventions: one on opium and one on other narcotics. Further conventions, in 1931 and 1936, introduced measures to control the production and consumption of drugs. The New York Protocol of 1953 introduced measures to control the cultivation of opium poppies. In 1961, 77 delegations signed the Single Convention on Narcotic Drugs, which was ratified by 133 states and applies to 118 plants and natural and synthetic substances. This was the start of an international ban on narcotics, amended by the 1972 Geneva Protocol. On 19 December 1988 a new United Nations convention against the illicit trafficking of narcotic drugs and psychotropic substances was signed in Vienna.

Prohibition did not reduce the consumption of narcotics, which grew steadily throughout the world. In the 1970s and 1980s heroin consumers totalled 2 million in the United States, 500,000 in Europe, 260,000 in Italy, over 1 million in Pakistan, 1 million in Iran and 500,000 in India and Thailand; cocaine consumers numbered 6 million in the United States and were rising sharply in Europe; in both the United States and Europe regular and occasional cannabis users totalled several million and consumption in the former communist countries has grown in recent years. Recent data published in the Ministry of Social Solidarity's report on drug addiction shows that the number of cannabis and cocaine users in Italy doubled from 2001 to 2005, while the number of heroin users fell. The number of cocaine users is currently about 2 million and there has been a steep rise in the consumption of hallucinogens and chemical mixtures with toxic effects. The European Monitoring Centre for Drugs and Drug Addiction puts the number of cocaine users in Europe at 12 million, users of ecstasy (a synthetic drug) at 9.5 million and users of amphetamines (stimulants) at 11 million. Heroin consumption, which had been falling, is rising again, with over 3 million users. There are at least 70 million occasional cannabis users and consumption of a variety of drugs has grown in recent years.

The criminal organizations controlling production and distribution secure enormous profits while the countries where the raw materials (opium, cannabis, coca) are produced are among the poorest in the world. Opium is produced in Burma-Myanmar, Laos, Thailand, Afghanistan, Iran and Pakistan; cannabis in a number of countries including Mexico, Colombia and Lebanon; coca in Bolivia, Colombia and Peru. It is estimated that the price of the finished product is some 2,000 times that of the basic substance. In the 1980s profits from drug trafficking were put at $400–800 billion per year. Drugs distributed in small doses are usually adulterated with dangerous substances, posing serious risks for consumers. In Italy, deaths from drug use stood at 239 in 1981, rising to 1,161 in 1990. In 2005 overdoses resulted in 603 deaths. Alcoholism accounted for a much larger number: 24,000 between 2001 and 2005.

As part of Progetto Droga – promoted in conjunction with CISS (International South-South Cooperation) and involving NGOs from three continents – the Centro Impastato has proposed the organization in schools and public places of an ongoing information campaign to highlight the harmful effects of psychoactive substances, both legal and illegal, from alcohol to tobacco and from drugs described as 'soft' to 'hard' ones.

## The Japanese Yakuza

The name of the Japanese mafia is derived from three figures: 8-9-3, pronounced *ya-ku-za*.[12] The Japanese criminal organizations also go back a long way, with roots in the eighteenth century; here, too, there is a founding myth that seeks to make its members descendants of the *ronin*, the samurai without lords, bandit-knights. In the nineteenth century these organizations formed links with the nationalist extreme right and took part in the opium trade. Their links with the Right continued later. At the beginning of the twentieth century the Yamaguchi-gumi emerged as the biggest criminal group in Japan and today boasts 13,000 members in the main cities.

The yakuza, with over 100,000 members, play a political role as electoral agents, collectors of funds and private guards. Their members are marked by the use of tattoos over their whole body and the amputation of fingers as a punishment for misdemeanours. Their activities include illegal gaming, extortion, including the use of *sokaya* – shareholders who use blackmail and corruption to control shareholder meetings – usury, through the *sarakin* (often the victims are forced to commit suicide), prostitution and the trafficking of drugs and weapons.

Until a few years ago the yakuza had offices open to the public with name plates and wore badges in their buttonholes.

The yakuza are to be found in a number of countries. They are engaged in drug trafficking, especially in east Asia, Korea, Taiwan, the Philippines and the United States, and have investments in Hawaii and California, South America and Europe, principally to recycle illegal capital.

Godfathers in the Japanese mafia (*kuromaku*) often have a devout and charitable image: an example is Ryoichi Sasakawa, an adviser to the Unification Church, a leading anti-communist and the man behind a foundation that finances cultural activities throughout the world.

Recent revelations about the yakuza have come from two women: Mitsuyo Ohira, the former wife of a criminal and later a lawyer and the author of a book in which she recounts her experiences, and Shoko Tendo, the daughter and wife of a yakuza boss and author of an autobiographical novel.[13] In the past women were leaders in organized crime in Japan but now they play an indirect role.

## The African Drug Route

In recent years Africa has become an integral part of the world drug-trafficking system. Its fragile institutions, widespread corruption and ever closer links with Europe make it an ideal transit zone. It is also both a producer of raw materials for the manufacture of narcotics and a consumer.

Nigerians have played an increasingly prominent role, first as drug couriers and later increasingly as principals. They have formed their own criminal network, which is represented, thanks to a large number of emigrants, in Britain and the United States. Lagos airport is the main terminal for air traffic in west Africa and Nigerians obtain drugs in Asia and transport them to Europe and the United States. In 1990 over 2,000

Nigerians involved in drug trafficking were arrested, 1,800 in the United Kingdom. Because they know they are being watched, Nigerian bosses often use couriers from other countries. Criminal gangs of Nigerians are also active in people trafficking, particularly women being sold into prostitution.

Early in October 2011, arrest warrants were issued in Palermo for 67 people involved in drug trafficking. The leaders of this group of traffickers and pushers are the Nigerian Francis Olabayo Wiwoloku and Salvatore Castigliola, from Palermo. The criminal band includes persons apparently beyond reproach and some women. A number of its members are also part of Cosa Nostra and the network extends as far as Catania and Messina.

## The Colombian Cartels

Starting in the 1970s South America saw the emergence of several groups engaged in the production and marketing of cocaine. Consumption of coca leaf is traditional among natives of the Andes and is linked to the cult of Mama Coca, where it plays the same role as does wine in Christianity. During the sixteenth century, the Spanish conquistadors encouraged its use by mine workers as a means of boosting energy. In the nineteenth century the chemical treatment of coca leaf resulted in the production of cocaine, a stimulant, use of which spread both as a medicine and as a luxury drug, first in limited circles and then among a growing public.

The best known of the groups involved in cocaine trafficking are the Colombian cartels, particularly those from Medellín and Cali.[14] These are informal groups of the criminal-business type. The Medellín cartel is the most notorious, partly because of the enormous number of attacks in the city, reputedly the most violent in the world, with thousands of murders every year. Linked to the cartel are bands of *sicarios* recruited among boys, who murder to order. This tidal wave of violence, which has struck at countless journalists and even candidates standing for the presidency, provoked a reaction that in 1993 led to the killing of Pablo Escobar, regarded as the leader of the cartel.

The Cali cartel operates more discreetly, although the US Drug Enforcement Administration (DEA) described it as 'the most powerful criminal organization in the world'. The dirty money is recycled by a multiplicity of means and underlies the development of Miami, in Florida, as one of most important international financial centres.

Drug traffickers are at the heart of a close-knit system of links, from the lowest levels of the population, who have no other sources of income, upwards to lawyers, magistrates, financiers, businessmen, journalists, writers and politicians.

In Colombia right-wing paramilitary groups operate and in some areas groups of left-wing guerrillas (the best known is the FARC: Revolutionary Armed Forces of Colombia) finance themselves by cocaine trafficking and kidnapping. In Peru, too, the Sendero Luminoso (Shining Path) group collects a sort of tax on the cultivation of coca and cocaine trafficking. The guerrilla groups are linked mainly with the peasant growers.

Groups of *narcos* (narcotics traffickers) also operate in Bolivia where they are linked to right-wing politicians and there has been talk of a 'narcocracy', where the traffickers exercise political power.

The links between South American criminal groups, particularly the Colombian cartels, and the Italian mafias are documented through judicial investigations that have resulted in the seizure of batches of cocaine. In October 1987, 596 kilos of cocaine were seized at Castellammare del Golfo from the merchant ship *Big John*. The consignment of drugs had been ordered by the Madonia mafia family. In 1991 the financial manager Giuseppe Lottusi was arrested in Milan after receiving payment for a consignment of cocaine and was described as the cashier for the Medellín cartel. There has also been talk of an exclusive pact between Sicilian mafia families and Colombian traffickers. Links between the Colombian cartels and the 'ndrangheta have grown closer in recent years.

Latterly, a large proportion of drugs trafficked have passed through Mexico, where particularly violent criminal groups operate. The drugs are produced in Mexico and trafficking turnover is put at $280 billion. There are seven drugs cartels: Los Zetas, the Gulf Cartel, Sinaloa, Familia Michoacana, Beltrán Leyva, Juárez and Tijuana. Recent years have seen a veritable drugs war, both between the cartels and with other parties, which has left 50,000 dead. Victims include magistrates investigating the traffic in drugs and journalists pursuing inquiries. Ciudad Juárez has gained the dismal title of the city where most women are murdered. The total in the past few years amounts to several hundred and none of those responsible have been found.

In countries where coca leaf is cultivated there are producer unions that fight against the compulsory eradication practices required by the United States, and for the legalization of cultivation (there are already areas where cultivation is legal for traditional purposes), for the production and marketing of derivatives (coca tea, toothpaste) and for development plans. The unions are organized on a community basis, meet in regional federations and are affiliated to national confederations. The producer unions have clashed with the bodies trying to implement the eradication plans, are supported by NGOs in various countries and in the early 1990s were involved in the Progetto Droga run by the CISS and the Centro Impastato. In December 2005 one of the leaders, Evo Morales, was elected president of Bolivia. He is the first president from the country's indigenous community.

## Mafias and Globalization

The term 'globalization' is used to mean the process of unifying the world market, with the growing interdependence of the various areas of the planet. These processes are not simply the by-product of technological progress and do not affect just the economy but have a political aspect, largely as a result of the fall of 'real socialism' and the expansion of the capitalist mode of production. And they do not mean that the whole world is single-mindedly pursuing progress. On the contrary, globalization appears to be a supermarket of abundance and waste for the few, about 20 per cent of the world's population, and a major engine of marginalization for the remaining 80 per cent.[15]

In this context there has recently been talk of 'transnational crime' – that is, criminals and forms of criminality that exist in several countries – which has given rise to initiatives intended to combat this sort of criminal globalization.

Most of the explanations given for these new forms of criminality related to a standpoint that can be summed up as follows: for a long time the capitalist countries have been supported by two pillars, the market and the law, while the newer countries have created a market without a state and without rules, a primitive capitalism, dominated by the illegal accumulation of wealth, a sort of jungle. Hence weak states and unregulated markets underlie crime. And some countries, where those in power and criminals are one and the same, or closely linked, are described as 'mafia States'. These include Turkey and the Balkan States, such as Serbia and Albania, which sprang out of the dissolution of communist regimes.

These explanations are based on the stereotype of the shortage of opportunities to which we have already referred, and ignore the fact that the criminal phenomena have taken place to no lesser an extent in countries such as the United States, which is regarded as the best example of mature capitalism, economic and social progress and consolidated democracy. They also disregard the point that the very processes of globalization help create crime; that is, they produce the conditions that generate crime and help it take root.

Some academics see globalization itself as a criminal means of regulation, since it is based on the five greatest modern-day crimes against humanity: (1) financial transactions based on the laundering of illegal gains; (2) trade in weapons and harmful goods; (3) trade in human organs; (4) trade in drugs; (5) the sack of nature. The danger of these theories is that they see criminal activity in generalized terms, as a mass with no distinctions. The problem of the relationship between capitalism and the mafia, and organized crime in general, arises again.

Generally speaking, we can distinguish three phases in the relationship between capitalism and the mafias. In the first, the transition from feudalism to capitalism, mafia-type organizations (mafia in Sicily, Triads in China, yakuza in Japan) were formed where the state was unable to impose its monopoly of force. In the second, in countries with a mature capitalist system we find mafia-type organizations where certain conditions prevail. These include immigration (which does not mean that all immigrants are criminals, but that among those who have arrived most recently some individuals use crime as a primitive way of accumulating wealth and establishing a path to social mobility that it is impossible or very difficult to achieve in other ways); and black markets originating in prohibition, from illegal immigration to the prohibition first of alcohol and then of drugs. In the third phase, the spread of mafia organizations is explained by the great opportunities offered by globalized capitalism.

I have already mentioned that criminality is produced by globalization, particularly when generated by two aspects that are organically linked with the processes in question: (1) increasing territorial imbalances and social gaps; (2) the system of making the economy dependent on finance.

Many areas of the planet are isolated from the logic of markets and there the illegal economy is the only possible, or at least the most suitable, one. Even in developed societies social differences are increasing, encouraging recourse to the illegal accumulation of wealth.

The growth of the financial and speculative economy corresponds to globalization itself. This is exemplified by one figure: over the last 30 years financial trades have increased exponentially. In 1970 they totalled $10–20 billion, by 1980 they had grown to $80 billion and in 1990 amounted to $500 billion. Capital movements have grown to some $2,000 billion per day, of which only a tiny fraction, 1–2 per cent of the total, concerns the real economy, the production of goods and services. Against this background it becomes increasingly difficult to distinguish between legal and illegal flows. Despite anti-money-laundering measures, banking secrecy continues to be the rule in many countries, tax havens and offshore centres (small countries and islands that offer tax exemption and encourage inflows of capital) abound, as do new ways of collecting and routing money: unusual bonds, fiduciary companies, futures, derivatives, hedge funds, etc.

In December 2000 there was a United Nations conference in Palermo that drew up a convention against transnational organized crime. On this occasion, some study centres and associations, including the Centro Impastato, held an international seminar on 'I crimini della globalizzazione' ('The crimes of globalization') and the papers were published in a volume under the same title.

In the field of the civil antimafia, the year 2008 saw the foundation of FLARE (Freedom, Legality and Rights in Europe), a network of NGOs from many countries right across Europe, the Mediterranean basin, Russian Federation, Caucasus and Balkans. FLARE's goals are to:

(1)  raise awareness of the diffusion and the influence of the organized crime phenomenon in Europe and in the surrounding areas, through social events, communication, youth engagement and consultancy;

(2)  become a point of reference for civil societies in countering transnational organized crime, through support actions to national and international institutions;

(3)  have the European Parliament proclaim 21 March 'European Day in memory of the victims of the mafias and for the commitment in countering organized crime';

(4) request the European Commission and the Council of Europe to legislate in the matter of reuse for social purposes of property and assets confiscated from international criminal organizations.

## Revenue Estimates

A Confesercenti (Organizzazione nazionale dei commercianti: National Retail Organization) report in 2009 put the total turnover of crime in Italy at €135 billion per year, equal to 6 per cent of GDP and equal to the budget for five financial years. Organized crime accounts for 45 per cent. Trafficking in drugs, people and arms, and smuggling amounts to €67.87 billion, mafia 'taxes' (racketeering and usury) to €24 billion, 'business activities' (contracts and supplies, agricultural crime, gambling, counterfeiting and exploitation) to €25 billion while the 'eco-mafia' accounts for €16 billion. The net profit totals €68 billion.

Recent estimates put drug trafficking as the major source of revenue worldwide for criminal organizations. The National Intelligence Council puts the figures at $100–300 billion, the United Nations at $400 billion and the World Bank at $1,000 billion.

In second place is trafficking in weapons at $290 billion, followed at some distance by trafficking in human beings ($31 billion) and toxic waste ($10–12 billion).

Money laundering accounts for between 2 and 5 per cent of global GDP, amounting to some $1.5 trillion per year.

The so-called 'eco-mafias' are concerned mainly with building without permission and trafficking in waste, works of art and animals. In 2000 their turnover in Italy was put at 26,000 billion lire. Illegal activities concerned with waste disposal, particularly toxic and dangerous waste, which often uses the same routes as weapons trafficking, are on the increase. What happened in Somalia is an example: the murder of the journalists Ilaria Alpi and Miran Hrovatin on 20 March 1994 has been linked to an investigation they were carrying out into these ties. Criminal organizations offer services to major multinationals that are trying to economize on their waste-disposal operations.

'Modern slavery' is also growing: men, women and children are sold into slavery to undertake exhausting work or for prostitution. Some sources put modern slavery at 27 million people, but others put the figure at 200 million. Children working in inhuman conditions total 250 million. Every year 600,000 slaves arrive in Europe and 50,000 women arrive in Italy from Africa and Eastern Europe for the purposes of prostitution.

### Tax Havens

Information from the Ministry of the Economy and the Italian Exchange Office states that the following territories have acted as tax havens:

*Europe*: Alderney, Andorra, Cyprus, Gibraltar, Isle of Man, Jersey, Liechtenstein, Luxembourg, Malta, Monaco, San Marino, Switzerland.

*Middle East*: Bahrain, Djibouti, United Arab Emirates.

*Africa*: Liberia, Seychelles.

*Americas*: Anguilla, Antigua and Barbuda, Bahamas, Barbados, Bermuda, British Virgin Islands, Cayman Islands, Costa Rica, Dominican Republic, Ecuador, Grenada, Montserrat, Netherlands Antilles, Panama, St Kitts Nevis, St Lucia, St Vincent and the Grenadines, Turks and Caicos Islands.

*Asia and Oceania*: Brunei, Cook Islands and Niue, Hong Kong, Marshall Islands, Nauru, Philippines, Samoa, Vanuatu.

The OECD (Organization for Economic Cooperation and Development) lists 40 tax havens but press sources put the figure higher. During 2009, a conference in Mexico City attended by 70 countries approved an agreement on cracking down on tax havens proposed by Western countries, including the United States, Germany, France and the United Kingdom.

## United Nations Convention against Transnational Organized Crime

The United Nations Convention against Transnational Organized Crime, approved in Palermo in December 2000, requires the signatory countries to introduce into their legislation a type of offence resembling mafia association in Italian law, rules against money laundering and corruption, and for the confiscation of illicit goods, and required the states not to oppose banking secrecy and to cooperate in judicial inquiries and assist victims.

Two additional protocols concern trafficking in persons, particularly women and children, and in migrants. The signature of a third protocol against the production of and trafficking in weapons was postponed to a later date.

## The European Committee on Organized Crime

In March 2012 the European Parliament established a Special Committee on Organized Crime, Corruption and Money Laundering.

The committee's main task is to analyse and evaluate the extent of organized crime, corruption and money laundering and its impact on the European Union and its member states, and to propose appropriate measures to enable the EU to forestall and counter these threats, including at international, European and national level.

# GLOSSARY

*Abigeato*. Theft of animals. There is ample documentation on this crime, demonstrating the complicity of butchers and the police with cattle thieves.

*Beati Paoli*. The mythical ancestors of the Sicilian mafia. They are claimed to be the descendants of a sect of *Vendicosi* (men of vengeance) active in the twelfth century. According to the legend, in the eighteenth century there was a sect in Palermo that dispensed justice to make up for the shortcomings and perversions of the official system.

*Composizione*. Demand for a sum of money in exchange for the release of a kidnapped person or the return of stolen goods or animals. The legislation in force allowed for composition in the form of money and the Roman Catholic Church's canon law permitted this practice in compensation for crimes (the *bolla di componenda*).

*Consigliere istruttore* (Chief investigating magistrate). Before criminal procedure was reformed in 1988, the preparatory materials for trials were collected and examined by the Ufficio Istruzione, headed by the Consigliere istruttore. For years this task was carried out by Rocco Chinnici, the founder of the antimafia pool, a group of investigating magistrates who acted together in respect of mafia crimes, which were considered as parts of a single criminal plan. Chinnici was killed by the mafia on 29 July 1983.

*Cosa Nostra*. The expression was first used in the United States, following the revelations of the mafioso Joe Valachi (1963), and in Italy after the revelations of Tommaso Buscetta (1984). There is no evidence that it was used earlier.

*Gabelloti*. Those leasing land forming part of a *latifondo*, the large landholdings in central Sicily. They were often members of the mafia or connected to it, and formed a buffer between the landowners and the peasants. They exercised a vital role in the management of agriculture and the exploitation of labour.

*Lupara*. A shotgun used to hunt animals and by the mafia to commit murders.

*Lupara bianca*. A murder involving the disappearance of the corpse.

*Omertà*. This term has two versions: *ominità*, the ability of a so-called *uomo d'onore* (man of honour) to keep secrets and exact revenge for wrongs inflicted on him; and *umiltà*, the acceptance by associates of the rules of a mafia association and scrupulous obedience to the orders of its leaders.

*Osso, Mastrosso e Carcagnosso*. Legend has it that in about 1412 three Spanish knights, who were members of a secret association in Toledo known as Guarduna or Garduña, avenged the rape of one of their sisters by killing the rapist. They then took refuge on the island of Favignana, where they founded the mafia, the 'ndrangheta and the camorra. This myth, designed to show the organizations in a good light, is particularly dear to the 'ndrangheta, which combines honour killings and religion. The knights are supposed to represent Jesus Christ, St Michael the Archangel and St Peter. The historical fact that may have given rise to the legend is the existence of criminal organizations within prisons, including the notorious one on Favignana.

*Papello*. The document containing the mafia leaders' demands for putting an end to the massacres of the 1990s. These demands would have formed the basis for negotiations between the mafiosi and the representatives of the state.

*Picciotto*. A Sicilian word meaning lad; the term was used for young Sicilians who accompanied Garibaldi on the expedition of the Mille and for members of criminal groups. The original name of the 'ndrangheta in Calabria was *picciotteria*.

*Pizzo*. A Sicilian word denoting the beak of a bird. The expression *vagnarisi u pizzu* (to wet one's beak) means to extort (to demand a sum of money by threatening to harm a person or his property in case of non-compliance) or to participate in the division of booty.

*Sicilianismo*. A pro-mafia mindset which seeks to defend the 'good name' of Sicily from 'denigrations' that portray it as a land subject to the mafia and *omertà*, and seeks the unity of all Sicilians to obtain finance and other concessions from the national government.

*Stidda*. A mafia-type organization established in certain provinces of Sicily (Agrigento, Caltanissetta, Enna) comprising deserters from Cosa Nostra and other criminals.

*Stuppagghieri*. The name of a group in Monreale tried in 1878. The name comes from *stuppagghiu*, stopper or cork, or fuse.

*Vicaria*. The Palermo prison used until the construction, under the Bourbons, of the Ucciardone (from *chardons*, wild thistles, which grew on the land where the prison was built). In Naples the building that houses the courts and jails has the same name.

# CHRONOLOGY

## Sicilian Mafia

1531. An official complained to Emperor Charles V that justice in Sicily applied only to the 'little people' and that the number of unpunished crimes was growing daily. These included the murder of a magistrate by thugs linked to a nobleman and protected by the viceroy. Because they had no faith in the justice system, a large number of people did not report crimes or give evidence and so criminals continued to operate without punishment.

1576. A document from the Sicilian parliament reported complicity between butchers and cattle thieves: 'virtually no meat is slaughtered in public slaughterhouses ... so allowing the criminals who steal these animals to cover their tracks.'

1591. King Philip II forbade the Sicilian barons to associate with the Inquisition and the trial of those accused of murder in this privileged court, but the practice of 'familiars' going unpunished continued. The Inquisition was abolished by Viceroy Caracciolo in 1782.

1628. A document referred to letters demanding money and containing threats if payment was not made.

1773. A document denounced the complicity of the *compagnie d'armi*, who acted as the police force at that time, with cattle thieves: 'The most usual, and safest, way of cattle rustling is based on the information provided by the thieves to the local captains into whose territory they bring the animals stolen elsewhere.' If the owners agreed to pay for the return of the stolen animals, this was 'normally divided between the thieves and the captain'.

**1838.** Report of the chief prosecutor of the Trapani High Criminal Court on unions or brotherhoods which act like government within the government.

**1861.** In a report on the conditions in Sicily to the Minister of the Interior, Bettino Ricasoli, the MP Diomede Pantaleoni stated that violence was used by political groups, particularly those in power, although the opposition groups were also accused.

**1862.** *January.* A revolt in Castellammare (Trapani) against the *cutrara*, the members of the bourgeoisie who had divided among themselves the *cutra* (the blanket – i.e. taken over land and the municipal administration). People who may be considered to belong to the mafia acted as mediators between the rebels and the authorities.

*1 October.* Twelve people stabbed in Palermo. Thanks to the evidence given by one of them, the thugs were identified and sentenced, although those giving the order remained hidden. This may be regarded as the first episode of the 'strategy of tension' (the use of violence to influence social and political life).

**1863.** The popular comedy *I mafiusi di la Vicaria di Palermu*, by Giuseppe Rizzotto and Gaspare Mosca, was first staged. The word *mafiusi* appears in the title while the text talks of an organized camorra inside the prison, carrying out extortion and murder.

*13 August.* Giovanni Corrao, once a general in Garibaldi's army, was killed near Palermo. This may be considered the first political crime carried out by the mafia.

**1865.** The prefect of Palermo, Gualterio, used the word *maffia* for the first time in an official text. The subject was a criminal association embracing felons and members of the political opposition (Bourbons, Garibaldini and supporters of Mazzini).

**1866.** *15–22 September.* Anti-unification riots in Palermo in which mafia and criminal elements participated. The parliamentary inquiry that followed paid little attention to the problem of the mafia.

1875. A parliamentary inquiry into social and economic conditions in Sicily concluded with a report by the MP Romualdo Bonfadini. In his view, there was no organized mafia and no 'social question' in Sicily.

1876. Alongside the official investigation, two young intellectuals, Leopoldo Franchetti and Sidney Sonnino, undertook a private inquiry; Franchetti looked at the mafia while Sonnino was concerned with the peasants. Franchetti, too, concluded that the mafia did not exist as a single organization, but the social context of the mafia phenomenon was identified: the mafiosi were the 'workhorses of the middle class', engaged in an 'industry of violence' to secure wealth and power; they formed the 'dominant class'. While the state took firm action against the lower classes, it could do nothing against the mafia and the better off.

1878. The trial in Palermo of the Stuppagghieri, a group from Monreale. The 12 accused of criminal association were first found guilty and then acquitted. The Stuppagghieri are regarded as the model for other associations such as the Fratuzzi of Bagheria (Palermo), the Fontana Nuova from Misilmeri (Palermo), the Oblonica from Agrigento and the Fratellanza from Favara (Agrigento).

1883. The trial in Palermo of the Amoroso brothers, leaders of the mafia group in Porta Montalto, near the River Oreto. The existence of a criminal association was acknowledged and nine people accused of a series of murders were sentenced to death.

1885. The trial in Agrigento of the Fratellanza from Favara: 168 people charged with criminal association. The association had spread to a number of places and had some 500 members, including workers in the sulphur industry, peasants, craftsmen and landowners. The association had a leader and rules governing initiation rites, an oath and recognition signs of Masonic origin. The trial returned guilty verdicts.

1886–8. In 1886 the book, *La maffia nei suoi fattori e nelle sue manifestazioni*, by the public order officer Giuseppe Alongi, was published. He argued that there were criminal associations with leaders and members but that the mafia was a way of being, feeling and acting rather than an organization. Another police officer, Antonino Cutrera, author of *La mafia e i mafiosi*, published in 1900, was of the same opinion.

In 1888 the folklore student Giuseppe Pitrè argued that the mafia was neither a group nor an association, and had no rules or constitution. It was about awareness of one's own being, and an exaggerated concept of individual power. The idea of an unorganized mafia would prevail for many years.

**1891–4.** The Fasci Siciliani was a movement for the reform of labour relations and the renewal of local administrations that came up against a power base centred on landowners and mafia tenants (*gabelloti*). They comprised some 300,000 people, peasants, workers in the sulphur industry and craftsmen, led by intellectuals and professional people. Most of the Fasci had socialist ideas, others sprang from local conflicts, and two were led by mafia members. An important feature was the participation of women. After some significant results, including signature of the Corleone Pacts on 31 July 1893, the concerns of the landowners led the government to intervene by arresting the leaders; later anti-tax demonstrations degenerated into attacks on town halls, which were met by armed forces and indeed massacres. Soldiers sent by Prime Minister Francesco Crispi and mafia gamekeepers opened fire. There were 108 deaths between January 1893 and January 1894. Orders were given to dissolve the Fasci and impose a state of siege, and the leaders received heavy sentences, although these were later commuted. After the defeat, about 1 million Sicilians out of a population of 3.5 million emigrated.

**1893.** *1 February.* Emanuele Notarbartolo, mayor of Palermo from 1873 to 1875 and director of the Banco di Sicilia from 1876 to 1890, was killed. The trials, held in Milan (1899), Bologna (1902) and Florence (1904), resulted in the acquittal of the mastermind, the MP Raffaele Palizzolo, who was connected with the mafia and returned in triumph to Palermo. Notarbartolo's son, Leopoldo, battled to secure justice and was supported by some of the city: on 17 December 1899 a demonstration in Palermo was attended by about 30,000 people.

**1898–1900.** In a series of reports the chief of police of Palermo, Ermanno Sangiorgi, reconstructed the chart of the mafia organizations in the city and its hinterland. This was the structure, with a 'supreme leader' at its head, which Tommaso Buscetta would reveal in the 1980s. In 1901 the trial of 51 accused, in response to Sangiorgi's reports, resulted in 32 guilty verdicts and 19 acquittals, but the idea that the mafia was a unified organization would be ignored for a long time.

**The early 1900s.** The peasant movement enjoyed a new lease of life. Its most important achievements were collective leases and the formation of alternative sources of credit. Farmers' cooperatives were formed to try to lease land and wrest its management from mafia tenants: this was a strategic option designed to eliminate the mafia's social role.

**1909.** *12 March.* The American police lieutenant Joe Petrosino, who had come to Palermo to investigate the role of the mafia in clandestine emigration, was killed there. The mafia boss Vito Cascio Ferro was accused of the crime but released during the investigation because he had an alibi: on the evening of the crime he had been at the house of the MP Domenico De Michele Ferrantelli.

**1911.** *16 May.* The socialist leader Lorenzo Panepinto was killed at Santo Stefano Quisquina (Agrigento).

**1915.** *3 November.* The peasant leader and socialist mayor Bernardino Verro was killed at Corleone (Palermo).

**1919.** *8 October.* At Riesi (Caltanissetta) the police opened fire on peasants, killing 15 and wounding 50.

**1920.** *29 February.* The mafia killed the peasant leader Nicolò Alongi at Prizzi (Palermo).

*14 October.* Giovanni Orcel, the secretary of the metal workers' union, was killed in Palermo: Alongi and Orcel were working to unify the struggles of the peasants and the workers.

**1922.** *10 June.* Sebastiano Bonfiglio, the socialist mayor of Monte San Giuliano (present-day Erice, Trapani), was killed.

**1925.** Cesare Mori was appointed prefect of Palermo. He would act against the mafia, making thousands of arrests, and also targeted people in high positions. In 1929 he was dismissed, and retired at the age of 57.

**1943.** *10 July.* Allied landings in Sicily, where the war finished in August. It has long been held that the mafia played a part in the landings and the conquest of the island, but more recent studies have demonstrated that the mafia played a decisive role subsequently in maintaining social control when political activities and the peasant struggles resumed.

**Early 1940s.** Landowners and the mafia headed the separatist movement, which employed armed bands, such as that led by Salvatore Giuliano, to promote the separation of Sicily from Italy. The real aim was to triumph over the parties of the Left and secure regional autonomy under their control. The strategy sought to check the influence of northern Italy, as represented by the formation of the national anti-fascist coalition comprising the Christian Democrats, the Socialist Party, the Communist Party and the Partito d'Azione, which governed from 1944 until May 1947, and the anti-fascist resistance in central and northern Italy.

**1944.** *16 September.* At Villalba, in the province of Caltanissetta, the mafia, led by Calogero Vizzini, attacked and wounded the regional secretary of the Communist Party, Girolamo Li Causi.

*19 October.* In Palermo officers ordered soldiers to fire on a demonstration against rising prices. Official sources put the casualties at 19 dead and 108 wounded but the Committee of Liberation put the dead at 30 and the wounded at 150, including women and children.

*October.* The Minister of Agriculture, the communist Fausto Gullo, issued decrees on the division of yields in favour of the peasants and the allocation of uncultivated and poorly cultivated land to peasant cooperatives. These decrees gave the green light to the peasant struggles.

**1947.** *4 January.* Accursio Miraglia, a trade unionist and Communist Party leader, was killed in Sciacca (Agrigento).

*20 April.* The Left coalition (Blocco del Popolo) won the first regional elections.

*1 May.* Portella della Ginestra massacre. This month also saw the fall of the anti-fascist national government and the formation of national and regional governments headed by the Christian Democrats in alliance with the parties behind the massacres.

**1948.** *2 March.* Epifanio Li Puma, a socialist and organizer of the peasant struggles, was killed in Petralia Soprana (Palermo).

*10 March.* The secretary of the Trades Council and socialist leader Placido Rizzotto was killed in Corleone.

**1950.** *December.* Regional law on agricultural reform: just over 99,000 hectares in over 17,000 lots were allocated by ballot. Only 11 per cent of the 154,000 applicants received a small area of land. Thanks to the Gullo decree on uncultivated and poorly cultivated land, over 86,000 hectares were allocated to 50,000 farmers organized in cooperatives.

The second half of the 1950s saw the start of a mass exodus from Sicily of around 1.5 million people out of a population of 4.5 million.

**1955.** *16 May.* The peasant leader and socialist activist Salvatore Carnevale was killed in Sciara (Palermo).

*13 August.* The communist mayor Giuseppe Spagnolo was killed in Cattolica Eraclea (Agrigento).

**1957.** *October.* A Sicilian-American summit to agree strategies to combat international drug trafficking was held in the Hotel delle Palme, Palermo.

**1959.** *26 June.* Fifteen-year-old Anna Prestigiacomo was killed in Palermo.

*18 September.* Thirteen-year-old Giuseppina Savoca was killed in Palermo during a mafia shoot-out.

**1950s and 1960s.** The years of the so-called 'sack of Palermo'. The Palermo council was headed by Mayor Salvo Lima, who was connected with the mafia, with Vito Ciancimino responsible for public works. The Antimafia Commission would describe him as the politician most closely connected to the mafia. In 1993 Ciancimino was found guilty of association with the mafia.

In the late 1950s and early 1960s, some monks in the monastery of Mazzarino (Caltanissetta) were tried and sentenced because of their links with the mafia. The journalist involved in reporting these events, Cosimo Cristina, was found dead in May 1960.

**1961–3.** Clashes between traditional mafia families, such as the Greco, and up-and-coming clans, like the La Barbera, leaving about 100 dead.

1962. Following the deaths of her partner and son, Serafina Battaglia broke the code of *omertà* and denounced the mafiosi responsible for the killings – she did not secure justice.

1963. Cars packed with dynamite were used in the mafia's internal battles.

*26 April.* Cesare Manzella, the uncle of Giuseppe Impastato, became the first victim; he was killed with his minder in Cinisi (Palermo).

*30 June.* In the Ciaculli district, Palermo, another car full of explosives aimed at certain mafia members killed seven policemen. Shortly afterwards, the parliamentary Antimafia Commission, which had been set up the previous year, began work. It finished its task in 1976, amassing a large quantity of documents but without suggesting how the mafia could be fought. Alongside the majority report, the Communist Party submitted a minority report, drafted in large part by Pio La Torre and the magistrate Cesare Terranova. This stressed the links between the mafia and politics. Another minority report was submitted by the Movimento Sociale Italiano.

1965. *December.* Franca Viola, aged 17, was raped by a mafia member in Alcamo (Trapani). She refused marriage 'to make amends' and had the rapist and his accomplices arrested.

1968. *22 December.* In Catanzaro, the trial against 114 mafia bosses ended with many acquittals.

1969. *10 December.* In Palermo, the massacre of Viale Lazio saw three mafia bosses and two other people killed.

1970. *16 September.* *L'Ora* journalist Mauro De Mauro disappeared in Palermo. He was probably investigating the death of the ENI (Ente Nazionale Idrocarburi: National Hydrocarbon Organization) president Enrico Mattei, or had information about an attempted fascist coup. The inquiry into his disappearance has recently been reopened, with Totò Riina in the frame.

1971. *5 May.* State Prosecutor Pietro Scaglione and his driver Antonino Lo Russo were killed in Palermo. This was the first *delitto eccellente* (eminent crime) after World War II.

1972. *28 October*. *L'Ora* correspondent Giovanni Spampinato was killed in Ragusa; the son of the president of the court would be found guilty of the crime.

1973. In Palermo, Leonardo Vitale, a young man belonging to a traditional mafia family, spurred by ethical and religious motives, accused himself and others of certain crimes carried out by the mafia in his area, and reported links with politicians, including a portfolio holder on the city council. Only part of his confession was believed and he was found guilty of the crimes committed and sent to a criminal asylum. When he returned to Palermo he received no protection and was killed in December 1984.

1978. *8–9 May*. A murder disguised as an act of terrorism in Cinisi led to the death of the New Left (Nuova Sinistra) activist Giuseppe Impastato. The organizers of the murder, the mafia leaders Vito Palazzolo and Gaetano Badalamenti, were convicted in 2001 and 2002, and in 2000 the parliamentary Antimafia Commission adopted a report on an inquiry into the investigation by representatives of the judiciary and the forces of law and order.

*22 May*. Mafia member Giuseppe Sirchia and his wife Giacoma Gambino were killed in Palermo. Sirchia travelled with his wife in the belief that the mafia would not kill him because of their respect for women.

1979. *26 January*. Mario Francese, a journalist on the *Giornale di Sicilia* who was investigating the mafia, was killed in Palermo.

*9 March*. Michele Reina, the provincial secretary of the Christian Democrats, was killed in Palermo.

*11 July*. The lawyer Giorgio Ambrosoli, who was liquidating the banks of Michele Sindona, a financier with mafia connections, was murdered in Milan. Sindona was sentenced to life imprisonment and in 1986 died in jail after drinking coffee laced with cyanide.

*21 July*. The deputy chief of police, Boris Giuliano, who was undertaking inquiries into the mafia and had unearthed drug trafficking between Sicily and the United States, was killed in Palermo.

*25 September*. The magistrate Cesare Terranova and Lenin Mancuso, who was working with him, were killed in Palermo. After carrying out some of the most important mafia investigations in the 1960s, Terranova had been elected to Parliament as an independent on the Communist Party list. He was preparing to rejoin the magistracy as head of the office of investigation.

**1980.** *6 January.* Regional President Piersanti Mattarella was killed in via Libertà, in the very heart of Palermo. He was striving to raise the moral tenor of public life and favoured bringing the Communist Party into the regional government. After the murder, a regional government headed by D'Acquisto, an associate of Salvo Lima, was formed, excluding left-wing parties. Some mafia leaders were convicted but the neo-fascist Giusva Fioravanti was acquitted of carrying out the murder.

*4 May.* The *carabinieri* captain, Emanuele Basile, was killed in Monreale (Palermo).

*6 August.* Chief Prosecutor Gaetano Costa was killed in Palermo. As the deputy prosecutors had refused to sign, he was the sole signatory on the arrest warrants of a number of mafia members, including the Inzerillo family.

**1981.** *23 April.* Stefano Bontate, the young heir to a mafia dynasty, was killed in Palermo.

*11 May.* The mafia leader Salvatore Inzerillo was killed in Palermo. This marked the beginning of the mafia war, provoked by mafia members from Corleone.

*10 September.* Marshal Vito Ievolella, who was engaged in inquiries into the mafia, was killed in Palermo.

**1982.** *30 April.* The regional secretary of the Communist Party, Pio La Torre, and his co-worker, Rosario Di Salvo, were killed in Palermo.

*17 June.* The banker Roberto Calvi, connected with the laundering of dirty money, was found hanging under Blackfriars Bridge in London. He was probably murdered by the mafia.

*11 August.* The university lecturer and police doctor Paolo Giaccone was killed in Palermo after refusing to help a mafia member by changing his statement.

*3 September.* The prefect, former *carabinieri* General Carlo Alberto Dalla Chiesa, his wife Emanuela and his bodyguard Domenico Russo, were murdered in Palermo. The antimafia law was passed ten days later.

*14 November.* The policeman Calogero Zucchetto, who was carrying out inquiries into mafia members in hiding, was killed in Palermo.

**1983.** *25 January.* The magistrate Giangiacomo Ciaccio Montalto was killed in Trapani.

*13 June.* Captain Mario D'Aleo and *carabinieri* officers Giuseppe Bommarito and Pietro Morici were killed in Palermo.

*29 July.* A car filled with explosives killed the chief investigating magistrate Rocco Chinnici, his bodyguards Salvatore Bartolotta and Mario Trapassi and the concierge of his apartment block, Stefano Li Sacchi. Antonino Caponnetto was appointed to replace Chinnici and placed the antimafia pool on a permanent footing.

*October.* Arrest of Tommaso Buscetta in Brazil. He was extradited to Italy.

**1984.** *5 January.* Giuseppe Fava, writer, dramatist and founder of the review *I Siciliani*, was killed in Catania.

*July.* The investigating judge Giovanni Falcone began to take the testimony of Tommaso Buscetta who, having found himself on the losing side in the mafia war, had decided to cooperate with the judicial authorities.

*18 October.* In Palermo, the massacre of Piazza Scaffa saw 8 butchers killed.

**1985.** *2 April.* An attack near Trapani on the magistrate Carlo Palermo killed the young twins Giuseppe and Salvatore Asta and their mother Barbara Rizzo.

*28 July.* The police inspector Beppe Montana, who was investigating mafiosi in hiding, was killed near Palermo.

*6 August.* The head of the flying squad, Ninni Cassarà, and police officer Roberto Antiochia were killed in Palermo.

*12 December.* Seventeen-year-old Graziella Campagna, who had found a diary belonging to the convicted mafia leader in hiding, Gerlando Alberti, was killed in Villafranca Tirrena (Messina).

**1986.** *10 February.* The so-called 'maxi-trial' began in Palermo. The 475 mafia leaders and members were accused of mafia association and a number of murders. The thrust of the accusation was that the main crimes were decided on by the *cupola* (commission), the body controlling Cosa Nostra. The trial at first instance ended in December 1987 with 19 life sentences, reduced to 12 on appeal. The substance of the accusation was upheld.

*7 October.* Eleven-year-old Claudio Domino was killed in Palermo.

**1988.** *12 January.* The former mayor Giuseppe Insalaco, who had spoken out about links between the mafia and politicians, was killed in Palermo.

*14 January.* The police officer Natale Mondo was killed in Palermo.

*19 January.* The Higher Council of the Magistracy rejected Giovanni Falcone's application to head the office of investigation and chose Antonino Meli, who dismantled the antimafia pool.

*25 September.* The judge Antonino Saetta, who was to preside over the Court of Appeal for the maxi-trial, and his disabled son Stefano, were killed near Canicattì (Agrigento).

*26 September.* Mauro Rostagno, the former leader of the student movement and of the left-wing group Lotta continua, was killed near Trapani. He was working in a community for drug addicts and had reported mafia activities on local television.

*28 September.* The mafia leader Giovanni Bontate and his wife Francesca Citarda were killed in Palermo.

**1989.** *29 June.* Attack on Giovanni Falcone, who was later transferred to the Ministry of Justice in Rome.

*5 August.* The police officer Antonino Agostino and his pregnant wife Ida Castelluccio were killed near Palermo.

*23 December.* Leonarda and Lucia Costantino and Vincenza Marino Mannoia, the mother, aunt and sister of the turncoat Francesco Marino Mannoia, were killed in Bagheria.

**1990.** *9 May.* The regional civil servant Giovanni Bonsignore was killed in Palermo.

*21 September.* The magistrate Rosario Livatino was killed near Agrigento by the Stidda.

**1991.** *29 August.* The businessman Libero Grassi, who had publicized his refusal to pay extortion in the press, was killed in Palermo.

**1992.** *January.* The Court of Cassation confirmed the sentences and procedure of the maxi-trial: Cosa Nostra was a single organization and the main crimes were decided on by the *cupola*. This was a victory for the Falcone approach.

*12 March.* Salvo Lima, Christian Democrat member of the European Parliament, was killed in Palermo.

*21 April.* The businessman Paolo Borsellino was killed in Lucca Sicula (Agrigento).

*23 May.* On the Punta Raisi–Palermo motorway an explosive device killed Giovanni Falcone, his wife Francesca Morvillo and their bodyguards Rocco Dicillo, Antonino Montinaro and Vito Schifani.

*19 July.* A car bomb in Palermo killed the judge Paolo Borsellino and the police officers Agostino Catalano, Walter Cosina, Emanuela Loi, Vincenzo Li Muli and Claudio Traina.

*26 July.* The 17-year-old Rita Atria, a witness who had cooperated with Borsellino, killed herself in Rome.

*17 September.* Ignazio Salvo, who had been convicted at the maxi-trial of mafia association, was killed near Palermo. With his cousin Nino, he had for years operated the concession to collect taxes in Sicily and headed a financial empire.

*28 September.* The former naval captain Paolo Ficalora was killed in Castellammare del Golfo (Trapani). Totuccio Contorno, who was cooperating with the judicial authorities, had stayed in his tourist village although Ficalora was ignorant of his identity.

*17 December.* Murder of Giuseppe, father of the businessman Paolo Borsellino, who was helping the judicial authorities investigate the killing of his son.

**1993.** *8 January.* The journalist Beppe Alfano was killed in Barcellona Pozzo di Gotto (Messina).

*15 January.* After 23 years on the run, Totò Riina, regarded as the supreme leader of Cosa Nostra, was arrested in Palermo. Following his arrest, no checks were made on the villa where he had been living, which was cleaned so as to remove any embarrassing evidence. The then Colonel Mario Mori and Captain Sergio De Caprio were tried for favouritism but acquitted.

*9 May.* In Agrigento Pope John Paul II condemned mafia murderers and invited them to repent. He had earlier met the parents of Judge Livatino, who was murdered in 1990.

*14 May.* In Rome, there was an attack on the TV presenter Maurizio Costanzo, who had made programmes about the mafia.

*27 May.* A car bomb near the Uffizi Gallery in Florence killed five people, including two children.

*27 July.* In Milan another car bomb killed five more people. This was the first time that mafia violence hit outside Sicily to such an extent. It was aimed at monuments in Florence, Milan and Rome, where some churches were damaged.

*15 September.* The parish priest of Brancaccio, Father Pino Puglisi, was killed in Palermo. He was engaged in education and improving social conditions in this traditional mafia stronghold.

*23 November.* The 11-year-old Giuseppe Di Matteo, whose father was cooperating with the judicial authorities, disappeared. He was held prisoner until January 1996, strangled and his body dissolved in acid.

**1995.** *1 September.* Carmela Minniti, the wife of the mafia leader Nitto Santapaola, was killed in Catania.

*26 September.* The trial of Giulio Andreotti, one of the most famous Christian Democrat leaders and many times prime minister, began in Palermo. He was accused of mafia association on the basis of statements by several of those cooperating with the judicial authorities. The first trial resulted in acquittal due to lack of evidence; on appeal he was found guilty of criminal association up to 1980, but the crime was time-barred. The acquittal for lack of evidence was confirmed in respect of the period after 1980. The judgement of the Appeal Court was confirmed by the Court of Cassation.

**1996.** Following a petition organized by Libera, a grouping of associations founded in 1995, Law No. 109 on the use of confiscated property by public bodies and associations was passed.

**1999.** *22 April.* Twelve-year-old Stefano Pompeo was killed in the ambush of a mafioso at Favara.

**2006.** *11 April.* Bernardo Provenzano, who had been on the run for 43 years, was arrested near Corleone.

*20 June.* Arrest of the boss Antonino Rotolo and 44 other mafiosi in Palermo.

**2007.** *5 November.* Arrest of the mafia boss Salvatore Lo Piccolo, his son Sandro and other mafiosi. Confiscated documents revealed a network of extortion centred on Palermo.

**2008.** *7 February.* Operation 'Old Bridge': the arrest in Italy and the United States of 73 mafiosi from the Inzerillo and Gambino families, the losers in the mafia war of the early 1980s. They were accused of mafia association and drug trafficking.

**2010.** *22 March.* Arrest in Palermo of Giuseppe Liga, architect, businessman and regional director of the Movimento Cristiano Lavoratori (Christian Workers' Movement), regarded as boss Lo Piccolo's successor at the head of the San Lorenzo-Tommaso Natale *mandamento*.

**2011.** *22 January.* Following confirmation by the Court of Cassation of his sentence for favouring the mafia, the former president of the Region of Sicily, Salvatore Cuffaro, was sent to prison.

*21 April.* Arrest of Massimo Ciancimino, son of the former mayor of Palermo, Vito Ciancimino, for slandering the police chief Gianni De Gennaro, whom he had accused of taking part in negotiations with mafia leaders.

*5 October.* The Florence Court of Assizes imposed a life sentence on the boss Francesco Tagliavia for the 1993 massacres. The statements by Gaspare Spatuzza, who cooperated with the judicial authorities and talked of 'negotiations' between mafia bosses and representatives of the institutions, were decisive. The heads of the *cupola* had already been sentenced for the massacres. Relatives of the victims sought the identification and punishment of the 'outside organizers'.

*27 October.* Following the statements by Gaspare Spatuzza, who had confessed to stealing the car used in the 19 July 1992 massacre, so contradicting statements by the false turncoat Vincenzo Scarantino, the Catania Court of Appeal ordered the release of those sentenced and agreed to review the trial for the massacre.

## Cosa Nostra in the United States

1890. *5 October.* Murder of the police captain David Hennessy in New Orleans. The trial of some immigrants of Sicilian origin resulted in their acquittal. On 14 March 1891 an enraged mob lynched ten Italian prisoners, including those who had stood trial for killing Hennessy.

1903. The corpse of a decapitated man was found in a barrel in Manhattan. The case was investigated by an Italo-American policeman, Joe Petrosino. There was talk of the existence of an organization of extortionists called the Black Hand.

1920. The Volstead Act (repealed in 1933) introduced the prohibition of alcoholic drinks. The mafia clans, led by Al Capone, engaged in the production and distribution of alcoholic drinks, making enormous profits.

1929. *14 February.* The St Valentine's Day massacre. In Chicago men from Al Capone's mob, wearing police uniforms, killed seven members of an opposing clan. This was the most famous episode in the battle for territory between criminal groups.

1930–1. The period of the 'Castellammarese War' – armed clashes between criminal groups from Sicily, including some natives of Castellammare, in the province of Trapani, led by Salvatore Maranzano and Joe Masseria. The most notorious criminals subsequently included Joe Bonanno and Lucky Luciano (Salvatore Lucania).

1943. Murder in New York of the trade unionist Carlo Tresca, an opponent of the fascist regime, by the clan headed by Vito Genovese, who was linked to Mussolini and appointed a commendatore by him.

After the fall of Fascism, Genovese worked as an interpreter for the army's intelligence service in Sicily and was linked with the bandit Giuliano.

1951. Senator Estes Kefauver's report on organized crime. The activities of a number of families were documented.

1957. *14 November.* Apalachin meeting: representatives of the mafia families met following the murder of the boss Albert Anastasia by Vito Genovese, with assistance from Carlo Gambino. Vito Genovese aimed to become the supreme boss. A police raid led to the arrest of 58 bosses, including Carlo Gambino.

1963. In testimony to the Senate Investigations Committee chaired by Senator McClellan, the mafia member Joe Valachi revealed the existence of the Cosa Nostra organization and described the activities carried out by the American mafia.

1970. The Organized Crime Control Act (OCCA) and the Racketeer Influenced and Corrupt Organizations (RICO) statute introduced the crime of conspiracy, the association of professional criminals.

1975. James R. Hoffa, former boss of the Teamsters Union, a powerful union of truckers, disappeared. He had been jailed for his links with organized crime.

1979. *July.* Murder in a Brooklyn restaurant of the boss Carmine Galante, from the Bonanno family.

1981–3. During a mafia war in Sicily, many of the 'losers' took refuge in the United States. These included associates of the Inzerillo family, who were related to the Gambino clan.

1984. Tommaso Buscetta cooperated with justice in the United States and drew up the organization chart of the American Cosa Nostra.

1985. *18 December.* Murder of the boss 'Big Paul' Castellano, godfather of the Gambino family.

1983–6. Presidential Committee on organized crime headed by Judge Irving R. Kaufman. The committee concluded with a report demonstrating how organized crime controlled four of the main unions: the International Longshoremen's Association, the Hotel Employees and

Restaurant Employees International Union, the International Brotherhood of Teamsters and the Laborers' International Union of North America.

**1987.** *22 June.* In the 'Pizza Connection' trial of mafia members involved in international drug trafficking, Gaetano Badalamenti and Salvatore Catalano received prison terms of 45 years. In 2002 Badalamenti was convicted in Italy of Giuseppe Impastato's murder. He died in 2004 in a US prison.

**1988.** US Senate report setting out the composition of the five New York families: Bonanno, Colombo, Gambino, Genovese and Lucchese.

**1992.** Life sentence for John Gotti, boss of the Gambino family. He was succeeded by his son, John Angelo Gotti, who was convicted of attempted homicide in 2004.

**2008.** *7 February.* Operation 'Old Bridge', with the arrest of 73 mafiosi in Italy and the United States.

**2011.** *20 January.* Arrest of 110 members of the Bonanno, Colombo, Gambino, Genovese and Lucchese families in New York.

## 'Ndrangheta

**1874.** Leopoldo Franchetti wrote that landowners in Calabria employed small armed forces made up of prisoners awaiting sentence.

**1876.** The owner of a factory producing lime was killed near Reggio Calabria. The killers belonged to an *'ndrina* that was trying to take over the firm.

**1884.** The Court of Appeal of the Calabrias sentenced prisoners who had already been warned on account of 'maffia and camorra'. One of them was accused of being the 'head of an association of maffiosi'.

**1890.** Trial of 66 accused in the province of Reggio Calabria. The association to which they belonged was called a *setta dei camorristi*. In another trial, the association was defined as an *associazione dei picciotti*. A third trial resulted in 34 convictions for membership of a criminal association, divided into a *società maggiore*, comprising *camorristi*, and a *società minore*, comprising followers.

**1892.** A trial of 219 accused in Palmi (Reggio Calabria) resulted in 156 convictions, including two women.

**1896.** A number of trials took place. There were 29 convictions in Reggio Calabria. The roles within the organization were identified as: head, deputy, treasurer, etc. Other trials resulted in 40 and 26 convictions, and the sentencing of a well-off group affiliated to an *'ndrina*.

**1897.** In Palmi 45 convictions. Reference was made to a code discovered in 1896 in Seminara (Reggio Calabria). Other codes were found in 1902 in Catanzaro, in 1936 in the Platì area and in 1963 at S. Giorgio di Morgeto (Reggio Calabria). Similar documents would be found in Canada and Australia. In Reggio Calabria, 61 convictions, including two women. The slang of the members was established.

**1900.** The trial in Palmi of 225 accused resulted in 221 convictions. The trial was based on the revelations of Francesco Albanese, a leader from Gioia Tauro (Reggio Calabria). Those convicted included a woman.

**1901.** There were 122 convictions in Palmi for organization of a criminal association involved in various activities. In Reggio Calabria, 61 convictions, including two women. The Court of Appeal of the Calabrias returned 230 guilty verdicts on 248 people sent for trial (317 had originally been accused). This was the largest trial in terms of numbers accused.

**1902.** Several trials in Palmi resulted in guilty verdicts.

**1903.** A trial in Reggio Calabria resulted in 45 convictions and one in Cosenza resulted in 86 convictions. Trials in Palmi resulted in 54 and 36 convictions. In Catanzaro 87 people were convicted.

**1905.** There were 47 convictions in Nicastro (Catanzaro) and 148 in Palmi.

**1908.** Trial of 126 people belonging to *'ndrine* in various villages in the province of Reggio Calabria following accusations by a mayor and a parish priest. Only 12 of the accused were convicted, but they were then acquitted.

**1920s.** Repression by the fascist regime, with thousands of arrests and large-scale trials. In 1923 one judge remarked that the *picciotti* relied on the 'acquiescence of the wealthiest class who often use the criminals to further their own goals of personal supremacy and to guard their estates'.

**1933.** The national secretary of the Fascist Party states that the party secretary in Reggio Calabria was 'notoriously affiliated to the organized crime that still infects the province'.

**1945.** *5–9 March.* Short-lived autonomous republic of Caulonia (Reggio Calabria).

**1946.** *28 November.* In the province of Crotone a gamekeeper killed 31-year-old Giuditta Levato, the mother of two children and a leader of the peasant struggles.

**1947.** *13 April.* At Petilia Policastro, in the province of Catanzaro, the *carabinieri* opened fire on peasants and killed Francesco Massaro and Isabella Carvelli.

**1949.** *29 October.* At Melissa (Catanzaro) the forces of law and order opened fire on peasants and killed Francesco Nigro, Giovanni Zito (aged 15) and Angelina Mauro.

**1950.** Approval of the Sila Law providing for partial agricultural reform.

**1955.** At Presinaci, in the province of Catanzaro, an agricultural worker, Serafino Castagna, kills five people. After capture, he reveals the secrets of the 'ndrangheta.

**1967.** *June.* Massacre in the market square in Locri (Reggio Calabria): three dead. Members of Cosa Nostra were also involved but those responsible were not convicted.

**1969.** *October.* A meeting of 130 *'ndranghetisti* held in the countryside near San Luca (Reggio Calabria) to unite the various *'ndrine* was broken up by the police. The area of San Luca is home to the Sanctuary of Our Lady of Polsi, a focus for popular devotion and a frequent choice for mafia summits. It is known as the Bethlehem of the 'ndrangheta.

**1970.** *July.* Movement to make Reggio Calabria the regional capital led by fascist groups aided by the 'ndrangheta. Following the movements in Reggio, funds were allocated for the construction of the port of Gioia Tauro.

*22 July.* The Freccia del Sud express derailed near Gioia Tauro, probably due to an explosive device on the track, leaving six dead and 50 injured.

*26 September.* Five young anarchists, who had investigated the attack and were taking the information they had collected on links between fascist groups and the 'ndrangheta to Rome, died in a road accident that could have been deliberate.

**1974–7.** First war between the *'ndrine*: There were 233 murders. These included front-line people such as Giovanni and Giorgio De Stefano, Antonio Macrì and Mico Tripodo. By the end of the 1970s there were more than 1,000 murders. This period saw the establishment of *la Santa*, the organization concerned with links with public institutions.

**1975.** *3 July.* Murder in Lamezia Terme (Catanzaro) of the state advocate-general, Francesco Ferlaino, a Mason who opposed links between Freemasonry and the 'ndrangheta.

**1977.** *12 March.* Murder in Gioiosa Jonica of the communist leader Rocco Gatto.

*15 July.* Disappearance in Australia of the liberal MP Donald Mackay, who had led a press campaign against drug trafficking controlled by 'ndrangheta members resident in Griffith, Queensland.

**1980.** *11 June.* Murder in Rosarno (Reggio Calabria) of the communist leader Giuseppe Valarioti.

*21 June.* Murder in Cetraro (Cosenza) of the communist town councillor Giovanni Losardo.

**1982.** *3 May.* Murder in Reggio Calabria of the businessman Gennaro Musella, who had resisted demands from criminals.

**1983.** *26 June.* Murder in Turin of Chief Prosecutor Bruno Caccia, who was investigating the 'Calabrian clans'.

**1984–91.** Second 'ndrangheta war, with some 600 deaths.

**1985.** *12 March.* Murder in Cosenza of Sergio Cosmai, the prison governor, who had refused requests for favours from 'ndrangheta bosses.

**1989.** *12 January.* Murder in Canberra, Australia, of Colin Winchester, assistant commissioner in the Australian Federal Police. A criminal band of 'ndrangheta members was operating in Australia.

*23 February.* Marcella Tassone, 10 years old, was killed during a shoot-out in the province of Reggio Calabria.

*26 August.* Murder near Reggio Calabria of the former Christian Democrat MP and former head of the Italian State Railways, Ludovico Ligato, as a result of a dispute over the allocation of business.

**1991.** *10 July.* Murder in Reggio Calabria of the landowner Antonino Cordopatri, who was resisting demands by the 'ndrangheta. His sister Teresa identified those responsible for the murder and continued to farm with the help of volunteers, since mafia intimidation meant that she could not hire labour.

*9 August.* Murder in the province of Reggio Calabria of the Court of Cassation prosecutor Antonino Scopelliti, who was to participate in the maxi-trial of Cosa Nostra. This was a favour by the 'ndrangheta to the Sicilian mafia.

**1992.** *4 January.* Murder in Lamezia Terme (Catanzaro) of the police superintendent Salvatore Aversa, who was carrying out investigations into the 'ndrangheta, and his wife Lucia Precenzano.

**1993.** Agatino Licandro, former mayor of Reggio Calabria, revealed 'Tangentopoli' dealings in the city and the links between politicians and the 'ndrangheta.

**1994.** *29 September.* An American child, Nicholas Green, was killed in the province of Catanzaro during a robbery by 'ndrangheta associates.

**2005.** *16 October.* During the centre-left primary elections, murder in Locri of the vice-president of the regional council, Francesco Fortugno. At his funeral young people held a banner that read 'E adesso ammazzateci tutti' ('And now kill us all').

**2007.** *14–15 August.* Murder in Duisburg, Germany, of six people as a result of a feud that had begun in the hamlet of San Luca, the home of one of the oldest and most powerful *'ndrine*.

**2008.** *18 February.* The arrest in Reggio Calabria of Pasquale Condello (the 'Provenzano' of the 'ndrangheta), who had been on the run since 1990.

*February.* Report of the parliamentary Antimafia Commission on the 'ndrangheta, which described it as the most dangerous organization, with national and international branches.

*July.* Operazione Crimine led to the arrest of over 300 people.

*12 December.* After two workers from Ivory Coast were injured at Rosarno, demonstrations were held to protest against racism, the 'ndrangheta and the exploitation of immigrant workers.

**2009.** *25 June.* 11-year-old Domenico Gabriele was wounded during a shoot-out in Crotone and died three months later.

*24 November.* Lea Garofalo, the state witness from Petilia Policastro, disappeared. She was tortured and killed.

**2010.** *18 May.* Sentencing in the trial resulting from 'Operation Missing', which reconstructed recent crimes in Cosenza. The public prosecutor asked for 37 life sentences but the court imposed only four, plus varying terms of imprisonment, and acquitted several major bosses, including Pasquale Condello.

**2011.** *19 November.* A court in Milan convicted 110 people, including some 'ndrangheta bosses operating in Lombardy in recent years. Charges include: mafia-type criminal association, drug trafficking and building speculation. There are some 500 'ndrangheta affiliates in Lombardy.

## Camorra

**1842.** Francesco Scorticelli, a member, collected the rules of a *società dell'umiltà* (humble society) in a *frieno* (code) with 26 articles.

**1848.** Following a failed liberal uprising, the Bourbon police used members of the camorra to keep public order; the liberals, too, negotiate with the *camorristi*.

**1860.** Following the arrival of Garibaldi in Naples and the fall of the Bourbon kingdom, Liborio Romano, the police chief and a former Bourbon minister, engaged *camorristi* to ensure public order.

1861. Silvio Spaventa, the chief of police, had several camorra members arrested. Repression continued in subsequent years as part of the campaigns against banditry.

1863. The Italo-Swiss writer Marco Monnier brought out the first book on the camorra.

1885. Law on cleaning up the city of Naples.

1893. Popular uprising in Naples headed by the camorra.

1901. Commission of inquiry into Naples headed by Senator Giuseppe Saredo: this talked of a lower camorra, active among the lower classes, and an administrative and political camorra, the high camorra, formed by members of the bourgeoisie.

1906. *June*. Murder of Gennaro Cuocolo, a *camorrista* who had cooperated with the judicial authorities, and his wife Maria Cutinelli, a former prostitute.

1911. The main camorra leaders went on trial for the murder of Cuocolo and his wife. The trial was followed with interest by the national and international press. They were accused by a turncoat *camorrista*, Gennaro Abbatemaggio, and convicted. Subsequently the camorra disappeared from Naples but survived in the wider province. Several years later, in 1927, Abbatemaggio admitted that his accusations were false. He had been induced to lie by the promise of avoiding prison and a bribe.

1926–8. Repression organized by Fascism, with the arrest of hundreds of (alleged) criminals.

1946. The Sicilian-American boss Lucky Luciano, expelled from the United States, established himself in Campania from where he organized drug trafficking.

1955. Murder of Pasquale Simonetti (Pascalone 'e Nola). His young widow, the 18-year-old Pupetta Maresca, killed his murderer, Antonio Esposito.

1960s and 1970s. The camorra groups focused mainly on contraband tobacco, in agreement with the Sicilian Cosa Nostra. They later moved into drug trafficking.

**1970.** Creation of the Nuova Camorra Organizzata, organized by Raffaele Cutolo, with 7,000 members. This declared war on the local bosses affiliated to Cosa Nostra and on independents. To oppose Cutolo the other camorra groups united in the Nuova Famiglia, led by Carmine Alfieri.

**1978–83.** War among *camorristi*, with some 1,500 dead. Defeat of Cutolo.

**1980.** Earthquake in Irpinia. Rebuilding would provide business for the various camorra clans.

*11 December.* Murder of Marcello Torre, the Christian Democrat mayor of Pagani (Salerno).

**1981.** The Red Brigades kidnapped the Christian Democrat regional councillor Ciro Cirillo, who was freed following mediation by Cutolo.

**1982.** *29 May.* An attack on the magistrate Alfonso Lamberti at Cava dei Tirreni (Salerno) killed his daughter Simonetta, aged 10.

**1984.** *24 August.* Massacre at Torre Annunziata (Naples), leaving eight dead. This was a clash between Carmine Alfieri, the Gionta clan and other camorra clans.

**1985.** *23 September.* Murder in Naples of the journalist Giancarlo Siani, who had investigated links between *camorristi* and politicians in building speculation following the Irpinia earthquake. The *camorristi* Angelo Nuvoletta and Valentino Gionta were found guilty of organizing the murder.

**Late 1980s–early 1990s.** The clans of Casal di Principe (Casalesi) in the province of Caserta became increasingly dominant, controlling territory and drug trafficking. In May 1988 the Schiavone, De Falco, Iovine and Bidognetti clans removed the head, Antonio Bardellino, who had taken refuge in the United States, and divided up the business. But there were other clashes between the various clans.

**1989.** *25 August.* Murder of the South African refugee Jerry Essan Masslo at Villa Literno (Caserta). This was followed by a strike by immigrant workers to protest against exploitation, and a national demonstration against racism in Rome. The following year a law on the position of foreigners in Italy was adopted.

**1993.** The bosses Carmine Alfieri and Carmine Schiavone began to cooperate with the authorities. They were followed by other Casalesi leaders.

**1994.** *19 March.* Murder at Casal di Principe of the parish priest Giuseppe Diana, who was engaged in education work against the camorra. After a number of failures the bosses of the Casalesi clan were convicted.

**1997.** *11 June.* In the centre of Naples, *camorristi* fired on the crowd, killing Silvia Ruotolo, who was returning home with her 5-year-old son. This was a clash involving a number of clans, leaving several dead, including passers-by.

**2000.** *12 November.* During a shoot-out in the province of Naples, 2-year-old Valentina Terracciano was killed.

**2004.** *27 March.* During the ambush of a *camorrista* in Naples, 14-year-old Annalisa Durante was killed.

**2008.** *20 June.* The Appeal Court in the Spartacus trial of *camorristi* from Caserta handed down heavy sentences (16 years to life imprisonment), confirmed by the Court of Cassation in January 2010.

*18 September.* A camorra squad killed six Africans at Castelvolturno (Caserta). One who was wounded helped the authorities, leading to the arrest of the camorra leader Giuseppe Setola, who was on the run. This was followed by demonstrations against racism and the camorra.

**2010.** *5 September.* Murder of the mayor, Angelo Vassallo, in Pollica (Salerno). He was trying to defend the town from speculation and had opposed drug trafficking there.

# APPENDIX

# ABOUT THE CENTRO IMPASTATO

Founded by Umberto Santino and Anna Puglisi in 1977, the Sicilian Centre of Documentation was the first study centre on the mafia in Italy. The name of Giuseppe Impastato, a new Left activist murdered by the mafia on 9 May 1978, was soon added to its masthead.

The Centre's purpose is to develop awareness of the mafia and other similar organizations at both a national and international level; to develop initiatives aimed at fighting such organizations; to debate and promote a culture of legality, development and a high level of democratic participation. To such an end, the Centre carries out the following activities: the collation of political, economic, historical and sociological data; the organization of research, the promotion of cultural initiatives (conferences, seminars, public meetings, exhibitions, etc); the publication of books, pamphlets and various material.

In the course of its activities the Centre, which is completely self-financed, has developed a specialised archive on the mafia and other forms of organized crime; it has published bibliographies, archive material and the results of research; it has engaged in educational work within schools and universities, both in Italy and abroad; it has initiated mobilizations (starting from the first national demonstration held in Italy against the mafia, which took place in May 1979) and acts of solidarity, as well as playing a key role in investigating the murder of Giuseppe Impastato. Through the 'Mafia and Society' project the Centre has developed a scientific analysis of the mafia, carrying out research on murders committed in Palermo, on mafia front companies, on international drug trafficking, on the links between the mafia and politics and on the antimafia movement and the activities of the women.

The Centre has also been active in both the peace movement and the movement against neo-liberal globalization, given that it stands for the globalization of democratic participation and human rights.

In the past year the Centre has proposed to build a 'Memorial centre for the struggle against the mafia', it will include a historical museum, library, research centre and meeting point for the citizens of Palermo.

All publications in English can be found on the website www. centroimpastato.com.

Address: Via Villa Sperlinga 15, 90144 Palermo,
phone number: 0039.6259789,
fax: 0039.7301490,
e-mail: csdgi@tin.t,
website: www.centroimpastato.com.

# NOTES

## Prelims

1. The Centre's website, which gives details of its many publications and activities, is at: www.centroimpastato.com (accessed 8 April 2015).
2. Umberto Santino has written a useful explanation of his own work, which is available in English as 'Studying mafias in Sicily', Sociologica, 2, 2011 (monographic issue *"Telling about the Mafia"*: *Research, Reflexivity, and Representation*, edited by Marco Santoro).
3. Peppino Impastato's story would become the subject of Marco Tullio Giordana's film, *I cento passi (The Hundred Steps)* in 2000.

## Chapter 1   Theories and Realities

1. There is a review of studies on the various forms of the mafia in Umberto Santino, *Dalla mafia alle mafie: Scienze sociali e crimine organizzato*, Soveria Mannelli: Rubbettino, 2006.
2. For a history of social struggles against the mafia, see Umberto Santino, *Storia del movimento antimafia: Dalla lotta di classe all'impegno civile*, Rome: Editori Riuniti University Press, 2000.
3. On mafia violence, see Giorgio Chinnici and Umberto Santino, *La violenza programmata: Omicidi e guerre di mafia a Palermo dagli anni '60 ad oggi*, Milan: F. Angeli, 1989, 1990.
4. On mafia economy, see Umberto Santino and Giovanni La Fiura, *L'impresa mafiosa: Dall'Italia agli Stati Uniti*, Milan: F. Angeli, 1990.
5. On the costs of crime, see Antonio La Spina (ed.), *I costi dell'illegalità: Mafia ed estorsioni in Sicilia*, Bologna: il Mulino, 2008.
6. On 'post-development', see Serge Latouche, *Survivre au développement*, Paris: Fayard, 2004, and Umberto Santino, *Mafia, crimine transnazionale e globalizzazione* in *Mafie e globalizzazione*, Trapani: Di Girolamo, 2007, pp. 213–24.

7. I consider the political activity of the mafia in Umberto Santino, 'La mafia come soggetto politico', in Giovanni Fiandaca and Salvatore Costantino (eds), *La mafia, le mafie: Tra vecchi e nuovi paradigmi*, Rome-Bari: Laterza, 1994, pp. 118–41. A more wide-ranging text with the same title was published in the series *Appunti* (Notes) by the Centro Impastato in 1994 and by Di Girolamo in 2013.

8. For further information, please refer to, Max Weber, *Economy and Society*, vol. 1, Berkeley, CA: University of California Press, 1978.

9. Emil Lederer considered the problem of the 'double state' in a 1915 essay on the impact of World War I on Germany, which was taken up by Ernst Fraenkel in *Der Doppelstaat*, Frankfurt am Main-Cologne: Europäische Verlagsanstalt, 1974. The subject has been addressed again in the Italian debate on the role of the secret services and the events surrounding the P2 Masonic lodge and Gladio, the anti-communist secret organization directly dependent on NATO, by the historian Franco De Felice, 'Doppia lealtà e doppio Stato', *Studi storici*, 3, 1989, pp. 493–563. On the discussion concerning this possible way of reading the situation in Italy see, Francesco M. Biscione, *Il sommerso della Repubblica: La democrazia italiana e la crisi dell'antifascismo*, Turin: Bollati Boringhieri, 2003, pp. 15–41.

10. The magistrates Giovanni Falcone and Giuliano Turone consider the three levels of mafia crime in the report on 'Tecniche di indagine in materia di mafia', published in *Il Consiglio Superiore della Magistratura*, supplement 2–3, May– June 1982, Rome, 1983, pp. 38–71, republished in G. Falcone, *Interventi e proposte (1982–1992)*, Florence: Sansoni, 1994, pp. 221–55.

11. On controversy with Giovanni Falcone, see Umberto Santino, *L'alleanza e il compromesso: Mafia e politica dai tempi di Lima e Andreotti ai giorni nostri*, Soveria Mannelli: Rubbettino, 1997, in particular pp. 102–16, and *Storia del movimento antimafia*, pp. 346–8.

12. On concepts of culture, subculture and transculture in Sicily, see Umberto Santino, *Dalla mafia alle mafie*, pp. 281–7.

13. The definition of subculture used in the text may be found in Luciano Gallino, *Dizionario di Sociologia*, Turin: UTET, 1983, p. 703.

14. On Henner Hess, see his book *Mafia: Zentrale Herrschaft und lokale Gegenmacht*, Tübingen: Mohr, 1970.

15. On crime in Chicago and juvenile delinquency see, Clifford R. Shaw, *The Jack-Roller. A Delinquent Boy's Own Story*, Chicago: University of Chicago Press, 1930; *The Natural History of a Delinquent Career*, Chicago: University of Chicago Press, 1931; Henri Mckay and Clifford R. Shaw, *Juvenile Delinquency and Urban Areas*, Chicago: University of Chicago Press, 1942. Edwin H. Sutherland's most famous work is *White Collar Crime*, New Haven, CT, and London: Yale University Press, 1983 (1st edn 1949). See also: Albert Cohen, *Delinquent Boys: The Culture of the Gang*, Glencoe, IL: Free Press, 1955; Robert K. Merton, *Social Theory and Social Structure*, Glencoe, IL: Free Press, 1957; Franco Ferracuti and Martin E. Wolfgang,

*The Subculture of Violence: Towards an Integrated Theory in Criminology*, London: Tavistock Publications, 1969.

16. For further consideration of the concept of a *società mafiogena* ('mafia-generating society'), see Umberto Santino *Dalla mafia alle mafie*, pp. 287–90.

17. On the lack of a sense of civic responsibility in the Mezzogiorno, see Robert D. Putnam, *Making Democracy Work: Civic Traditions in Modern Italy*, Princeton, NJ: Princeton University Press, 1993.

18. There is an investigation of forms of association in the Mezzogiorno in Carlo Trigilia (ed.), *Cultura e sviluppo. L'associazionismo nel Mezzogiorno*, Rome: Donzelli, 1995.

19. Umberto Santino, *La mafia interpretata: Dilemmi, stereotipi, paradigmi*, Soveria Mannelli: Rubbettino, 1995. Umberto Santino, *Dalla mafia alle mafie: Scienze sociali e crimine organizzato*, Soveria Mannelli: Rubbettino, 2006.

20. Umberto Santino, *La cosa e il nome: Materiali per lo studio dei fenomeni premafiosi*, Soveria Mannelli: Rubbettino, 2000.

21. Giorgio Chinnici and Umberto Santino, *La violenza programmata: Omicidi e guerre di mafia a Palermo dagli anni '60 ad oggi*, Milan: F. Angeli, 1989, 1990. Various authors, *Gabbie vuote: Processi per omicidio a Palermo dal 1983 al maxiprocesso*, Milan: F. Angeli, 1992.

22. Umberto Santino and Giovanni La Fiura, *L'impresa mafiosa: Dall'Italia agli Stati Uniti*, Milan: F. Angeli, 1990.

23. Umberto Santino, 'The financial mafia: The illegal accumulation of wealth and the financial-industrial complex', *Contemporary Crises*, 12/3, Sept. 1988, pp. 203–43.

24. Umberto Santino and Giovanni La Fiura, *Behind Drugs: Survival Economies, Criminal Enterprises, Military Operations, Development Projects*, Turin: Edizioni Gruppo Abele, 1993.

25. Umberto Santino, 'La mafia come soggetto politico' in Giovanni Fiandaca and Salvatore Costantino (eds), *La mafia, le mafie: Tra vecchi e nuovi paradigmi*, Rome-Bari: Laterza, 1994, pp. 118–41. Umberto Santino, *L'alleanza e il compromesso: Mafia e politica dai tempi di Lima e Andreotti ai giorni nostri*, Soveria Mannelli: Rubbettino, 1997.

26. Felicia Bartolotta Impastato with Anna Puglisi and Umberto Santino, *La mafia in casa mia*, Palermo: La Luna, Palermo, 1986. Anna Puglisi, *Sole contro la mafia*, Palermo: La Luna, 1990. Anna Puglisi, *Storie di donne*, Trapani: Di Girolamo, 2007. Anna Puglisi, *Donne, mafia e antimafia*, Trapani: Di Girolamo, 2005, 2012.

27. Umberto Santino, *La democrazia bloccata: La strage di Portella della Ginestra e l'emarginazione delle sinistre*, Soveria Mannelli: Rubbettino, 1997. Umberto Santino, *Storia del movimento antimafia: Dalla lotta di classe all'impegno civile*, Rome: Editori Riuniti, 2000; Editori Riuniti University Press, Rome, 2009.

28. Augusto Cavadi (ed.), *Il vangelo e la lupara: Materiali su chiese e mafia*, Bologna: Edizioni Dehoniane, 1995. Umberto Santino, *Mafie e globalizzazione*, Trapani: Di Girolamo, 2007.

29. Augusto Cavadi (ed.), *A scuola di antimafia: Materiali di studio, criteri educativi, esperienze didattiche*, Palermo: Centro Impastato, 1994; Trapani: Di Girolamo, 2006. Umberto Santino, *Oltre la legalità: Appunti per un programma di lavoro in terra di mafie*, Palermo: Centro Impastato, 1997–2002. Anna Puglisi and Umberto Santino (eds), *l'Agenda dell'antimafia 2011*, Trapani: Di Girolamo, 2010.

## Chapter 2   Premafia Phenomena

1. The text referred to in this chapter is Umberto Santino, *La cosa e il nome. Materiali per lo studio dei fenomeni premafiosi*, Soveria Mannelli: Rubbettino, 2000.
2. On the Sciacca case: Francesco Savasta, *Il famoso caso di Sciacca*, Palermo: Felicella e Magrì, 1726, reprinted Palermo: Sigma Edizioni, 2000.
3. On the early mafia in Palermo and the role of the Inquisition, see Orazio Cancila, *Così andavano le cose nel secolo sedicesimo*, Palermo: Sellerio, 1984. This book contains the letters from a Palermo magistrate to Emperor Charles V complaining of the conditions under which justice was administered in Sicily. Many crimes went unpunished because those responsible enjoyed powerful protection.
4. On extortion in Palermo, see Argisto Giuffredi, *Avvertimenti cristiani*, manuscript in the Palermo municipal library, printed in Luigi Natoli (ed.), *Documenti per servire alla storia della Sicilia*, 4/5, Palermo, 1896.
5. On armed bands, see Enzo D'Alessandro, *Brigantaggio e mafia in Sicilia*, Messina-Florence: G. D'Anna, 1959.
6. On Mario de Tomasi, see Giovanni Marrone, *Città, campagna e criminalità nella Sicilia moderna*, Palermo: Palumbo, 1995.
7. The report by Pietro Calà Ulloa, *Considerazioni sullo stato economico e politico della Sicilia*, in Santino, *La cosa e il nome*, pp. 215–27.
8. On banditry: Giovanna Fiume, *Le bande armate in Sicilia (1819–1849): Violenza e organizzazione del potere*, Palermo: Facoltà di Lettere, 1984.
9. On the 'world-systems theory': Immanuel Wallerstein, *The Modern World System: Capitalist Agriculture and the Origins of the European World Economy in the Sixteenth Century*, New York: Academic Press, 1974.
10. On the apologetic myth: Luigi Natoli, *I Beati Paoli*, Palermo: Flaccovio, 1971 (original edn 1909–10) and Francesco Renda, *I Beati Paoli. Storia, letteratura e leggenda*, Palermo: Sellerio, 1988.

## Chapter 3   Mafia and Antimafia in an Agricultural Society

1. On the revolt in Castellammare, see Salvatore Costanza, *La Patria armata: Un episodio della rivolta antileva in Sicilia*, Trapani: Corrao Editore, 1989.
2. Giuseppe Rizzotto and Gaspare Mosca, *I mafiusi di la Vicaria di Palermu*, Palermo: Editrice Reprint, 1994.
3. On Diego Tajani's measures, see Paolo Pezzino (ed.), *Mafia e potere: Requisitoria, 1871*, Pisa: Edizioni ETS, 1993.

4. The Bonfadini Report was published in Salvatore Carbone and Renato Grispo (eds), *L'inchiesta sulle condizioni sociali ed economiche della Sicilia (1875–1876)*, 2 vols, Bologna: Cappelli, 1969, pp. 1037–186. The report by the prefect of Palermo, Rasponi, appears on pp. 30–3. The memorandum by Gaspare Galati is on pp. 999–1016. The most recent works include: Salvatore Lupo, *History of the Mafia*, New York: Columbia University Press, 2009. Francesco Renda, *Storia della mafia: Come, dove, quando*, Palermo: Sigma Edizioni, 1997. Giuseppe Carlo Marino, *Storia della mafia*, Rome: Newton & Compton, 1998. John Dickie, *Cosa Nostra: A History of the Sicilian Mafia*, London: Hodder & Stoughton, 2004 and *Blood Brotherhoods. The Rise of the Italian Mafias*, London: Hodder & Stoughton, 2011.

5. The Franchetti inquiry, published as *Condizioni politiche ed amministrative della Sicilia*, Florence: Barbera, 1877, was reprinted Rome: Donzelli, 1993. See also *L'inchiesta in Sicilia di Franchetti e Sonnino: La Sicilia nel 1876*, Palermo: Kalòs, 2004.

6. On Napoleone Colajanni, see *Nel regno della mafia: La Sicilia dai Borboni ai Sabaudi*, Palermo: Ila Palma, 1971 (1st publ. 1900). Gaetano Salvemini's *Il ministro della mala vita* is published in the first volume of part 4 of his *Opere*, Milan: Feltrinelli, 1966. Salvatore Francesco Romano, *Storia della mafia*, Milan: Mondadori, 1966.

7. On Stuppagghieri, see Amelia Crisantino, *Della segreta e operosa associazione: Una setta all'origine della mafia*, Palermo: Sellerio, 2000.

8. On the Favara brotherhood, see Paolo Pezzino, *Una certa reciprocità di favori: Mafia e modernizzazione violenta nella Sicilia postunitaria*, Milan: Franco Angeli, 1990, pp. 205–18.

9. On the Notarbartolo trial, see the evidence of his son Leopoldo, *La città cannibale: Il memoriale Notarbartolo*, Palermo: Novecento, 1994 (1st publ. 1949).

10. Of Giuseppe Pitrè's works, see *Usi e costumi, credenze e pregiudizi del popolo siciliano*, Palermo: il Vespro, 1978 (1st publ. 1887–8).

11. The reports by the chief of police, Sangiorgi, are kept in the Central State Archives. The Centro Impastato has a photocopy.

## Chapter 4  Mafia and Antimafia in the 1960s and 1970s

1. The Antimafia Committee has published a volume with the *Relazione conclusiva* and *Relazioni di minoranza*, Rome: Tipografia del Senato, 1976. It subsequently published *Documentazione allegata* in 5 vols, some in several parts. On Henner Hess, see *Mafia: Zentrale Herrschaft und lokale Gegenmacht*.

2. Franco Ferrarotti's report was published in the volume *Rapporto sulla mafia: Da costume locale a problema dello sviluppo nazionale*, Naples: Liguori, 1978.

3. Francesco Brancato's report was published in *La mafia nell'opinione pubblica e nelle inchieste dall'Unità d'Italia al fascismo*, Cosenza: Pellegrini, 1986. On Michele

Pantaleone, see *The Mafia and Politics*, London: Chatto & Windus, 1966; *Mafia e droga*, Turin: Einaudi, 1966.

4. On Danilo Dolci's work, see the bibliography in Umberto Santino, 'Nonviolenza, mafia e antimafia' in Vincenzo Sanfilippo (ed.), *Nonviolenza e mafia: Idee ed espertienze per un superamento del sistema mafioso*, Trapani: Di Girolamo, 2005, pp. 77–106.

5. On 1968 in Palermo, see Umberto Santino, *Il '68 e il '77 a Palermo*, Palermo: Centro Impastato, 2008.

6. On the work of Giuseppe Impastato, see Umberto Santino (ed.), *Lunga è la note: Poesie, scritti, documenti*, Palermo: Centro Impastato, 2002–8. Felicia Bartolotta Impastato, *La mafia in casa mia*, in Anna Puglisi and Umberto Santino (eds), Palermo: La Luna, 1986–2003. Salvo Vitale, *Nel cuore dei coralli, Peppino Impastato, una vita contro la mafia*, Soveria Mannelli: Rubbettino, 1995–2008. Umberto Santino (ed.), *Chi ha ucciso Peppino Impastato: Le sentenze di condanna dei mandanti del delitto Vito Palazzolo e Gaetano Badalamenti*, Palermo: Centro Impastato, 2008. Tom Behan, *Defiance: The Story of One Man Who Stood up to the Sicilian Mafia*, London: I.B.Tauris, 2008. The report of the Antimafia Committee is published in *Peppino Impastato: Anatomia di un depistaggio*, Rome: Editori Riuniti, 2001, 2006, Rome: Editori Riuniti University Press, 2012.

7. On the work of the Centro Impastato, visit the website: www.centroimpastato. com (accessed 8 April 2015), which includes links to the sites of institutions and associations.

## Chapter 5    Mafia and Antimafia from the 1980s to the Present Day

1. On state witnesses, see Sandra Rizza, *Una ragazza contro la mafia: Rita Atria, morte per solitudine*, Palermo: La Luna, 1993. Pietro Calderoni, *L'avventura di un uomo tranquillo: Storia vera di Piero Nava, supertestimone di un delitto di mafia*, Milan: Rizzoli, 1995. Antonino Miceli, *Io, il fu Nino Miceli: Storia di una ribellione al pizzo*, Milan: Edizioni Biografiche, 2007.

2. On the role of the Church, see Augusto Cavadi (ed.), *Il vangelo e la lupara*, Bologna: Edizioni Dehoniane, 1995 and, by the same author, *Il Dio dei Mafiosi*, Cinisello Balsamo: Edizioni San Paolo, 2009.

3. On the role played by women, see Renate Siebert, *Secrets of Life and Death: Women and the Mafia*, London: Verso, 1996. Clare Longrigg, *Mafia Women*, London: Chatto & Windus, 1997. Anna Puglisi's, *Donne, mafia e antimafia*, Trapani: Di Girolamo, 2005, discusses this topic. She also wrote *Sole contro la mafia*, Palermo: La Luna, 1990, and *Storie di donne*, Trapani: Di Girolamo, 2007. There is important evidence in Giusy Vitale, with Camilla Costanzo, *Ero Cosa loro: L'amore di una madre può sconfiggere la mafia*, Milan: Mondadori, 2009, and in Carla Cerati, *Storia vera di Carmela Iuculano: La giovane donna che si è ribellata a un clan mafioso*, Venice: Marsilio, 2009.

4. On work in schools, see Augusto Cavadi, *A scuola di antimafia*, Trapani: Di Girolamo, 2007. Umberto Santino *Oltre la legalità: Appunti per un programma*

*di lavoro in terra di mafie*, Palermo: Centro Impastato, 1997–2002, is intended in particular for use by teachers.

5. On the anti-racketeering movement: Tano Grasso, *Contro il racket: Come opporsi al ricatto mafioso*, Rome-Bari: Laterza, 1992.

6. On the antimafia activities in the last years, see Alison Jamieson, *The Antimafia. Italy's Fight against organized Crime*, London: MacMillan Press Ltd, 2000. Jane C. Schneider and Peter T. Schneider, *Reversible Destiny: Mafia, Antimafia and the Struggle for Palermo*, Berkeley, Los Angeles, London: University of California Press, 2003.

## Chapter 6   Other Mafias

1. The most recent books on the mafia in the United States include: Selwyn Raab, *Five Families*, New York: St Martin's Press, 2006. Salvatore Lupo, *Quando la mafia trovò l'America: Storia di un intreccio intercontinentale, 1888–2008*, Turin: Einaudi, 2008. See also Alan Block, *East Side – West Side. Organizing Crime in New York 1930–1950*, Cardiff: University College Cardiff Press, 1980.

2. US Senate Permanent Subcommittee on Investigations, *Hearings on Organized Crime: 25 Years after Valachi*, Washington, DC: US Senate, 1988.

3. On the mafia in Canada, see Lee Lamothe and Antonio Nicaso, *Bloodlines: Project Omertà and the Fall of the Mafia's Royal Family*, Toronto: HarperCollins, 2001.

4. On the 'ndrangheta: Enzo Ciconte, *'Ndrangheta dall'Unità a oggi*, Rome-Bari: Laterza, 1992. Nicola Gratteri and Antonio Nicaso, *Fratelli di sangue*, Cosenza; Pellegrini, 2006, Milan: Mondadori, 2009. In February 2008 the Antimafia Commission, chaired by Francesco Forgione, adopted a report published in: *'Ndrangheta: La relazione dell'Antimafia*, Palermo: La Zisa, 2008, and *'Ndrangheta: Boss, luoghi e affari della mafia più potente del mondo*, Milan: Baldini Castoldi Dalai, 2008.

5. On the camorra, see Tom Behan, *See Naples and Die. The Camorra and Organised Crime*, London: I.B.Tauris, 2002. Isaia Sales, with Marcello Ravveduto, *Le strade della violenza: Malviventi e bande di camorra a Napoli*, Naples: L'ancora del Mediterraneo, 2006. Roberto Saviano, *Gomorra, Viaggio nell'impero economico e nel sogno di dominio della camorra*, Milan: Mondadori, 2006 (a very successful narrative that cites no documentary sources). Gigi Di Fiore, *L'Impero: Traffici, storie e segreti dell'occulta e potente mafia dei Casalesi*, Milan: Rizzoli, 2008. Francesco Barbagallo, *Storia della camorra*, Rome-Bari: Laterza, 2010.

6. On the mafia in Apulia: Monica Massari, *La Sacra Corona Unita*, Rome-Bari: Laterza, 1998.

7. On the mafia in Basilicata: Pantaleone Sergi, *Gli anni dei Basilischi: Mafia, istituzioni e società in Basilicata*, Milan: F. Angeli, 2003.

8. Information on the various mafias and their role in drug trafficking may be found in Umberto Santino and Giovanni la Fiura, *Behind Drugs*, Milan: Edizioni Gruppo Abele, 1993, research by the Centro Impastato and the CISS (International South-South Cooperation) published in four languages. On the

Corsican clans: Jaques Follorou, Vincent Nouzille, *Les parrains corses*, Paris: Fayard, 2004; Jean-Michel Verne, *Main basse sur Marseille et...la Corse*, Paris: Nouveau Mond éditons, 2012.

9. On the mafia in Russia, see Arkadij Vaksberg, *The Soviet Mafia*, London: Weidenfeld & Nicolson, 1991; Cesare Martinetti, *Il padrino di Mosca*, Milan: Feltrinelli, 1995.

10. On the mafia in the countries of the former socialist bloc, see *Gli Stati mafia*, a special edn of 'Limes', 2000.

11. On the Triads, see Martin Both, *The Triads: The Chinese Criminal Fraternity*, London: Grafton Books, 1990. On the presence of Chinese criminal groups in Italy, see Stefano Becucci and Monica Massari (eds), *Mafie nostre, mafie loro*, Turin: Edizioni di Comunità, 2001.

12. The most accessible work on the Japanese yakuza is David E. Kaplan and Alec Dubro, *Yakuza: Japan's Criminal Underworld*, Berkeley-Los Angeles, CA: University of California Press, 2003.

13. See also Mitsuyo Ohira, *So can you*, Tokyo: Kodansha English Library, 2000; Shoko Tendo, *Yakuza Moon*, Tokyo: Kodansha International Ltd, 2004. I am grateful to Tomoko Takahashi, a friend of the Centro Impastato who died prematurely in 2007, for this information.

14. On drug trafficking in Colombia, see C. G. Arrieta, L. J. Orjuela, E. Sarmiento Palacio and J. G. Tokatlian, *Narcotráfico en Colombia*, Bogotá: Ediciones Uniandes, Tercero Mundo Editores, 1990. Antonio Mazzeo, *Colombia: L'ultimo inganno*, Rome: Palombi Editori, 2001.

15. On the relationship between organized crime and globalization: Marco Antonio Pirrone and Salvo Vaccaro (eds), *I crimini della globalizzazione*, Trieste: Asterios, 2002, and Umberto Santino, *Mafie e globalizzazione*. On the international connections of the Italian mafias: Francesco Forgione, *Mafia export: Come 'ndrangheta, Cosa nostra e camorra hanno colonizzato il mondo*, Milan: Baldini Castoldi Dalai, 2009.

# BIBLIOGRAPHY

Arrieta, C. G., L. J. Orjuela, E. Sarmiento Palacio and J. G. Tokatlian, *Narcotrà fico en Colombia*, Bogota: Ediciones Uniandes, Tercero Mundo Editores, 1990.

Barbagallo, Francesco, *Storia della camorra*, Rome-Bari: Laterza, 2010.

Bartolotta Impastato, Felicia, Anna Puglisi and Umberto Santino, *La mafia in casa mia*, Palermo: La Luna, Palermo, 1986.

Becucci, Stefano, and Monica Massari (eds), *Mafie nostre, mafie loro*, Turin: Edizioni di Comunità, 2001.

Behan, Tom, *See Naples and Die. The Camorra and Organised Crime*, London: I.B.Tauris, 2002.

—— *Defiance: The Story of One Man Who Stood up to the Sicilian Mafia*, London: I.B.Tauris, 2008.

Biscione, Francesco M., *Il sommerso della Repubblica: La democrazia italiana e la crisi dell'antifascismo*, Turin: Bollati Boringhieri, 2003.

Block, Alan, *East Side – West Side. Organizing Crime in New York 1930–1950*, Cardiff: University College Cardiff Press, 1980.

Both, Martin, *The Triads: The Chinese Criminal Fraternity*, London: Grafton Books, 1990.

Cancila, Orazio, *Così andavano le cose nel secolo sedicesimo*, Palermo: Sellerio, 1984.

Carbone, Salvatore, and Renato Grispo (eds), *L'inchiesta sulle condizioni sociali ed economiche della Sicilia (1875 – 1876)*, 2 vols, Bologna: Cappelli, 1969.

Cavadi, Augusto (ed.), *A scuola di antimafia: Materiali di studio, criteri educativi, esperienze didattiche*, Palermo: Centro Impastato, 1994.

—— (ed.), *Il vangelo e la lupara: Materiali su chiese e mafia*, Bologna: Edizioni Dehoniane, 1995.

—— (ed.) *A scuola di antimafia*, Trapani: Di Girolamo, 2007.

—— *Il Dio dei Mafiosi*, Cinisello Balsamo: Edizioni San Paolo, 2009.

Cerati, Carla, *Storia vera di Carmela Iuculano: La giovane donna che si è ribellata a un clan mafioso*, Venice: Marsilio, 2009.

Chinnici, Giorgio and Umberto Santino, *La violenza programmata: Omicidi e guerre di mafia a Palermo dagli anni '60 ad oggi*, Milan: F. Angeli, 1989, 1990.

Ciconte, Enzo, *'Ndrangheta dall'Unità a oggi*, Rome-Bari: Laterza, 1992.

Cohen, Albert, *Delinquent Boys: The Culture of the Gang*, Glencoe, IL: Free Press, 1955.

Colajanni, Napoleone, *Nel regno della mafia: La Sicilia dai Borboni ai Sabaudi*, Palermo: Ila Palma, 1971; Milan: Rizzoli, 2013 (1st publ. 1900).

Costanza, Salvatore, *La Patria armata: Un episodio della rivolta antileva in Sicilia*, Trapani: Corrao Editore, 1989.

Crisantino, Amelia, *Della segreta e operosa associazione: Una setta all'origine della mafia*, Palermo: Sellerio, 2000.

D'Alessandro, Enzo, *Brigantaggio e mafia in Sicilia*, Messina-Florence: G. D'Anna, 1959.

Dickie, John, *Cosa Nostra: A History of the Sicilian Mafia*, London: Hodder & Stoughton, 2004.

—— *Blood Brotherhoods. The Rise of the Italian Mafias*, London: Hodder & Stoughton, 2011.

Di Fiore, Gigi, *L'Impero: Traffici, storie e segreti dell'occulta e potente mafia dei Casalesi*, Milan: Rizzoli, 2008.

Falcone, Giovanni, *Interventi e proposte (1982–1992)*, Florence: Sansoni, 1994.

Ferracuti, Franco, and Martin E. Wolfgang, *The Subculture of Violence: Towards an Integrated Theory in Criminology*, London: Tavistock Publications, 1969.

Ferrarotti, Franco, *Rapporto sulla mafia: Da costume locale a problema dello sviluppo nazionale*, Naples: Liguori, 1978.

Fiume, Giovanna, *Le bande armate in Sicilia (1819–1849): Violenza e organizzazione del potere*, Palermo: Facoltà di Lettere, 1984.

Forgione, Francesco, *Mafia export: Come 'ndrangheta, Cosa nostra e camorra hanno colonizzato il mondo*, Milan: Baldini Castoldi Dalai, 2009.

Franchetti, Leopoldo, and Sidney Sonnino, *Inchiesta in Sicilia*, Florence: Vallecchi, 1974 (original edition 1877).

Grasso, Tano, *Contro il racket: Come opporsi al ricatto mafioso*, Rome-Bari: Laterza, 1992.

Gratteri, Nicola, and Antonio Nicaso, Fratelli di sangue, Cosenza; Pellegrini, 2006; Milan: Mondadori, 2009.

Gunnarson, Carina, *Cultural Warfare and Trust: Fighting the Mafia in Palermo*, Manchester: Manchester University Press, 2008.

Hess, Henner, *Mafia: Zentrale Herrschaft und lokale Gegenmacht*, Tübingen: Mohr, 1970.

Impastato, Giuseppe (ed. Umberto Santino), *Lunga è la notte: Poesie, scritti, documenti*, Palermo: Centro Impastato, 2002–14.

Jamieson, Alison, *The Antimafia. Italy's Fight against organized Crime*, London: MacMillan Press Ltd, 2000.

Kaplan, David E., and Alec Dubro, *Yakuza: Japan's Criminal Underworld*, Berkeley-Los Angeles, CA: University of California Press, 2003.

Lamothe, Lee, and Antonio Nicaso, *Bloodlines: Project Omertà and the Fall of the Mafia's Royal Family*, Toronto: HarperCollins, 2001.

La Spina, Antonio (ed.), *I costi dell'illegalità: Mafia ed estorsioni in Sicilia*, Bologna: il Mulino, 2008.

Longrigg, Clare, *Mafia Women*, London: Chatto & Windus, 1997.

Lupo, Salvatore, *Quando la mafia trov ò l'America: Storia di un intreccio intercontinentale, 1888–2008*, Turin: Einaudi, 2008.

—— *History of the Mafia*, New York: Columbia University Press, 2009.

Marino, Giuseppe Carlo, *Storia della mafia*, Rome: Newton & Compton, 1998.

Mckay, Henri, and Clifford R. Shaw, *Juvenile Delinquency and Urban Areas*, Chicago: University of Chicago Press, 1942.

Marrone, Giovanni, *Città, campagna e criminalità nella Sicilia moderna*, Palermo: Palumbo, 1995.

Martinetti, Cesare, *Il padrino di Mosca*, Milan: Feltrinelli, 1995.

Massari, Monica, *La Sacra Corona Unita*, Rome-Bari: Laterza, 1998.

Mazzeo, Antonio, *Colombia: L'ultimo inganno*, Rome: Palombi Editori, 2001.

Merton, Robert K., *Social Theory and Social Structure*, Glencoe, IL: Free Press, 1957.

Miceli, Antonio, *Io, il fu Nino Miceli: Storia di una ribellione al pizzo*, Milan: Edizioni Biografiche, 2007.

Notarbartolo, Leopoldo, *La città cannibale: Il memoriale Notarbartolo*, Palermo: Novecento, 1994 (1st publ. 1949).

Ohira, Mitsuyo, *So can you*, Tokyo: Kodansha English Library, 2000.

Pantaleone, Michele, *The Mafia and Politics*, London: Chatto & Windus, 1966.

Pezzino, Paulo, *Una certa reciprocità di favori: Mafia e modernizzazione violenta nella Sicilia postunitaria*, Milan: Franco Angeli, 1990.

—— (ed.), *Mafia e potere: Requisitoria, 1871*, Pisa: Edizioni ETS, 1993.

Pirrone, Marco Antonio, and Salvo Vaccaro (eds), *I crimini della globalizzazione*, Trieste: Asterios, 2002.

Puglisi, Anna, *Sole contro la mafia*, Palermo: La Luna, 1990.

—— *Donne, mafia e antimafia*, Trapani: Di Girolamo, 2005.

—— *Storie di donne*, Trapani: Di Girolamo, 2005, 2012.

Putnam, Robert D., *Making Democracy Work: Civic Traditions in Modern Italy*, Princeton, NJ: Princeton University Press, 1993.

Raab, Selwyn, *Five Families*, New York: St Martin's Press, 2006.

Renda, Francesco, *Storia della mafia: Come, dove, quando*, Palermo: Sigma Edizioni, 1997.

Rizza, Sandra, *Una ragazza contro la mafia: Rita Atria, morte per solitudine*, Palermo: La Luna, 1993.

Rizzotto, Guiseppe, and Gaspare Mosca, *I mafiusi di la Vicaria di Palermu*, Palermo: Editrice Reprint, 1994.

Romano, Salvatore Francesco, *Storia della mafia*, Milan: Mondadori, 1966.

Sales, Isaia, and Marcello Ravveduto, *Le strade della violenza: Malviventi e bande di camorra a Napoli*, Naples: L'ancora del Mediterraneo, 2006.

Umberto Santino *La mafia interpretata: Dilemmi, stereotipi, paradigmi*, Soveria Mannelli: Rubbettino, 1995.

—— *L'alleanza e il compromesso: Mafia e politica dai tempi di Lima e Andreotti ai giorni nostri*, Soveria Mannelli: Rubbettino, 1997.

—— *La democrazia bloccata: La strage di Portella della Ginestra e l'emarginazione delle sinistre*, Soveria Mannelli: Rubbettino, 1997.

—— *La cosa e il nome: Materiali per lo studio dei fenomeni premafiosi*, Soveria Mannelli: Rubbettino, 2000.

—— *Storia del movimento antimafia. Dalla lotta di classe all'impegno civile*, Rome: Editori Riuniti, 2000.

—— *Dalla mafia alle mafie. Scienze sociali e crimine organizzato*, Soveria Mannelli: Rubbettino, 2006.

—— 'Mafia, crimine transnazionale e globalizzazione' in Umberto Santino (ed.), *Mafie e globalizzazione*, Trapani: Di Girolamo, 2007.

—— (ed.), *Chi ha ucciso Peppino Impastato: Le sentenze di condanna dei mandanti del delitto Vito Palazzolo e Gaetano Badalamenti*, Palermo: Centro Impastato, 2008.

—— *L'altra Sicilia: Caduti nella lotta contro la mafia e per la democrazia dai Fasci siciliani ai nostri giorni*, Trapani: Di Girolamo, 2010.

Santino, Umberto, "Mafia e maxiprocesso" in Various authors, *Gabbie vuote: Processi per omicidio a Palermo dal 1983 al maxiprocesso*, Milan: F. Angeli, 1992.

—— *La mafia interpretata: Dilemmi, stereotipi, paradigmi*, Soveria Mannelli: Rubbettino, 1995.

—— *L'alleanza e il compromesso: Mafia e politica dai tempi di Lima e Andreotti ai giorni nostri*, Soveria Mannelli: Rubbettino, 1997.

—— *La democrazia bloccata: La strage di Portella della Ginestra e l'emarginazione delle sinistre*, Soveria Mannelli: Rubbettino, 1997.

—— *La cosa e il nome: Materiali per lo studio dei fenomeni premafiosi*, Soveria Mannelli: Rubbettino, 2000.

—— *Storia del movimento antimafia: Dalla lotta di classe all'impegno civile*, Rome: Editori Riuniti, 2000; Editori Riuniti University Press, 2009.

—— *Dalla mafia alle mafie: Scienze sociali e crimine organizzato*, Soveria Mannelli: Rubbettino, 2006.

—— 'Mafia, crimine transnazionale e globalizzazione' in Umberto Santino, *Mafie e globalizzazione*, Trapani: Di Girolamo, 2007.

—— (ed.), *Chi ha ucciso Peppino Impastato: Le sentenze di condanna dei mandanti del delitto Vito Palazzolo e Gaetano Badalamenti*, Palermo: Centro Impastato, 2008.

—— *L'altra Sicilia: Caduti nella lotta contro la mafia e per la democrazia dai Fasci siciliani ai nostri giorni*, Trapani: Di Girolamo, 2010.

—— *La mafia come soggetto politico*, Trapani: Di Girolamo, 2013.

Santino, Umberto, and Giovanni La Fiura, *L'impresa mafiosa: Dall'Italia agli Stati Uniti*, Milan: F. Angeli, 1990.

—— *Behind Drugs: Survival Economies, Criminal Enterprises, Military Operations, Development Projects*, Turin: Edizioni Gruppo Abele, 1993.

Saviano, Roberto, *Gomorra, Viaggio nell'impero economico e nel sogno di dominio della camorra*, Milan: Mondadori, 2006.

Shaw, Clifford R., *The Jack-Roller. A Delinquent Boy's Own Story*, Chicago: University of Chicago Press, 1930

—— *The Natural History of a Delinquent Career*, Chicago: University of Chicago Press, 1931.

Schneider, Jane C. and Peter T., *Reversible Destiny. Mafia, Antimafia and the Struggle for Palermo*, Berkeley, Los Angeles, London: University of California Press, 2003.

Sergi, Pantaleone, *Gli anni dei Basilischi: Mafia, istituzioni e società in Basilicata*, Milan: F. Angeli, 2003.

Siebert, Renate, *Secrets of Life and Death: Women and the Mafia*, London: Verso, 1996.

Sifakis, Carl, *The Encyclopedia of American Crime*, New York: Factis on File, 1982.

Sutherland, Edwin H., *White Collar Crime*, New Haven, CT, and London: Yale University Press, 1983 (1st edn 1949).

Tendo, Shoko, *Yakuza Moon*, Tokyo: Kodansha International Ltd, 2004.

Vaksberg, Arkadij, *The Soviet Mafia*, London: Weidenfeld & Nicolson, 1991.

Varese, Federico, *The Russian Mafia. Private Protection in a New Market Economy*, Oxford: Oxford University Press, 2001.

Vitale, Giusy, with Camilla Costanzo, *Ero Cosa loro: L'amore di una madre può sconfiggere la mafia*, Milan: Mondadori, 2009.

Vitale, Salvo, *Nel cuore dei coralli, Peppino Impastato, una vita contro la mafia*, Soveria Mannelli: Rubbettino, 1995–2008.

Wallerstein, Immanuel, *The Modern World System: Capitalist Agriculture and the Origins of the European World Economy in the Sixteenth Century*, New York: Academic Press, 1974.

Weber, Max, *Economy and Society*, vol. 1, Berkeley, CA: University of California Press, 1978.

# INDEX

**Plate 1** Frontispiece to Francesco Savasta, *Il famoso caso di Sciacca*, published 1726. The Sciacca case is the most famous example of a clash between noble families. The Luna and Perollo families (crests shown above) clashed first in 1455 and then again in 1529.

**Plates 2–3** The manuscript by the Marquis of Villabianca, written in the eighteenth century, describes the measures taken against bandits who had no protection. The other document, from 1843, is a list of outlawed bandits from the scrubland around Palermo.

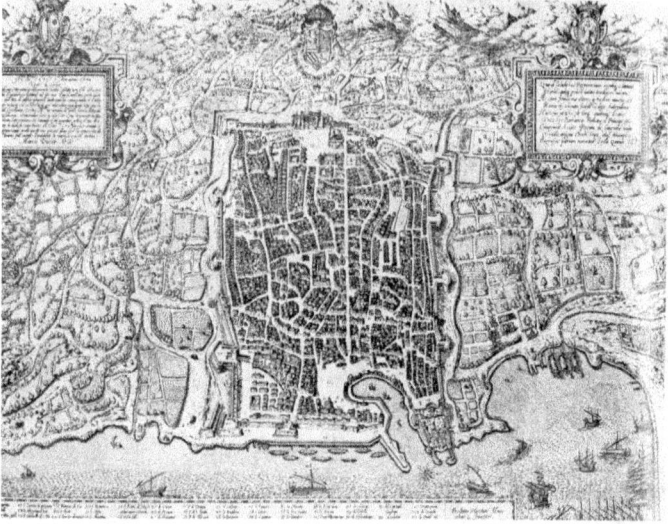

**Plate 4**  Map of Palermo, printed in Rome in 1580. The presence of *'bravacci'* who killed in broad daylight, raped women and lived by robbery, demanding a ransom for surrendering their ill-gotten gains, is documented. Their leader was Girolamo Colloca, known as the 'king of the *Bocceria*' (the *'Vucciria'* was the meat market).

**Plate 5**  A recent photograph of the *Vucciria* market. Demands for 'protection money' in the market are documented as long ago as the fifteenth century.

**Plates 6–8**  The cover of the novel *The Leopard* by Giuseppe Tomasi di Lampedusa, in it he notes that the unification of Italy meant that the jackals had replaced the leopards, that is, the bourgeoisie had replaced the aristocrats. However, one ancestor of the Tomasi was more jackal than leopard. Mario de Tomasi, who lived in the sixteenth century, started out as a foot guard, chosen from a pool of poor, dangerous individuals, later becoming a captain at arms and making his fortune from crime. He then married the noble Francesca Caro, so founding the line of the *Gattopardi*, which includes saints and other religious figures.

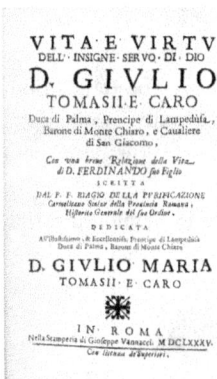

**Plate 9**  Cover of Orazio Cancila, *Così andavano le cose nel secolo sedicesimo* containing letters sent by Antonio Montalto, prosecutor at the High Royal Court, to the Emperor Charles V. In a letter of 1531 he wrote that justice applied only to the 'little fish' and that the number of unpunished crimes was growing every day. A magistrate who had given judgement against the Count Luna had been killed by his men, but there could be no justice because the murderers were protected by the viceroy.

L'ATTO
PUBBLICO DI FEDE
SOLENNEMENTE CELEBRATO NELLA CITTA'
DI PALERMO.
à 6. Aprile 1724.
DAL TRIBUNALE DEL S. UFFIZIO DI SICILIA.
DEDICATO
ALLA MAESTA' C. C. DI
CARLO VI.
IMPERADORE.
E III. RE DI SICILIA.
DESCRITTO DAL D. D. ANTONINO MONGITORE
Canonico della Cattedrale Metropolitana Chiefa della ftefsa
Città, Confultore, e Qualificatore di detto S. Uffizio.

IN PALERMO, M.DCC.XXIV.
Nella Regia Stamperia d'Agoftino, ed Antonino Epiro, Familiari, ed Imprefsori
del moderno Tribunale.
CON LICENZA DE' SUPERIORI.

**Plates 10–11** Frontispiece to Antonino Mongitore, *L'atto pubblico di fede solennemente celebrato nella città di Palermo, à 6 aprile 1724.* The Inquisition, set up to root out heretics who were regarded as a threat to the public, was a political organisation used for repression by the Spanish government. Those who aligned themselves with the Inquisition as 'familiars' were subject to special courts and escaped official justice. They included nobles and rich criminals. This gave rise to a culture in which illegal behaviour went unpunished. The engraving showing the burning at the stake of two alleged heretics is taken from the book describing the *Auto da fé* of 6 April 1724.

# I BEATI PAOLI

**Plate 12**  Cover of Luigi Natoli, *I Beati Paoli*. The founding myth of mafia organisations seeks to portray them founded on justice and honour. The mafia in Sicily appears to originate from the *Beati Paoli*, a group dispensing justice and whose distant ancestors were the *Vendicosi*, mentioned in 1186. The novel by Luigi Natoli makes use of this myth and is regarded as a kind of Bible for mafia members.

**Plate 13**  The Spanish knights Osso, Mastrosso and Carcagnosso are regarded as the mythical founders of the mafia, 'ndrangheta and camorra. They are supposed to have landed in 1412 on the island of Favignana, where they drew up the rules for these three organizations. The mafia have used these legends and a series of references to religious symbols in an attempt to improve their standing in the eyes of their members and in general.

**Plate** 14 Garibaldi's entry into Palermo. The battle of the Ponte dell'Ammiraglio.

NINO BIXIO

**Plate** 15 During the riots in Palermo in 1820 and 1848, groups of ordinary people faced bands comprising aristocrats and members of the bourgeoisie. Both included criminal elements. In 1860, 'lads' drawn from the former groups fought alongside the supporters of Garibaldi, but the views of the property owners found a sympathetic ear even among officers in Garibaldi's army. In August 1860, Nino Bixio, a leading member of Garibaldi's *Mille*, bloodily put down a revolt in Bronte seeking the distribution of State land.

Plate 16   On 1 October 1862, 12 people were stabbed in Palermo. The confessions of one of the attackers resulted in a trial which sentenced the perpetrators to death or imprisonment but failed to identify those behind the attack (the name of the Prince of Sant'Elia, a senator, was mentioned). This is regarded as the first example of the 'strategy of tension'. The anonymous drawing shows the execution of one of those condemned.

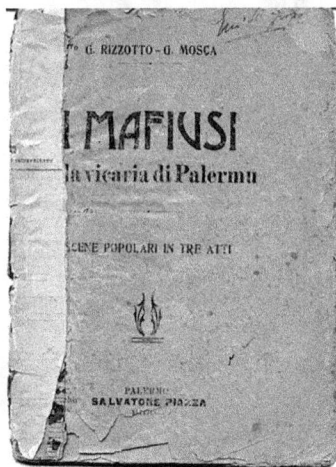

Plates 17–18   An old edition of the popular comedy *I mafiusi di la Vicaria di Palermu*, staged in 1863 and a poster with some scenes from the play. This was the first time the word 'mafiusi' had been used in literature.

**Plate 19** Bust of Giovanni Corrao, a general in Garibaldi's army. He was killed in Palermo on 3 August 1863. Of humble origins, he had taken part in the expedition of the *Mille* in 1860 and in 1862 had accompanied Garibaldi in his attempt to conquer Rome, which came to an end when Garibaldi was wounded in Calabria. Regarded by his political opponents as being on the side of the Bourbons and a mafia boss, Corrao was killed because he had a large following.

**Plates 20−21** Cover of Giuseppe Pitrè, *Usi e costumi, credenze e pregiudizi del popolo siciliano*. Student of folk traditions Pitrè stated that the words 'mafia' and 'mafioso' were used in Palermo in the nineteenth century in a positive sense. For example, a beautiful girl was described as 'mafiosa'. According to Pitrè, following the success of the play *I mafiusi di la Vicaria* the word then became synonymous with banditry, the camorra and criminality. Pitrè regarded the mafia as 'an exaggerated concept of individual force' which had nothing to do with criminal activity.

— PROGETTI DI LEGGE E RELAZIONI

TITOLO II.

**Inchiesta sulla Sicilia.**

Art. 23.

È ordinata un'inchiesta sulle condizioni sociali ed economiche della Sicilia e sull'andamento dei pubblici servizi.

Art. 24.

L'inchiesta sarà fatta da una Giunta composta di nove membri, dei quali tre saranno nominati dalla Camera dei deputati, tre dal Senato del regno, e tre con decreto reale, sentito il Consiglio dei ministri. La Giunta eleggerà fra i suoi membri il proprio presidente.

Art. 25.

Sono applicabili ai testimoni chiamati dalla Giunta le disposizioni di cui agli articoli 306, 364, 365, n° 3, 368, 369, n° 4, 370, n° 4, del Codice penale.

Se il testimonio ritratta la falsa testimonianza o palesa il vero dinanzi alla Giunta, prima che contro di lui sia istituito procedimento penale, la pena alla quale avrebbe dovuto soggiacere sarà diminuita di uno a tre gradi.

Art. 26.

Entro un anno saranno presentati al Governo i documenti e la relazione dell'inchiesta, la quale verrà trasmessa alle due Camere del Parlamento e pubblicata.

Art. 27.

Per provvedere a questa inchiesta sarà stanziata nel bilancio 1875 del Ministero dell'interno, capitolo 53, la somma di lire 100,000.

**Plate 22** The Palermo Prosecutor Diego Tajani had a violent clash with the chief of police Giuseppe Albanese, whom he accused of having criminal connections. After resigning from the judiciary, he became an opposition MP and in 1875 made a speech in parliament arguing that the mafia was an instrument of 'local government'.

**Plate 23** The text of the bill on the parliamentary inquiry in Sicily in 1875.

**Plate 24** From the cover of Leopoldo Franchetti and Sidney Sonnino, *Inchiesta in Sicilia*. On the left Sidney Sonnino, on the right Leopoldo Franchetti, in the middle Enea Cavalieri, who accompanied them during the private investigation of 1876.

**Plate 25**  Emanuele Notarbartolo, the mayor of Palermo and a director of the Banco di Sicilia, was known for his rectitude as an administrator and for his opposition to speculation on the bank. He was killed on 1 February 1893.
**Plate 26**  Leopoldo Notarbartolo waged a long battle against those accused of his father's murder.

**Plate 27**  Raffaele Palizzolo, a Member of Parliament with links to the mafia, was charged with being behind Notarbartolo's murder. He was first found guilty but then acquitted.
**Plate 28**  The Marquis Antonio di Rudinì, the mayor of Palermo and later prime minister, was a friend of Emanuele Notarbartolo's. When Notarbartolo's son Leopoldo sought his help, he advised him to take matters into his own hands by hiring an assassin to kill Palizzolo.

**Plates 29–31**  The cover of Salvatore F. Romano, *Storia dei Fasci siciliani*. The period from 1891 to early 1894 saw the growth in Sicily of a large-scale mass movement known as the 'Fasci siciliani', which included peasants and workers. Women were also involved, forming 'Fasci femminili'. The movement was bloodily repressed by the forces of law and order, with the help of mafia gamekeepers. The trials against the leaders of the Fasci resulted in heavy sentences. The engraving shows the women of Piana dei Greci in the province of Palermo, who took part in the peasant struggles.

**Plate 32**  Francesco Crispi, a leader of the Italian Risorgimento and prime minister, ordered the dissolution of the Fasci siciliani as requested by the landowners and sent the army to put down the movement.

**Plate 33**  Palermo police chief, Ermanno Sangiorgi, between 1898 and 1900 drew up a series of reports on the mafia at that time. He described it as a vast association of evil-doers, organized in sections and divided into groups, each with its own leader and with the whole company of evil-doers subject to a supreme head. This was the organizational structure which Tommaso Buscetta would describe in the 1980s. After the trial held in 1901 the idea of a mafia organized hierarchically was consigned to oblivion.

**Plate 34**  The first page of the report by Ermanno Sangiorgi, 1898.
**Plate 35**  The trial based on Sangiorgi's reports, From *L'Ora*, 3–4 May 1901.

**Plate 36** Joe Petrosino, the Italian-American policeman killed in Palermo in 1909.
**Plate 37** Lorenzo Panepinto, the socialist leader killed in 1911.

**Plate 38** Bernardino Verro, the socialist mayor of Corleone killed in 1915.
**Plate 39** Giuseppe Rumore, the socialist activist killed in 1919.

**Plate 40** Nicolò Alongi, the socialist leader killed in 1920.
**Plate 41** Giovanni Orcel, the socialist trade unionist killed in 1920.

**Plate 42** Sebastiano Bonfiglio, the socialist mayor of Monte San Giuliano killed in 1922.
**Plate 43** A peasant demonstration in the 1920s.

**Plates 44–46** Cesare Mori, the prefect of Palermo from 1925 to 1929, who waged a campaign against the mafia. The pictures show him during a demonstration in the countryside around Roccapalumba, in the province of Palermo, at the swearing of the gamekeepers' oaths on 13 May 1926.

**Plate 47**  Allied landing in Sicily, 10 July 1943. Recent studies have revised the role of the mafia in the military operations. Later it was to prove decisive for the social control of the territory as it led the repression of the peasant struggle.

**Plate 48**  Calogero Vizzini, the mafia leader at Villalba (Caltanissetta). On 16 September 1944 he organized an attack on the regional secretary of the Communist Party, Girolamo Li Causi, during a meeting in the town square.

**Plate 49**  Special issue of *La Voce Comunista* and *La Voce Socialista*.

**Plate 50**  Mafiosi leading a separatist demonstration in Palermo.

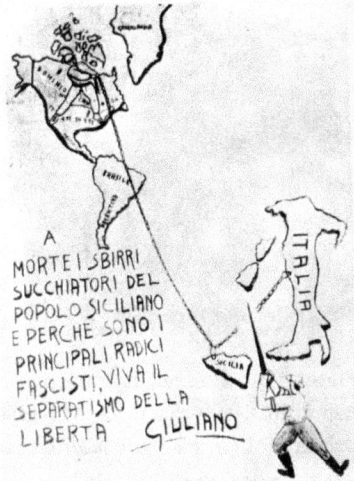

**Plate 51** The bandits Salvatore Giuliano and Gaspare Pisciotta. The Giuliano gang was employed by the separatist movement to engage with the forces of the left who were leading the peasant struggles.

**Plate 52** A manifesto, signed by Giuliano.

**Plates 53–54** The Minister of Agriculture, the communist Fausto Gullo, issued decrees which opened the way to a relaunch of the peasant struggles through the occupation of uncultivated or badly cultivated land.

**Plates 55–56** Leaders of the peasant struggles killed by the mafia: Nicolò Azoti, in 1946; Accursio Miraglia, in 1947 (under the photograph is written: '*Meglio morire in piedi che vivere in ginocchio*': 'Better to die on your feet than live on your knees').

**Plates 57–58** May Day 1947: the massacre at Portella della Ginestra. The elections for the Regional Assembly of Sicily ten days earlier had seen a triumph for the forces of the Left making up the *Blocco del popolo* list.

Bandits from the Giuliano gang were found guilty of the murders but those ordering it remain unknown.

# Questi i risultati delle elezioni in Sicilia

| CIRCOSCRIZIONI | Blocco del popolo | Democrazia Cristiana | Liberali e qualunq. | Separatisti | Partito monarchico | Socialisti lavor. ital. | Partito repubbl. |
|---|---|---|---|---|---|---|---|
| PALERMO | 90.426 | 62.340 | 71.093 | 44.286 | 70.834 | 10.261 | 25.340 |
| CATANIA | 72.395 | 79.052 | 54.049 | 53.375 | 43.920 | 27.136 | 4.199 |
| MESSINA | 66.624 | 49.155 | 70.297 | 27.174 | 33.675 | 11.438 | 13.475 |
| AGRIGENTO | 98.911 | 60.455 | 29.011 | 4.652 | 8.821 | 3.306 | 2.242 |
| TRAPANI | 66.611 | 30.699 | 20.101 | 10.761 | 13.130 | 6.803 | 23.975 |
| SIRACUSA | 53.404 | 23.537 | 35.119 | 10.937 | — | 10.603 | 6.315 |
| CALTANISSETTA | 55.250 | 37.287 | 30.850 | 2.103 | 4.618 | 953 | 1.917 |
| RAGUSA | 52.729 | 32.029 | 25.532 | 4.282 | — | 5.420 | 2.526 |
| ENNA | 34.531 | 24.628 | 11.824 | 13.282 | 9.846 | 6.261 | 6.628 |
| **TOTALI** | 590.881 | 329.182 | 287.588 | 170.852 | 184.844 | 82.181 | 82.418 |
| **TOTALE SEGGI** | 29 | 19 | 14 | 8 | 9 | 4 | 4 |

**Plates 59–62** Leaders of the peasant struggles killed by the mafia: Epifanio Li Puma, Placido Rizzotto, Calogero Cangelosi in 1948; Salvatore Carnevale in 1955.

**Plate 63** The mother of Salvatore Carnevale, Francesca Serio, with the writer Carlo Levi, author of the book *Words are Stones*.

**Plate 64** The funerals following the Ciaculli massacre of 30 June 1963.

**Plate 65** Cardinal Ruffini and Pope Pius XII gave priority to the struggle against communism.

**Plate 66** The Waldesian Pastor Pietro Panascia. Immediately after the Ciaculli massacre Cardinal Ruffini entered into an argument with him, playing down the role of the mafia.

**Plates 67–68** Salvo Lima and Vito Ciancimino promoted building speculation through the 'sack of Palermo'.

**Plates 69–71** Giuseppe 'Peppino' Impastato, a *Nuova Sinistra* activist killed in 1978; the journalist Mario Francese, killed in 1979; Deputy Police Chief Boris Giuliano, killed in 1979.

**Plates 72–74** The magistrate Cesare Terranova, killed in 1979, with the *carabinieri* officer Lenin Mancuso; President of the Region of Sicily Piersanti Mattarella, killed in 1980; the communist leader, Pio La Torre, killed in 1982, with Rosario Di Salvo.

**Plates 75–76** Prefect Carlo Alberto Dalla Chiesa and his wife Emanuela Setti Carraro, killed in 1982, with the police officer Domenico Russo; the magistrate Rocco Chinnici, killed in 1983, with the police officers Salvatore Bartolotta and Mario Trapassi and the doorman Stefano Li Sacchi.

**Plates 77 and 78** The *pentito* Tommaso Buscetta. His statements were used in the 'maxi-trial' in 1986–87, which was held in a bunker in Palermo prison and resulted in the conviction of leaders and ordinary members.

**Plates 79–82** The magistrate Giovanni Falcone and his wife Francesca Morvillo and Paolo Borsellino, killed along with their escorts in the massacres at Capaci on 23 May 1992 and Via D'Amelio on 19 July 1992.

**Plate 83**  The businessman Libero Grassi, killed in 1991 for refusing to pay 'protection money'.

**Plate 84**  Rita Atria, who gave evidence for the State but killed herself after the murder of Paolo Borsellino.

**Plate 85**  The parish priest Pino Puglisi, killed in 1993.

**Plate 86**  The arrest of the mafia leader Totò Riina in January 1993 after 25 years on the run.

**Plate 87**  The massacre in Florence on 27 May 1993 which left five dead. The massacre in Milan on 27 July killed a further five people. The massacres outside Sicily were designed to persuade the State to relax the antimafia legislation and review some trials.

**Plate 88**  The arrest of the perpetrator of the Capaci massacre, Giovanni Brusca, in May 1996.

**Plate 89**  The arrest of the mafia leader Antonino Giuffrè in April 2002.

**Plate 90**  The arrest of the supreme leader Bernardo Provenzano in April 2006, after 43 years on the run.

**Plate 91**  The arrest of the mafia leader Salvatore Lo Piccolo in November 2007.

**Plate 92**  The mafia members involved in the 'Old Bridge' operation in February 2008.

**Plate 93**  The mafia leader Matteo Messina Denaro, still on the run.

**Plate 94** A national demonstration against the mafia to mark the first anniversary of the murder of Giuseppe Impastato, 9 May 1979.

**Plate 95** Antimafia initiatives in Sicilian schools.
**Plate 96** On fields confiscated from the mafia.
**Plate 97** Anti-racketeering demonstration.

**Plate 98** The bandit Salvatore Giuliano and the Italo-American mafia leader Vito Genovese.
**Plate 99** Lucky Luciano in Palermo.

**Plate 100** Cinisi (Palermo) in the 1950s. From left to right: Mayor Leonardo Pandolfo, mafia leader Cesare Manzella, the father of Giuseppe Impastato, two mafia members and Gaetano Badalamenti. Badalamenti was convicted in the 'Pizza Connection' trial and found guilty of the murder of Giuseppe Impastato.
**Plate 101** The mafioso Joe Valachi, who revealed the secrets of Cosa Nostra in America in 1963.

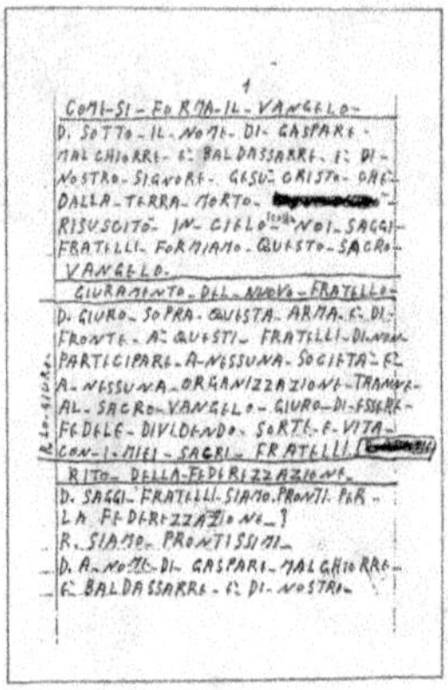

**Plate 102**  The first page of the 'ndrangheta code seized in Reggio Calabria in 1987.

**Plate 103**  A page from the code seized by the Canadian police from the home of an 'ndrangheta member.

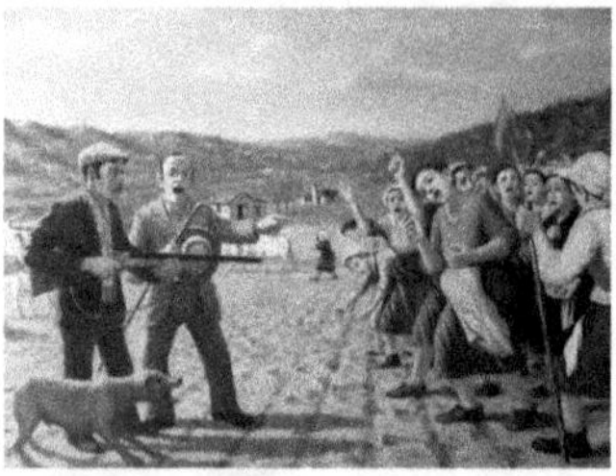

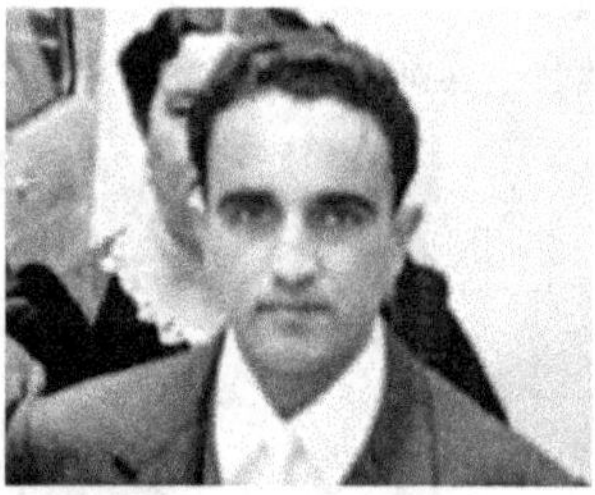

**Plate 104**  The murder of Giuditta Levato, a leader of the peasant struggles in Calabria in the 1940s.

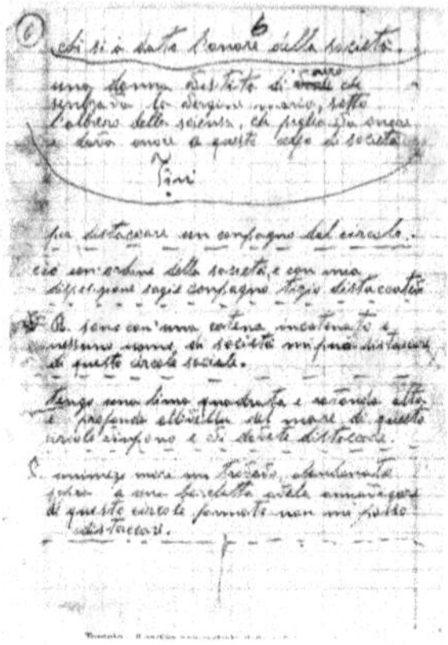

**Plate 105**  The communist activist Rocco Gatto, killed in 1977.

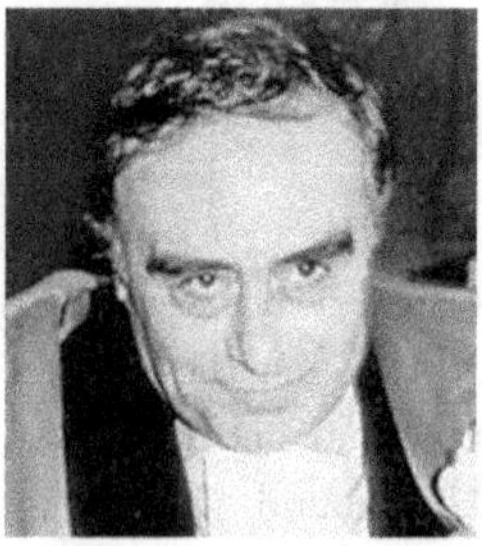

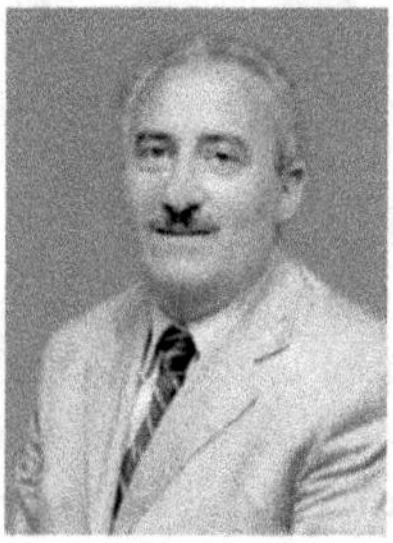

**Plate 106**  The magistrate Antonino Scopelliti, killed in 1991.

**Plate 107**  Francesco Fortugno, vice-president of the Regional Council of Calabria, killed in 2005.

Plate 108   Raffaele Cutolo, head of the 'Nuova camorra organizzata'.
Plate 109   Carmine Alfieri, head of the 'Nuova famiglia', which fought with the Cutolo clan. Alfieri later cooperated with the forces of law and order.

Plate 110   The Christian Democrat Mayor of Pagani (Salerno), Marcello Torre, killed in 1980.
Plate 111   The journalist Giancarlo Siani, killed in 1985.
Plate 112   The priest Giuseppe Diana, killed in 1994.

Plate 113   Silvia Ruotolo, killed during a camorra shootout in 1997.
Plate 114   The mayor of Pollica (Salerno), Angelo Vassallo, killed in 2010.

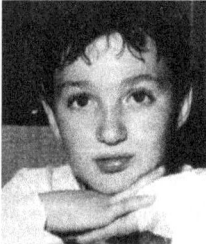

**Plates 115–125**  Mafia violence has hit children several times. These are pictures of some of those killed: Giuseppina Savoca (1959). Simonetta Lamberti (1982). The twins Giuseppe and Salvatore Asta killed with their mother in 1985. Claudio Domino (1986). Marcella Tassone (1989). Nicholas Green (1994). Giuseppe Di Matteo (1996). Stefano Pompeo (1999). Valentina Terracciano (2000). Annalisa Durante (2004). Domenico Gabriele (2009).

**Plate 126** Following the deaths of her partner and son, Serafina Battaglia broke the code of *omertà* and denounced the mafiosi responsible for the killings – she did not secure justice.

**Plate 127** Franca Viola, aged 17, was raped by a mafia member in Alcamo (Trapani). She refused marriage 'to make amends' and had the rapist and his accomplices arrested.

**Plate 128**  Felicia Bartolotta, the mother of Peppino Impastato.

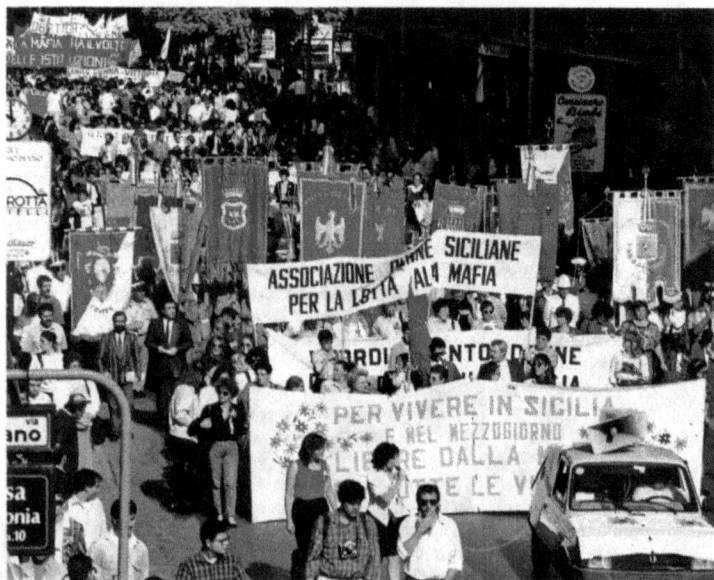

**Plate 129**  A demonstration of the Associazione delle donne siciliane per la lotta contro la mafia (Association of Women in Sicily against the Mafia).